JOHN WALSH

WITH SUSAN SCHINDEHETTE

TEARS
OF
RAGE

From Grieving Father
to Crusader for Justice:
The Untold Story of the
Adam Walsh Case

POCKET BOOKS
New York   London   Toronto   Sydney   Tokyo   Singapore

Originally published in hardcover in 1997 by Pocket Books

POCKET BOOKS, a division of Simon & Schuster Inc.
1230 Avenue of the Americas, New York, NY 10020

ISBN: 0-671-00669-X

First Pocket Books paperback printing July 1998

10 9 8 7 6 5 4 3 2 1

For Adam, Meghan, Callahan, and Hayden.
And all the children we'll never meet.

Acknowledgments

Revé and I would like to thank the people who have loved and supported us:

The friends and family who suffered with us during unbearable grief.

The volunteers whose time, money and effort fueled the battle for children's rights.

The caring politicians who drafted the laws.

The members of the law enforcement community who protect me in the streets.

The victims of violence who have opened their hearts.

And the untold thousands who have regarded Adam as their own.

A simple child,
That lightly draws its breath,
And feels its life in every limb,
What should it know of death?

—WILLIAM WORDSWORTH

Contents

Contents
Book Four

Appendix

Prologue

AND WHEN THEY ASK, AS I'M SURE THEY WILL, WHY I HAVE decided to speak about these things, I will have an answer for them:

My hope is that these words will stand as a testament to the many sacrifices that were made.

My wife, Revé, and I did not make all of these sacrifices ourselves. There were others who helped carry the burden. We did not respond, for example, to the particular request that I am about to relate. We were spared little over the whole course of events. But we were saved from this, at least. The request was for someone close to us, a friend. A family member would have been ideal, but was judged, ultimately, to be unwise.

And so a friend, one who knew us well, went instead. Years before, I had done him what he regarded as a great favor, and now he believed that, as difficult as it might be, it was time to repay the kindness.

1

He left, accompanied by a detective, and drove recklessly in his white convertible up the divided concrete highway at an irresponsible speed. The August sun beat down on him, and the hot, dry tarry smell of the road swirled around them both. They did not speak. He was marshaling his strength, focusing himself, concentrating on the task at hand.

And finally, after an hour, they came to the place.

For some time, I did not know about what happened next. I was later told some of it because I asked to be told. I did not want to know all of it, and still do not. But it is important for these unspeakable things to be spoken of, because they actually happened in this world.

My friend remembers walking up what seemed like an endless flight of wooden stairs, to a set of swinging doors, scuffed at the bottom by impatient technicians who had kicked them open with their feet. Panes of frosted glass in these doors let light through, but obscured the things that took place within. He remembers the odor of disinfectant and formaldehyde. Cold, fluorescent light was reflected on ceramic tile, and rows of stainless steel instruments lay precisely on countertops beneath the overhang of metal cabinets. In the center of the room was a wheeled, stainless steel table.

A man wearing a clinical, white, knee-length smock walked up to him.

"Can you do this?" my friend was asked.

"Yes," he replied.

Then they brought out something swaddled in white towels, like a newborn, and laid it in front of him.

The warm, brackish water had done its work, transforming something once known intimately into something that could not exist even in the darkest imagination. But it did exist. It was now irrefutable.

The eyes, once clear, were not fully open. They were clouded, unseeing. The soft blondish hair, always straight, was now tangled and matted. The unblemished skin, the kind that had never deeply tanned, was taut, like a thin sheathing of plastic that no longer contained anything.

Beneath that, below the thin neck, where T-shirts had once covered the muscles of a small chest, and where fingers and feet had once been held in loving hands, there was now—nothing.

What was presented for identification in this strange, unfamiliar setting was all that remained.

The day before, two workers from the citrus fields who had cast their lines for brim and catfish had been walking along a fetid drainage canal not far from the Florida turnpike when they saw something floating in the still water, among the saw grass and pepperweeds. They later said that, at first, they thought it was the head of a little girl's life-size doll.

Now there was only this procedure of official identification. And so my friend asked, in a single breath . . . if he might be shown . . . if they could please . . . part the lips?

They did.

Only then did he see again what he had seen and remembered, just days, a lifetime ago: there, in the delicate gap, was a small, emerging tooth.

And then he knew.

All these years later, he still dreams of it. The face, he says, appears out of the darkness while he is sleeping. The image still comes to him when he cannot protect himself from it, during the night. And sometimes when it comes, he says, it is wearing a child's red baseball cap.

It is fitting that these things are called "the remains." Those words describe what still exists when all that has gone before it no longer does. The deed, the chosen action that would come to be called "the crime," had taken away everything that had been and had left in its place something that could not be comprehended or understood, something that, sixteen years later, we still cannot believe.

There had been promise, and now there was none. There had been an endless wellspring of hope and future, and now it was gone. What we had once loved with all of our beings, and believed we would always continue to love, that which we had cherished above all else, no longer existed. This was all that remained of a little boy.

The child on that autopsy table was my six-year-old son, Adam.

Book
One

1

Auburn

ON SUNDAY MORNINGS WHEN MY FATHER, "GENTLEMAN" Jack Walsh, genuflected in his best blue serge suit and took his seat in the front pew of St. Mary's Roman Catholic Church for Mass and Holy Communion, he was sometimes not accompanied by his boys.

It's not that there was any antipathy on our part. It was just that his sons—my younger brother Jimmy and I—were ordinarily in the back row with the old women and nuns, wearing the black eyes and split lips that we'd picked up in fistfights the Saturday night before.

It was not right, my father said, that his sons approach the altar in that unholy condition. "You can give God one hour of your life each week and thank Him for what you have," he would say. "And you can be presentable while you're doing it. That's not too much to ask."

That dictum was pretty hard to argue with, but there were stretches when it was not uppermost in mind. My nose was broken at least four times by the year I graduated from college, and it was usually at least partly my doing.

7

I fought over girls, I fought for my honor. I fought to protect Jimmy. And sometimes I fought for the love of fighting. My good friend John Monahan, an erudite Irishman, thinks that it has everything to do with heritage. You can't understand me, he says, unless you understand my Irish pride. It's not so much about ego; it's just that I can't abide anything derogatory being said about my family. That's even worse than someone attacking me. I'll fight to my last breath to protect my family's honor—and my own. I couldn't care less.

Once in the 1970s Monahan and I were in New York City on business and went to a great Spanish restaurant at Fifty-second and Broadway. We were walking along and four guys tried to roll us. I went for the first guy, whacked him on both ears—*crack!*— and he went down for the count. Then I turned on the second guy, who was a lot bigger than me, and almost put him through the window of Gallagher's steak house. Monahan and I both spent time in the ring. And neither one of us backs down.

I did not learn to fight from my father. His given name was John, like mine, but he was known either as Gentleman Jack, or, more often, by his nickname, which was Adam. It was always "Good morning, Adam" and "There goes Adam Walsh." I don't really know why that name stuck—maybe because it seemed as if he was such a premier guy. First in everything. He had been drafted out of Notre Dame when he was twenty to serve in the air force in World War II, and he went on to become a B-24 bomber pilot in the Pacific, the first lieutenant in a crew of twelve.

The B-24s were behemoths—big, dangerous targets in the sky, with gunner's stations in the nose and tail. My father rarely talked about the war, but he did tell us about how, over the radio, he heard his buddies being hit and going down. And he told us that the important thing to remember was that nothing was more dangerous in the world than a disorganized crew. Being disorganized could kill you.

Once, when he was listening over the radio to a plane going down, all the crew members were fighting over the parachutes, screaming and trying to jump out of their burning plane. My father always said that the reason he survived the war was because his own crew had been so disciplined. He had made them drill and rehearse constantly, just constantly. What if this happens? What if that goes wrong? What do we do? What's the plan? My Dad was a hero. He had medals, lots of them, for bravery under fire. And what he told me was to always be prepared.

Later he entered Tokyo with the Army of Occupation and I'm sure saw a number of things that he would rather not have seen. When he finally came home from the war in 1946 to our hometown of Auburn, a pristine town in the Finger Lakes in upstate New York, my father never wanted to leave. He had seen the violent side of the world and wanted no part of it brought into the big clapboard house on Lake Avenue. Sometimes he would go to see the World Series or to a Yankees game or the fights in New York City. But mostly he didn't want to spend even a single night away from home.

My dad was a role model for all of us: me, the oldest, born the day after Christmas, 1945 (my wife, Revé, who would not enter the picture for quite some time, says that I consider it an affront that I was not born on December 25). Then there was Jimmy, a year and a half younger; my younger sister, Jane; and our late-in-life, Irish Catholic–mistake baby brother, Joe, who wasn't born until Jane was in third grade.

Jane was beautiful, an all-around great girl. Dad always said, "Don't ever lay a hand on your sister, Jane, or you will pay ten times the penalty." And we did. My brother and I tormented this girl. We tied her to a tree and cut off big chunks of her hair. But that was just what you did to your sister: you teased and tormented her. To this day we love her, and she loves us, and it all worked out in the end. She gets to blame us for the rest of our lives.

It's not fashionable these days to remember happy childhoods, but that's the way mine was. Mostly what I remember is that my father loved my mother, and that she loved him back. They had a respect for each other, and even when they were older, they would still go out to dinner together and hold hands. I do not remember him ever yelling at her. My father was a member of the Holy Name Society at church, which was made up of men who did not take the name of the Lord in vain.

He was a tall, handsome guy with black, curly hair, and he loved to wear nice clothes. "Put your best foot forward," he'd always say, "because you never know who you'll run into when you go out on your way." He wasn't flamboyant, but he was elegant, and a bunch of his friends tried to get him into politics. He just never had that kind of ambition. All he was ever interested in, really, was staying at home and spending time with the family.

It was easy enough to see that all the women loved him. Whenever he'd go into a store, they would all turn and smile. As for women in general, we were taught to respect them absolutely. My father said that they were creatures who had to be defended and protected, and that also included my mother. "Your mother is my partner," my dad would say, "and the way you talk to her is the way you're talking to me. If you give her any teenage lip, you'll have to answer to me."

My mother was too nice a person ever to be the family disciplinarian. She had grown up in "the big house" on North Street, where a lady made doll clothes for her dolls, and her family had an English cook and gardener, and formal gardens with lilacs and a little pond with goldfish in it. The Callahans were lace-curtain Irish. My grandfather James Francis Callahan had owned a lot of real estate, and a paint company and a country club by the lake, but mainly he owned a big building company, Callahan Construction. He had poured the concrete for the huge prison in Auburn, the first one in the area, and when the time came for the first electrocution there, my grandpa Callahan was invited to be a witness to it because he had helped build the place.

My mother used to show us pictures of him, handsome, sitting in a raccoon coat in his big, elegant, polished automobiles. And then, when he was in the middle of all his success, a blood vessel burst in his head, and Grandpa Callahan died of a stroke at age forty-five.

Not long after that, his wife, Grandma Callahan, died when her three kids were still teenagers. They couldn't run the estate by themselves, so it was handed over to lawyers, who promptly ran it into the ground. By the time the war was over, everybody was broke. But my uncles started the business up from scratch again, beginning with one truck. Callahan Trucking. It was always a big deal when they'd go to Pennsylvania to get each new truck—only the best Mack trucks. And of course, all the trucks had kelly green shamrocks painted on them. You had to hand it to them: they built the business back up again from nothing into a huge concrete-making company.

My mother's family had had its rough spots, but it was still refined compared to my father's. He grew up on Tipperary Hill in Syracuse, an Irish neighborhood where the traffic lights are green on top instead of red. His father was a rough-and-tumble guy who had a cash-register store and four Irish sons. Maybe that's where Jimmy and I inherited it; we were always just such hell-raisers.

Outside the house, Jimmy and I always stuck up for each other. But inside, we tried to kill each other every day. Mom used to called us Cain and Abel. Once we got into a fight in the kitchen and just about destroyed it—knocked the roast on the floor and broke some plates that had been handed down for generations. But fighting was the thing in those days. It's a testosterone thing, a male-bonding thing that women will never in a million years understand. We just loved to roughhouse. We called it "roughing up." In those days, you didn't have guns and you didn't have knives. You had your fists. And you definitely settled your scores of honor.

There was always some guy who'd have one too many beers and decide he wanted to take on the Walsh brothers. Those were epic fights. And then there were the fights over girls. I don't know why girls wanted to hang around us, but they did, especially the pretty ones. Girls love bad boys, and I'd get caught all the time, sneaking out of their houses, parking with them in cars, bringing them into the living room. Their fathers wanted to kill me, as did their brothers, and there were lots of "You keep your son away from my daughter" confrontations. But those never worked. It only made the girls want to see you more.

In those days there was always something going on at our house. It was full of people all the time, usually around the dining-room table, eating. My mother baked something nearly every day, and she fed legions of kids—pot roast, meat loaf, spaghetti. My dad's big hobby was befriending kids who had nonparticipatory parents. His philosophy was that it was better having everybody at our house, and knowing what was going on, than worrying about us at somebody else's house, unsupervised.

For a long time I wasn't aware of much that took place beyond our house. I was so wrapped up in puberty that I didn't really pay attention to what was going on in the rest of the world. But I do remember the day that my father brought home Eddie Miles.

Eddie Miles was a poor kid who lived in the downtown part of Auburn. It was not far from my father's office, where he had taken over the cash-register business from his father. There was one house on that street. This little boy lived in there, and the whole family was so poor. Of course, Eddie would always be out in front of my father's store, and my dad would notice him and take him for an ice cream.

He felt so sorry for that little boy who had no chance in life. "Nobody really cares about him," Dad would say. Of course the Miles's had no car, so Dad would always take Eddie for a ride with him. That's how Eddie got up to our house. My dad would say, "Eddie, would you do an errand for me?" And then he would just sort of take Eddie along.

Eddie Miles's father was always trying to work, and always losing his job. Eddie was the oldest. He was dirty and poor—not the type of kid we associated with. Then one day Eddie Miles did something incredibly stupid: he jumped into the river off the big Lake Avenue bridge. Not only did he not know how to swim, but he also broke both of his legs. Somebody fished him out of the water, and the doctors put him in a body cast. Eddie was going to live all right, but after that, things really went downhill. You can't take a shower with a body cast on, and nobody was taking care of Eddie. On top of everything else, he was really starting to stink.

So one day when my brother Jimmy and I were about ten and eleven, my dad brought Eddie Miles out to our house. We couldn't figure it out. We thought it was really an intrusion—this kid from the city coming into our nice house and my dad showing him all our sports trophies. Jimmy and I went out of the room and started talking about it: "What the hell is Dad bringing that kid in here for? He stinks, and he's showing him all our personal stuff."

Evidently, my father overheard us. Because about two minutes later he found us and took us out of Eddie's earshot and really let us have it. "Let me tell you two something," he said, as angry as I'd ever seen him. "I'm going to tell you right now that you don't know how lucky you are. You live on this lovely street by the lake not because of anything *you've* done, but because of the luck of the draw. But for the grace of God, my boys, you could be Eddie Miles yourselves. You had nothing to do with being born into this family. And this boy had nothing to do with the fact that he was born into the situation he was. I don't ever want to hear you talk that way again!"

As stupid as we were, the lesson sank in. For the first time in my life that I can remember, I felt ashamed. My brother and I had been self-centered and arrogant. Selfish, arrogant little boys.

I don't really know how I got from that point to the way I later became. Somewhere along the line I began to feel that I was supposed to take care of everything, that it was my job to look out for the family and my brothers and sister. It's a feeling that has stayed with me my whole life. I don't know if it comes from being Irish or Catholic or both. Maybe I just believed that I was better than anybody at almost everything, so if anyone was in trouble or something was going wrong, no one would be able to fix things the way I could. That everything was my responsibility. That it was my job to be in charge of the world. I don't really know where it all came from, but it was there. And it was apparently pretty obvious, even early on.

My mother remembers that not long after Joe was born, when I was about fourteen, she was driving with me in the car someplace and I said to her, "You know, Mom, you and Dad are a little older, a little old to be having a kid. And I just want you to know that if anything happens to you both, I'll take care of Joe."

My father wasn't some kind of religious nut, but in retrospect, I'd have to say that I learned more about values and morality at home than I ever did in school, despite the parochial education. I attended Our Lady of Mount Carmel, a high school run by the Carmelite fathers. Boys separated from girls, and priests in monk's robes who believed in serious corporal punishment. If you were out in the hall when you weren't supposed to be, they'd slam your fingers in your locker. If you mouthed off, they'd take you out into the hall and hit you with a belt. All that, and you also had to wear a sport coat and tie. The unbelievable thing is that you paid good money to go there, and if you screwed up, you got kicked out. The academics were top-notch, and some of the priests were great guys, but they ran that school with an iron hand.

I had really high scores on my admissions tests, so I spent four years in the advanced classes with the same twenty-five eggheads. We were the guys who took Latin and all the accelerated courses, and they expected a lot from us. But it was always easy for me. I never studied, ever. I was the only jock in the group, and all I wanted was to get away from the eggheads and be with regular guys.

After the War, my father had never had the chance to finish at Notre Dame. By that time, he was married and a veteran and had a family to support. So of course when I graduated from high school, he wanted me to go to his alma mater. But by then I had my fill of Catholic school. I decided instead to go to Auburn Community College, a junior college near town, where I played soccer and loved it. I was trying to save some money, so I got a job working constuction during the summers. Callahan Trucking was all Teamsters by then, so I couldn't drive the trucks. But my uncle Jim had a friend, a successful Italian guy named Joe Pedergrass, who owned a big equipment company. Every year he would hire one college-bound kid, so I started working there and learned how to drive heavy equipment.

It was brutal, hard work in those days, but I made great money. I saved up enough to put myself through college, and I bought an old black Jaguar. Then I transferred to the University of Buffalo. It wasn't a state school at the time, it was private. It had a football team and a great English department. The writer John Barth was there, so I decided to major in English.

I loved college. The first thing I realized was that I could have an apartment off campus. That's exactly what I wanted to do. I just had the greatest time. I loved the parties. I loved the sports. I loved the independence. I loved the camaraderie. I would work hard all summer, save my money and pay my own bills. I had this beautiful car and a zillion beautiful girls. Michael Quinn and I were the best dressers on campus. Revé later used to say that I was the only college guy she ever knew who insisted on sending all his shirts out to the cleaners and having the collars starched. All the guys from the Jewish fraternities called me and my crowd the Gentile Jocks.

My friends were preppy then, and athletes. We pledged the big jock fraternities, the Animal House types. Tom Roche was a big basketball player, six feet four. Michael Quinn was a defensive halfback, tough as hell and good-looking. Quinn was a killer, a Golden Gloves boxer, and one day he hit me so hard when we were sparring at the Y that he blew out my eardrum and knocked me unconscious. I later got drafted three times, and I failed all three physicals. So you could say that Quinn was the one who kept me out of the army.

We were all part of the same clique—the big men on campus. We would meet girls from other colleges and take trips to visit them. We were great partyers. We kept up in school, though. The only D I ever got in college was for a Red Cross class in lifesaving. I was a great swimmer and I got an A on the final, but I had never showed up for class. The instructor said, "You never came to class the whole term. I'm going to give you a D."

I told him, "I know more than you do about swimming. Why should I come here and sit, freezing my ass off in this pool in the morning?"

He said, "Because I say so. That's why. And you still get the D."

During my final year at Buffalo I switched majors

from English to history. I don't know; maybe I was Englished-out. All I remember is all of a sudden being really interested in German history. It was the sixties and drugs were happening big time, but I was never into them. We were mostly into drinking, but never during the week. Later on, Students for a Democratic Society took over the Buffalo campus, and it was the beginning of the hippie movement. Being in a fraternity wasn't cool anymore, so all of my friends and I de-pledged.

Everybody was into love beads, love-ins, and being a hippie. When I went home that summer, Joe Pedergrass said he might not employ me that year because I was a longhair and against the war. My dad was the greatest guy in the world about it. He said, "World War II was totally different, John. I fought for this country because it was a terrible threat. You know, the Japanese and the Germans wanted to kill us. But this Vietnam business is senseless. I'll do anything I can. You and your brother Jimmy are not going to die in Vietnam."

As college kids, what we were most into was working out at the gym all the time. We cared about what we looked like on the beach, or to girls. I always had girlfriends, usually a couple at a time. I didn't think I was ever going to settle down; I was just enjoying everything too much. We used to go to Brunner's, a college bar that was packed with all kinds of girls— Rosary Hill girls, University of Buffalo girls, sorority girls. It was a fun bar, no band, no disc jockey, and a lot of noise. My friend Reggie Eyre was the doorman. He was a big man on campus, too. Older, but one of those guys who just couldn't seem to get his diploma. He was handsome, and the bartenders were Irish, and the bouncers were all football guys.

One night at Brunner's, Reggie was trying to pick up this girl named Barbara Whitman, talking to her all night. Barbara was there with a girlfriend—the quiet type, just kind of tagging along. Reggie took me over to meet Barbara's girlfriend, and I said hello. She looked about twenty. She was beautiful, and she had a body. Boy, this incredible centerfold body.

I asked her what her name was and she said, "Revé."

Re-*vay,* with the accent on the second syllable, a name her father had picked out. From a French word.

Revé. Like *reverie.*

From a word that means "to dream."

2

Revé

I NEVER GAVE MUCH THOUGHT TO HOW OLD REVÉ WAS. She was pretty, and she dressed sharp. And there was also that body. We were starting to kind of hang around together. She took me horseback riding, and we went skiing. She was always into her own thing, and I liked that. Then one night Tom Roche was sitting around at my place and picked up a copy of that day's *Buffalo Evening News*. In it was a picture of Revé, who had just won an art contest. "Holy Jesus, Mary, and Joseph," Tom said. "There's a picture of Revé in the paper, John, and she's sixteen years old."

But you know, she had this way about her. She had a certain presence. And after a while I just got over how young she was. She was way more sophisticated than anybody in her high school and she always dated older guys. She had a fake ID. That's how she got into Brunner's. She was bored with high school. She was into art and her horses. And even then, she always seemed very . . . I don't know, serene.

We weren't madly in love with each other. But we had a good time together, and I relaxed a little after she turned seventeen. She was beautiful, and she was caring, and she was up for anything. I was a wild child and I would go downtown when no one else would. I'd be the only white guy at James Brown concerts, and I'd go to the Pine Grill to listen to black bands because I loved the music and I loved to dance. I'd just go in and say hello to everybody and buy drinks, and everyone treated me really well. Revé loved that. She thought it was cool. She would watch Tom Roche and me go into these after-hours bars and bet a couple of bikers ten bucks at the pool table. She'd say, "You're going to get beaten to a bloody pulp." But we didn't. We'd win. We would hustle money playing pool all the time. She loved it. Tom and I were the only white guys on campus who could dance. In retrospect, I think that that was a big part of our allure.

Up until that time, even though my given name was officially John, for as long as I could remember everyone had always called me Jack. By then, even Revé's dad had heard that she was going out with this guy named Jack. Someone in college who was therefore a barbarian and way too old for her. Mr. Drew was thinking, "Well, she hasn't brought him home yet, which means he must be fifty-eight years old and married with children."

For a long time I would drop Revé off down the block, do anything not to be seen around her house. But when the time finally came that her dad wasn't going to let her out of the house at all anymore, she figured it was time to take me over to meet him. After all the negative advance publicity, it went like this: "Dad, I'd like you to meet my new friend, John Walsh."

A different guy entirely.

Revé had changed my name, and I never got it back. But it's like I always said. She was quick on her feet.

I graduated from UB in 1965 and wasn't really sure what I wanted to do next. I did know, however, what I didn't want. I had already been to the Virgin Islands

once, and also to Florida over spring break. I hated
those upstate New York winters more than anything,
so I talked Revé's brother Cliff into moving with me
to Florida. It was no big deal that Revé and I were
going to be so far apart. We were already both seeing
other people. We were both young and had other
things to do without getting tied down. Still, I decided
to keep in touch with her. After all, there was no
reason not to.

She wound up coming down to visit me in Florida,
and we had a great time. People liked her. Or as one of
my friends put it, she was John Walsh with longer hair.

And I would see her when I went up North to visit.
After a while Cliff decided to move back to upstate
New York, and when he did, I got my own apartment
and a job at the Diplomat Hotel. It was a gorgeous
place on the beach in Hollywood, Florida, a town
right next to Fort Lauderdale. My friend Jeff O'Regan
had by then come down, too. I knew Jeff from
Cornell, where he was a big football player. The
minute we met, we became instant great friends. He
was a daredevil, and we both liked dangerous sports.
He was a barefoot water-skier and we both loved
scuba diving and deep-sea diving and spearfishing.
Whenever we were together, it was The Saga of Jeff
and John. He was six foot four, a big, handsome Irish
boy and the wildest guy I ever met.

The Diplomat was a huge luxury hotel right on the
ocean, and I was a cabana boy working on the beach.
Then head cabana boy. My job was to set up a hundred
or so beach chairs in the morning and take care of all
the guests. I made great money—a few hundred bucks
a day in tips. I got to swim in the ocean every day and
party every night. It was the most fun I had ever had in
my entire life, including college. I wasn't a beach bum.
I was a former college guy taking a break.

There was always a bunch of little kids hanging
around, bothering me. One of them, who belonged to
one of the hotel's top executives, John Monahan Sr.,

was little Michael Monahan, about ten years old. Michael and his brother, Johnny, were just a couple of little squids. I'd take them surfing and diving, and up to the Sportatorium drag strip with me every once in a while. So to them I was a big hero.

One day Johnny, who was eleven at the time, and Michael were playing around in a huge drainage pipe that led from the hotel out into the surf along a jetty. It was about six feet in diameter, and they were playing Batman in the cave inside it. Somehow Johnny got stuck underneath the pipe, between it and the sand, and then the tide started coming in. Michael tried to pull him out, but he was really stuck, and then the water started coming up around his mouth and they started screaming. Michael ran back up to the main pool deck where I was, crying, "John, John, you've gotta come. My brother's stuck and he's gonna drown!"

At first, I said, "Yeah, yeah, right. Stop playin' with me. I'm busy." But I finally realized that Michael wasn't kidding. "Where is he?" I screamed.

I ran down to where Johnny was and immediately got the picture. There was no way to get him out before the water got over his head. By this time a crowd was gathering around, and old ladies were starting to panic, but nobody seemed to know what to do. I was screaming, "Would someone go and get me a goddamn regulator!" but nobody really did anything. So I ran back up to the hotel myself and broke into the scuba stand and grabbed a regulator and a tank. I ran back down to where Johnny was and leaned down to him and in a real quiet voice said, "Now, Johnny, remember what I taught you. Don't panic here. I want you just to breathe. Breathe." I stuck the regulator in his mouth, and Johnny started to breathe when the water came over his head, like I had always showed him in the pool.

Then I started digging with my hands in the sand underneath Johnny and somehow got both my arms around him, and when the water flowed out, I just grabbed him really tight and pulled as hard as I could, and all of a sudden he popped out like a cork.

I do not honestly recall that episode as such a huge deal, but nobody ever forgot about it. Especially John Monahan. Monahan used to say that he had always liked me, right from the start. But now, thinking that I had saved his son's life, well, you can imagine. I am not trying to minimize what happened that day, or what might have happened had not cooler heads prevailed. But to me, more than anything it was an object lesson about practicing what my father had always preached: Stay organized. Don't panic.

The Walsh brothers were known for surprises. At my house, we were always giving our mother a heart attack. So one night Revé came home from a date and there I was, standing in her foyer. Right there on her doorstep—the hallway, actually—telling her that I loved her and that I wasn't going back to Florida without her. I didn't bother giving her any time to make up her mind, because in my mind the decision was already made.

I asked her to marry me, and I went up to her hometown, Clarence, New York, to give her a ring. She picked me up at the airport in her father's car, and as she was backing out of the parking space, she ran into a big, cement lamppost and totaled the back end of the car. "Well, we can either go home and tell my dad about it," she said, "or else we can just go out and have a good time."

So we headed out for the evening, and later on that night Revé also managed to lock her keys in the car. At that point, the car was already wrecked, so she just figured what the hell, and we kicked in the wing window of her father's beautiful new silver Ambassador.

I guess you could say things have kind of been that way ever since.

It wasn't too much later that Revé finally packed up

her sewing machine and her cheerleading pom-poms, and we drove her car down to Florida. We got married on July 10, 1971, in a big wedding where everybody had a fine time except all the old ladies, who were scandalized because I wore brown-and-white spectator shoes without socks. A great wedding. An even better honeymoon. This was back in the days before frequent-flyer programs, and John Monahan gave us two round-trip plane tickets to Europe.

We took off and I remember sitting on the plane with Revé and me just looking at each other, and it was kind of like, "Well, here we go." We decided that we would travel for as long as the money lasted—England, Italy, France, Spain. We felt like we were heading off on some great adventure, someplace that we had never been. I think that's the thing that I have always loved most about Revé. I mean, she's a good person and everything. She's loyal. She's loving. But mostly, she's game.

We got to England and went to Bournemouth to visit our friends, the Maidments. Bill was a high diver and his wife, Sonja, was an Aqua Belle. We had met them in Florida where they came to work the water shows during the summer. We eventually wound up spending two months traveling all over Europe. We saw Revé's relatives in Germany, and we went all over the place. But the Maidments were the ones who told us to go to Majorca. When I think of our honeymoon, that's what I think of. A beautiful island off the coast of Spain where we rented a motor scooter and went up into the hills. We saw cactus fields and little old men with donkey carts. I even took Revé to the bullfights. She thought I was a Renaissance guy.

After we got back to the States, we moved into our first little house in Miami Shores. I got a job as a cabana manager at one of the big high-rises on the beach. I think the boss wondered what a college graduate was doing even applying for the job. But the money was good, and I got to do a lot of diving. I knew that I'd be working serious jobs soon enough. We had a lot of fun in those years. John Monahan had always liked me, but after what happened with Johnny, he was really interested in helping me out. After a while, I finally decided that it was time to get a real job, and he gave me one.

Monahan worked for a huge company called the Gulf American Corporation, a big land-development company that owned nearly a million acres in Florida, Arizona, and California. GAC had gotten into a lot of trouble earlier on because they had built cities out in the middle of nowhere to help sell their land off—mini-cities like Coral Gables, River Ranch, and one in the Bahamas called Cape Eleuthera. These were all self-contained resorts with restaurants, drugstores, and everything so that when you went there, you'd think, "Jeez, this is really great. I'm going to buy some land around here." Except that there was nothing else around but the resort.

When GAC got into trouble, it was finally bought out, but the new company still had huge debts. Monahan had been managing hotels around Miami since he was a kid, so he got hired to revive these half dozen hotels. Hotels in places no one had ever heard of—Remuda Ranch in the Everglades, River Ranch up in the middle of Florida, and Cape Coral—that were all decrepit and losing money. He was called in by the bankruptcy courts and asked if he could take over these six hotels.

Monahan said that I was the kind of guy who drove my motorcycle too fast and wanted to see the whole world in fifteen minutes. He liked that, so he hired me. He was my mentor, and that's how I started my career in the hotel-marketing business.

John Monahan opened up the world for me and Revé. He was educated and sophisticated. His wife, Peggy, was beautiful, and they knew everybody in town. Monahan loved Revé. One afternoon, John and Peggy's only daughter, Lizanne, slipped out and wandered off, the way little kids do. She was probably four or five at the time. The Monahans lived across the street from a golf course, and Lizanne somehow made her way over there. Revé found her in the service barn where all the tractors were. Lizanne had just been having a little look around. Revé took her by the hand and walked her back over to the house. It wasn't like she had been in any real danger or anything. But it was scary for Peggy. She had gotten hysterical. And Monahan always remembered that it was Revé who had brought Lizanne back.

Monahan was a widely traveled sophisticate, and he and Peggy introduced us to a lot of things. Revé was impressed once when Monahan had to make a phone call at a restaurant. Instead of going over to the pay phone, he just snapped his fingers and the maître d' brought a Princess phone to the table.

In those years, the midseventies, Monahan and I did a lot of traveling—London, Berlin, all across the States. Anywhere we could get business for our hotels. We'd go all over the place selling the hotels to travel agents and making on-site visits. And it was great. All the old GAC properties had their own airstrips, and Monahan had a DC-3 for his personal use. We arranged bus tours and airboat rides. We had stables and fishing boats at our disposal. Anything to keep the guests coming.

I worked for John Monahan for about two years, and when he left GAC, I quit, too, and took a job with the Bahamian Out Islands Promotion Board, whose job it was to promote tourism in all the little, remote islands beyond Freeport and Nassau that no one had ever even heard of. My career was on a fast track, and I knew I was going places. Everyone was saying it: John Walsh was a success story waiting to happen.

The best part of the job was the people I met. I got to be great friends, for instance, with a guy named Garfield McCartney, a six-foot-four Bahamian diver with huge, broad shoulders. Garfield was a religious guy who owned a little rickety dive boat and lived on Tarpon Bay. He loved diving as much as I did. He could free dive seventy feet, go down without a tank, holding his breath for seventy feet. I had never seen a human being who could do that. So Garfield taught me how to free dive and I taught him how to scuba. He and his friends, and basically everyone down there, were wonderful, gentle people. This was twenty years ago, around the time that the Bahamas won their independence. Everybody on the island knew who I was. I would bring clothes and things down there for them when I came, and they opened up their homes to me. I'd be invited to all the funerals and weddings.

These were the really early days of pleasure diving. Hardly anyone was doing it, and there were no pressure gauges to tell you how much air was left in your tank. As part of our promotion effort, I came up with the idea of the Island Picnic, a great way to make money off the tourists. Garfield and I would take people out to a deserted island and then head out with the dive boat and spearfish all afternoon, bringing back bushels of fish and lobster for a big cookout dinner on the beach. I was the one hotel executive who actually took clients over there and got them in the water and took them snorkeling. I would put them in the boat with Garfield, give them snorkel gear and then drag them around so they could watch us spearfishing.

I was just starting out in the hotel-marketing business, and I was damn good at it. At the time, there was no air service to Eleuthera, and I got two airlines to start flying in. I was having a great time, and I was making money for these people. Pretty soon the government started hearing about it, but it didn't make them happy. The big honchos were used to being treated like kings, but I was one guy who refused to pay homage. And that led to a huge confrontation with a particular official. He summoned me into his office, waved his finger in my face, and told me to get off his island and never come back.

I split for a few days, flew back in, and then just went about my business as usual.

What I loved more than anything in those days was the diving. Jeff O'Regan would come down and hook up with me and Garfield for dive trips. If you're a weekend diver from Detroit, you use the buddy system, where you go out together and hold hands. But old professionals like us weren't afraid of going out by ourselves. One day we were all out of the boat, each going his separate way. I was carrying a beautiful, brand-new dive knife, and an arbolette, a big, triple-banded spear from Australia. Also a Hawaiian sling, which is a steel spear that has a wooden barrel and a big sort of rubber band on it. I also had a couple of bang sticks, CO_2 cartridges with a .38 slug on the tip, which is what you use if a shark is harassing or bumping you.

It was already pretty late in the afternoon, and I already had a big bag of lobster and grouper. Then I saw one last huge rock grouper and decided I'd take him, too. I shot him with the spear, which didn't quite kill him, so I went over and stuck him the way you're supposed to, between the eyes in the brain. I was trying to figure out how to hang on to everything and haul this forty-five-pound fish out of the area without hanging around too long—which is not a good idea, because sharks can smell blood—when all of a sudden the grouper just swam off with my brand-new dive knife stuck in the middle of his forehead. I wanted that fish, and I wanted my dive knife. So I followed them both for probably half an hour, which was a little risky because I was wearing a forty-five-minute tank. I was dragging all my gear and the dead fish, and every time I got close to the grouper, he would skitter away. I finally caught up to him and wrestled my knife out and speared him a few more times.

Then I collected everything and headed up toward the surface, which is when I first saw the turbulence. I knew what that meant. A big storm had come up while I was underwater. That's how it is in the Bahamas; the sky can be a beautiful clear blue, and all of a sudden, out of nowhere, it's nothing but huge black thunderclouds. When I made it to the surface, there were three- and four-foot waves. And I knew I was a long way from the boat.

Just a few weeks before, I had been swept away in the Keys when I was out on a dive trip with O'Regan. I dove off the stern to try to help somebody who was floundering in the water. Somehow I got swept away in the current, and I was out in the shipping lanes until dusk. Just floating. I was ready to spend the night in the water. I figured no one would be able to find me in the dark. At one point, I waved my fin at a huge tanker going by, but I knew there was no way on earth they could see me. Finally, an old lobster fisherman on his way home came by in a little boat and stopped. As he was hauling me in, he kept saying, "What are you doing out here? You could get killed by sharks."

So I had been through this kind of thing before and knew I could make it. This time, like the last one, I knew I'd just have to hang on. I was about twelve miles from shore, out in the middle of the ocean on a sixty-foot deep reef.

Step one was realizing that I would have to drop everything—my beautiful tank, my mask, the lobsters, the grouper, everything. Down they went. Then I stuck the biggest lobster on the prong of my four-and-a-half-foot Hawaiian sling and held it up as high as I could out of the water in the middle of all those waves.

Things were not the best, and I swallowed some water. But I didn't panic. And then, after I don't know how long, somewhere in the distance I finally heard the faint buzz of an engine. Jeff and Garfield had gotten back into the boat and tied the steering wheel so that it traveled in ever-larger concentric circles. Then Jeff, who's six foot four, climbed up on the shoulders of Garfield, who is also six foot four.

That's how you find someone who's lost out in the middle of the ocean.

Later on, Jeff told me that Garfield was sure I was going to be dead. He kept telling Jeff, "He's drowned. We're never going to find him. It's a huge storm, and he's miles from the boat." But Jeff had his own theory. He told Garfield that I was too mean to drown. Jeff said that I was out there, and that they would find me. And they did.

Jeff was my closest friend, and we knew that no matter what kind of trouble we got ourselves into, we would survive. Because we were always so calm, even in the worst panic situation. We would never be anything less than all right because we were so unrelentingly ice-cold-blooded.

Whether you have a $50,000 wedding, or do it at a justice of the peace, or go for a six-week honeymoon in Europe the way Revé and I did, marriage is still basically a verbal agreement between two people who are already pretty set in their ways. You're adults, you have similar interests, and you're in love. But let's face it: you're still just cohabiting. There are all the grandiose notions about love, the poetry, and how wonderful it is. But until you have a child, it's not the real deal. I know lots of married people who don't have kids. They each have their hobbies. They go on vacations together. They go out to dinner together. They do or don't talk.

When Revé and I first got married, I thought we weren't ready for kids. We both agreed that we had a lot of things we wanted to do first. Travel. Find careers. We wanted to wait to make sure that we had the income and the discipline. And we wanted to know for sure that the marriage was going to work.

We had both come from big families that revered children, and we knew that having them was more than some kind of hobby. I never understood how people could have kids and then treat them so badly.

One day in a mall parking lot, Revé and I were walking back to the car and we saw a guy with his little boy, about five or six years old. The guy was screaming at the kid and waving his arms. And then, all of a sudden, the guy started slapping the little boy across the face. I ran over to this guy, and shoved him into a parked car. I was screaming at him. "Don't you know any better than to hit your son that way? You wanna hit somebody, you hit me. People like you shouldn't be allowed to have kids!"

Later on, I regretted it. But only because I had scared the little kid. He was going, "Please don't hit my daddy. Leave my daddy alone."

The guy had told me to mind own goddamn business. As if that were something I was really going to do.

Revé and I did finally decide that we had been married long enough to know that we were going to stick together, and that we both loved children and were maybe mature enough to have a child. I don't remember if we actually sat down and said, "Now's the time to do it." I think we were just doing it. A lot.

It was pretty great out there in the moonlight on all those deserted islands, with the ocean and no people around. I don't know where or when exactly, but somewhere along the line Revé told me she was pregnant.

Our lifestyle didn't change immediately. Except that for the first time, Revé started getting seasick.

Right around that time, she and I were down on a trip to the Islands. I had managed to finagle a brand-new dive boat for Garfield, and he and I were out to spear as many groupers as we could. There were also some tourists along, including this woman who couldn't swim and was absolutely petrified. I told her that if she was going to do one thing before she died, she had to go underwater and see a living coral reef.

So we got this woman into a life vest, and I put Revé in charge of her. "Just get her into the water," I said. "She'll be fine." Then Garfield and I strapped on our tanks and went off for the kill. Leaving Revé, pregnant, in the middle of nowhere on a snorkeling trip with a terrified woman who didn't know how to float, let alone breathe through a snorkel.

As Revé tells it, the woman nearly drowned the both of them. She was hanging on to Revé for dear life, wondering how she had ever been stupid enough to let a bunch of lunatics talk her into this.

The way I always looked at things was that if something was easy for me, then everyone else should be able to do it, too. A dive magazine once came down to do a story on Garfield and me, because we were night-diving and doing three-hundred-foot dives where you see gnarly-looking things like mutants that only live way down deep. And cave-diving, where you go into little holes that are so pitch-dark that you have to hold on to a rope to find your way back out. Just the thought of it made Revé claustrophobic.

But not too long after that snorkel trip, Jeff O'Regan and I did get Revé down on a dive. She had on the mask and the flippers and the regulator, double-hosed back then. We were killing fish right and left. Fish blood looks green underwater, so there was all this green stuff emanating from an ever-larger pile of dead fish. Revé was pregnant enough to be pretty buoyant by then, so she was on the sidelines, just sort of floating. Then Jeff and I decided to move farther out, and I motioned for Revé to protect the pile from any sharks while we were gone. She was motioning with her head, "No way. Forget it. I'm going up."

But I kept saying, "No, no, no." I backed her up against this coral reef and handed her one of my Hawaiian slings. Now, I figured, nothing could get her from behind. And she could just use the sling to poke at anything that attacked her from the front.

Jeff and I took off, and there was Revé. By herself. Out in the middle of the ocean, not a human being in sight. Remora fish—big fish with suction cups—were all over the place, and she knew why. They always show up when sharks are around.

As she remembers it, the remora fish were sucking on her mask. She couldn't see anything. Green fish guts were all over the place. She figured the sharks had heard the dinner bell. She was totally out of her league. And I was just expecting that she could handle all of it.

That was the last time Revé ever went diving. Six months pregnant and she finally put her foot down.

3

Adam

REVÉ WAS A BEAUTIFUL PREGNANT WOMAN. IF YOU LOOK at pictures of her from that time, you can see it. She became even prettier than she already was. She had gotten into bodybuilding, was very disciplined about it, and was into being healthy. When she was pregnant, she took extremely good care of herself.

Closer to her due date, she started having baby showers with her family and girlfriends. We didn't want to come home from the hospital and not have the changing table set up, so we spent a lot of time getting ready for the big event. The baby's room was going to be the front bedroom.

I was doing a lot of work in the Bahamas and still flying over there all the time. And we were getting some important publicity. Burt Reynolds was supposed to be coming over with a film crew because someone had told him about this crazy diving operation that Garfield and I had. It would have been a big, big break for the resort—me being filmed teaching Burt Reynolds how to snorkel. But it was too close to Revé's due date. I turned it down.

Then, finally, came the day we had waited for. Revé went into labor and we drove, pretty calmly as I recall, to North Shore Hospital in Miami Shores. Back in those days fathers weren't allowed into the delivery room. I tried, but they made me wait outside. And at 12:15 P.M., November 14, 1974, a nurse came out to tell me that our baby had been born.

I remember that day as a blur of happiness, all of us in the waiting room, going into the nursery and seeing him for the first time. He was the only grandchild on my entire side of the family. The first in a whole big family of Irish Catholics.

We named him Adam, after my father. Adam John Walsh. How could it have been anything other than one of the most joyous days of my life? It's a boy. I'm a father. Holy mackerel.

I had created a new member of the species and I would now have a legacy. My genes would be carried on along with the Walsh name. I hadn't thought I would care whether it was a boy or girl, but any male is lying who doesn't admit he's happy that his first-born is a son. The male ego. Any man wants to have a son he can play ball with, get all that out of the way so that he can go on to have a little daughter to pamper. Seeing your very own offspring in the tribe. A *human* thing. I was so proud.

To this day, I shout in the car when good things happen. People always think you're nuts if you talk to yourself, but I never thought it was strange in the least. I remember riding in the car and blasting the radio and yelling at the top of my lungs, "I'm a father!"

And of course Revé came through like a champ.

Revé always said that I was not the demonstrative type, because I never sent her a lot of gifts and flowers and things. But it was different on the day Adam was born. She hadn't taken a Lamaze class. I don't think there even were those classes back then. It was truly natural childbirth. Your wife just did it.

At the time, like all the local divers, I used to wear

wooden clogs. Revé says she remembers lying in her hospital bed and hearing the sound of the clop, clop, clop as I came walking down the hospital corridor to her room. The echo of those footsteps on the tile, hearing me coming. I was so ecstatic.

We couldn't afford luxuries back in those days, but on the nightstand by her bed were a dozen red carnations. And in the center of all those red flowers was a single one, white. That was what I sent her. The white one was for Adam.

The day that Adam was born was like no other day of my life. We were happy beyond words. I remember calling everybody up and screaming and yelling. I was delirious, elated beyond measure. As of that day, my life was perfect. Revé and I were fine. Work was going great. And now we had a little baby. A boy. I went to look at him in the nursery and he was the handsomest. Of all the other little babies, some were splotchy, others a little misshapen. Adam was the perfect little baby everyone was looking at.

It was a different kind of love. Something that we ourselves had created. Our own flesh and blood. It's not like the love you have for your wife or your brother and sisters or the mother and father who you know will die someday.

While Revé was in the hospital, I got the house all cleaned up. I couldn't wait for this new little glorious person to come home.

For all of the joy, though, there was also something terribly sad going on in our family. Not too long before Adam was born, my father had started to not feel very well, and he seemed to be getting weaker and weaker. Once on a visit to the family upstate, we were all playing football out in the front yard. Like the Kennedys—cousins, friends, the whole gang. My dad, who had always been such an athlete, went out for a pass. I was defending him and accidentally knocked him down. He was hurt, he crumpled up, and it turned out that he had broken two of his ribs. I felt terrible because I thought I caused it. What we didn't know was that my father was sick. The diagnosis was multiple myeloma. Bone cancer.

We thought we were going to lose him.

My dad's bones got so brittle they would snap at nothing. My mom and my youngest brother, Joe, would have to call the ambulance that took him over to the VA hospital in Syracuse. It was the best in central New York, but it was thirty miles away from the house in Auburn, and he would have to endure that painful ride. My mother seemed, I don't know . . . lost. And then there was Joe. Only fifteen years old, younger than all the rest of us. After Jimmy and Jane and I had all left home, it was Joe who stayed, feeding my dad, washing and carrying him to the bathroom when he couldn't do it for himself. Joe, more than anyone else, was brokenhearted.

The only thing I wanted was for my father to hang on long enough to see my first baby born. It was going to be a great testament to him, a real feather in his cap. He had always talked about how he couldn't wait to be a grandfather, because he was going to take the kid to ball games and spoil him. Neither my brothers nor my sister was married at the time, but Dad was happy that at least one of us had been smart enough to settle down and give him a grandchild.

When Adam was born, there was such joy. I talked Revé into letting me borrow him when he was still an infant so I could take him up to New York to show my dad. I was desperate to have my father see Adam before he died. He was hurting so bad. And when someone's got cancer, you never know. They could get pneumonia and be gone in two days. So Joe and I went up to the ward and asked one of the nurses if we could bring Adam in. She said, "Because of the possibility of wiping out a whole ward, because children are so prone to colds and viruses and babies are not immune to certain viruses, it's totally against the rules to bring a child in here."

So I figured that with Joe and Jimmy, we could get Adam up the fire escape.

It was frigging ten degrees out, but if one brother went ahead, checked the hallway to make sure the coast was clear, we could do it. Operation Walsh. My Dad had hung on long enough to see his first grandchild. The least we could do was sneak this little baby in and put him on my father's bed so that he could see him and hold him. Once the head nurse came in and saw what was going on, and she just turned around and walked back out. Never told a soul.

We have pictures of my dad with Adam when Adam was four months old. My father had been feeling up to it, so he came down with my mother to Florida for a visit. Adam was in his stroller, and we all went to Disney World and dragged my dad all over the place. He had a body brace on and was sickly. Things weren't getting any better, but he was still laughing a lot.

Later, when things got worse and my dad couldn't get out of bed, we went to Auburn for a visit. We put Adam's playpen in Dad's bedroom, so that Adam could pull himself up and stand, holding the rail. The little guy would take his head all the way back, stretch his neck, make a round circle with his mouth, and then finally let out a little "Oooh, oooh, *o-o-o-h* . . ." It made us all laugh so hard that he'd just do it more. My family gives nicknames to everybody, and because of that, Adam's was the Rooster.

Which became Rooster McCooster.

And then, finally, Cooter.

Which was his nickname until the day he died.

My father had always talked about how he was going to spoil his grandkids. The only thing was, he never got the chance to. In those days the hospitals didn't know how to administer morphine the way they do now. He went down to ninety pounds and was in terrible pain. But he never once asked, "Why me?" The nurses used to remark about what a champion he was. How in spite of everything, he never complained. He died at age fifty-four. Even on his deathbed, he had such class.

Afterward, my mother was devastated. The lovely, gentle man she had loved almost all of her life was now gone. It broke my heart to have her so far away, all the way up in New York. So Revé and I asked her to be nearer to us, to come down to Florida to live. Jimmy was then in California, and Jane was gone a lot. She had gotten a job as a singer with a well-known sax player, Stan Getz. But Joe and Jane moved down with my mom, into a little house in a town called Dania not far from us. Revé loved my mom. She said my mother had way too much class to ever say anything bad about anybody. She called her "the silent majority."

After Adam was born, my mom's nickname became Gram. Later on, when he started talking, he was the first one to call her Gram Crackers. We knew right away that this little grandson was going to save her.

By that point, we were living in a little three-bedroom house at 2801 McKinley Street in Hollywood, Florida, which was right next to Fort Lauderdale. Three bedrooms, two baths. Adam's room in front, the master bedroom in back. I did the yard. Revé decorated the house. We had wicker and bamboo furniture, lots of plants, and an antique writing desk in the living room. The house was on the corner, next to an elementary school, not far from the golf course and a ball field.

Adam was the big event in all of our lives. Jane was his godmother, Joe his big brother. Our little kid was the center of Planet Walsh in Florida Universe.

Of course it's a tremendous change in anyone's life, from getting up in the middle of the night to change diapers because your wife has been up all night breast-feeding, to putting in the extra hours at work because the bills have to be paid. But now you aren't just saving up for a motorcycle or a nice car. Now you have responsibilities.

Right from the start, Adam was really mellow. He had a gentle, calming presence. I know that he had a maturing effect on me. I had always dreamed of being a dad like my dad. And now I was responsible for this little baby. We watched him constantly. He couldn't make a move without us studying him. He slept with us, in our bed, because we couldn't seem to put him down in his bassinet.

Then he started to smile, and we really went crazy. All the experts in the world can tell you that it's gas. But you know why it's happening. It's because he loves you.

I always used to think that women smelled great. Nowhere near as great as the smell babies have.

Adam never had the terrible twos or the unruly threes. He was always spoken to respectfully, like a person with a brain and feelings. We took him to restaurants because he never threw a tantrum. People would always comment on what a well-behaved little kid he was. We didn't believe in keeping him locked up in the house until he turned seven and then suddenly exposing him to the world.

Once, during one of our sales trips to Eleuthera, everyone decided to bring their kids along. There was a flotilla of three big boats—two for adults, and all the kids on the third. But we wouldn't do that to Adam. He came on board with us, the only child on the big persons' boat. I went down for cocktails one evening and found him sitting on a stool at the bar, surrounded by people. All the grown-ups were sliding over to talk to him.

Buddhists believe that some people have what they call old souls, as if they have already been here on earth many times. Adam was like that.

He was a little old soul.

There were always people in and out of our house in those days, such as O'Regan, my brother Joe, and

Jimmy Campbell, a friend of Michael and Johnny Monahan who worked the sailboat rental concession at the Diplomat. Jimmy more than anyone spent a lot of time at our house.

If someone has a really beautiful dog, like an Afghan, and everyone else wants to take it for walks—that's how all our friends were about Adam. "Can I take him to the ball game?" "Can he come to the movies with me?" He was the first little kid in our crowd, and everybody was always asking to borrow him. Gram used to say that she would rather have a conversation with Adam than with any grown-up in the room. He was just a lot of fun to have along.

One day Michael Monahan was over visiting Revé around dinnertime. Adam knew that I was going to be home in a few minutes, so he started gearing up. He liked to dress up like monsters and cartoon characters, and that day he put on his little Batman cape. He listened for the sound of my car pulling into the driveway, and when he heard it, he ducked behind a door.

I came in, and as I got to the end of the hall, *boom*, Adam flew out and tackled me, grinding his little teeth and trying to be scary: *"Oooh! Oooh! I'm the evil monster!"*

I was trying so hard to act scared—"Coots! Coots! Oh, no! Don't hurt me!"—and not to bust out laughing. But I guess it was pretty obvious that I had just had one of those grueling days at work. Because all of a sudden, Adam stopped cold, looked up at me, and in the most serious, adult, concerned-sounding way said, "Oh, Daddy, what's the matter? Did you have a hard day at work?"

Michael Monahan said that you could always tell when I was *really* laughing by the way my eyes would crinkle up. And that's the way he remembers me laughing that day.

Even when he was tiny, Adam had sharp clothes. On the playground all the other kids looked kind of scruffy compared to him. No matter how small he was, he always had a sport coat and dress shirts. He looked like the miniature version of an older prep-school kid. He wore, not sneakers, but Top-Siders. And small Izod shirts instead of regular tee's. His favorite hat was a captain's hat that I had bought him, an expensive one with black braid and a visor.

All in all, he was a mature, grown-up little guy. But in a lot of ways, he was also a typical little boy. He loved to do little-kid things. Revé tried to follow Dr. Spock about how kids should sleep in their own beds to get used to the routine of it. But Adam just went around to my side of the bed because he knew his dad would always sneak him in.

We had pets—a white rabbit named Hocus Pocus, because of all the magic shows that Adam staged. And a gray tiger cat named Tigger that he talked us into keeping after we came home one day and found the stray kitten in the yard. Adam loved to draw spiders and monsters and ghosts—things that were scary, but not too scary. Creepy-crawly things. His favorite hand puppet was a spider with long, hairy legs, whose name, of course, became Harry Spider. That was the one toy that didn't get covered with finger paints.

But the biggest thing of all was *Star Wars*. He had a Chewbacca doll and sandstorm trooper vehicles and he loved Princess Leia. He had every *Star Wars* toy ever made. But other than those, we never really bought Adam many plastic toys. Revé had a special name for stuff like that: landfill.

We always read to Adam from the time he was little, although lately he was beginning to want to read to us. And he loved to draw—not scribblings and gibberish, but big crayon drawings that were only a little bit scary. Whether these creatures were ghosts or were-wolves or sharks, they all seemed to have one thing in common: big, dangerous teeth and nails. That was something he and I cooked up ourselves.

With me in the house, of course, there were always

pranks and foolishness going on. Halloween was a huge deal at our house. We prided ourselves in doing costumes big time. But never store-bought ones. Only homemade. One year, when he was really little, Adam was Mickey Mouse. Next, he wanted to be a mummy. And the year after that, a skeleton.

That was the costume that Revé remembers best. She put Adam into a black leotard and laid him down on the living room floor and started painting little skeleton bones freehand. She wasn't using a picture as a guide. Just, "Let's see now. The foot bone's connected to the anklebone . . ." She fudged it a little and got engrossed in the painting. Finally, by the time she was done, Adam had fallen sound asleep, right on the floor, with all those little skeleton bones painted on his black leotard. Softly, she woke him. "Adam, Mommy's done. It's time to trick or treat. Open your eyes."

He did, and Revé says she'll never forget the look on his face. He peered down past his chin, seeing what she had done, and his eyes got as wide as saucers. "That's so cool, Mommy. That's just so cool . . ."

And there was the year he was the werewolf, a great one, like Lon Chaney, who always wore a banged-up suit that was a little too tight and had too-short sleeves. Revé took a little khaki-colored polyester suit of Adam's and put it in hot Rit dye—black—just long enough to shrink it and turn it all streaky and awful-looking. My brother Joe bought a miniature werewolf costume mask that covered Adam's whole head. Then we cut up a Halloween wig and glued the hair from it onto the backs of Adam's hands and the tops of his feet. He wore flip-flops to show them off.

But that wasn't the reason that Adam took first place in the costume contest at school that year. It was because when he lined up in the schoolyard with all the other kids, he never once broke character. He just struck a pose and held it. All hunched over and growly.

An elementary school was next door to our house, but instead of sending him to it, we enrolled him at St. Mark's, a private Lutheran school about a half mile away. His birthday was in November, so he was one of the youngest in his class, but he had done well in first grade and was looking forward to second. One of his teachers was Sue Hofman, whose son, Clifford, was one of Adam's best friends. The two of them played T-ball and, later, Little League together.

In fact, probably the only thing that Adam liked more than baseball was the water. He had a wet suit, a surfboard, and even a dive knife, just like mine. When I was at work, Revé used to take him to the beach every day at the Diplomat. I wasn't working there anymore by that time, but everyone else was: John Monahan and Billy Maidment and Jimmy Campbell. They were all pool attendants or cabana managers. Adam was learning how to surf, so he and Revé would go from one pool to another, visiting everybody on their rounds.

We have pictures of Adam in a diaper at about two years old, down in the Bahamas with me and Garfield, on the docks with lobsters everywhere. And another of him around six, in his mask and snorkel, smiling. Holding his dive knife in one hand, and—by the antennae—a big lobster in the other. He was still little, but he was already learning about diving. How to poke at things with a knife instead of your finger so that nothing can sting you.

Once we had him, we couldn't imagine what things had been like before. It was as if everybody had been waiting for him to come along. It wasn't that we were overly protective or that we smothered him. It was just that I don't remember him ever being "in the way." If he wanted to go to the playground or for a ride or an ice cream, that's what we did.

It was as if we were all kind of following him around.

I think the hardest thing for me at the time was the

traveling, having to leave Adam to go on business trips. In 1976 I left my job with the Bahamian Out Islands Promotion Board and started a company called Diversified Marketing, in partnership with a guy named Warren Binder. Binder was trying to develop a little regional car company by the name of Alamo, and I was working to help market it. At the time, Delta Airlines was hooked up with Hertz, and we managed to move in on them, placing Alamo instead. It was an intense time, and Binder was a complete workaholic. I was pulling down seventy-hour weeks, under a lot of pressure, and it was beginning to take a toll.

I had to travel a lot and work late hours, and I hated being away from Adam. One night he said to me, "Dad, what can I do so you don't have to work so hard?" It was tough on him and tough on my marriage. Probably a lot tougher than I realized at the time. It wasn't so much that there was tension between Revé and me. It was more that, after being married for ten years, things between us were just kind of going along.

The brightest spot in my life was our little boy. I would read to him as soon as I got home from work and tell stories. That's how Bobby and Sparky came to be. Bobby, with his trusty dog, Sparky, was a little kid about Adam's age, a brave little boy who did the right thing. I always made Bobby just a little bit older than Adam, so that he would have someone to look up to, someone who could face challenges. Not weird, dangerous ones that would terrorize him before he went to sleep. Just kind of exciting ones. If a grandma in the park was being harassed, or a timber wolf was trying to scare them in the woods, Bobby and his little dog would always face the challenge and stay calm and do the right thing.

That was the lesson. That no matter what happens, use your brain because it's your best tool. Conserve your energy, use your strength, and do the right thing.

Don't start screaming and running around, hysterical. Because the biggest thing was that, no matter how scary or weird things got for Bobby and Sparky, their dad would show up just in time to rescue them.

No matter what happened, Dad would always be there to save them in the night.

Adam was cautious by nature, not one of those loud, gregarious kids. He was never deer-in-the-headlights scared, just cautious. Reserved, even timid. But also very sure of himself when he had something on his mind.

I had almost been killed so many times from one thing or another. Crashed a couple of times on my motorcycle, got swept away in the ocean, and mugged. I had probably had forty broken bones and all kinds of stitches in the emergency room. But each and every time, I had gotten fixed up.

I knew the rough side of life, but I thought I was immortal. I figured I'd die in a rocking chair when I was eighty-five years old. That's probably not the healthiest way to live. But I loved dangerous sports, and I felt protected. Call it youthful invulnerability or whatever. I truly believed that I could not be killed.

But that was just for myself.

With Adam, things were different. When he was born, everything changed. I had a new fear, and it was now my greatest one. It was that something might somehow happen to him. I was completely unprepared for that feeling. I had always felt as if nothing could touch me. And now I knew that it could.

I always worried about him. Later on, someone said that he had been sheltered. What's that supposed to mean? He was six years old. We took him to school and picked him up every day. He wasn't allowed to go to the park by himself, or to ride his bike in the street. We didn't even let him cross by himself—we always held his hand. And we taught him landmarks—the golf course, the grocery store—so that if he ever got lost, he could find his way home.

He loved the water. He was always a water bug. But there were a lot of drainage canals in our neighborhood, and I worried about him falling into one. So I spent hours drown-proofing him in the pool. I would dunk him in the water and then bring him up, sputtering. I taught him how to hold his breath, starting when he was just an infant, nine or ten months old.

I had seen some strange things in my life, some violence when I was working as a cabana boy. There will always be people on the fringes of society who try to exploit other people. One good friend of ours knew a guy who had adopted several kids, boys, and used to show them porno films. It was creepy and weird, and without ever being extremely conscious of it at the time, I think we were always trying to protect Adam.

We lived across the street from a playground, but he never went over there alone. Either Revé would take him or I would, after work. Revé drove him to school every day. He wanted to walk, but he wasn't allowed to. Other people might let their kids run wild, but Adam wasn't like that. Revé and I had waited and waited to have him.

He was only a little kid. He was our only child.

It's not that Adam stayed locked up in the house or anything. He had his friends, like Jeremy, who lived just a few doors down. Adam couldn't really pronounce his name. It would come out "Germy." Revé would say, "No, Adam, *germy* means yucky stuff. It's Je-re-my." And Adam would say, "I know, Mom. That's what I'm saying. *Ger-my.*"

He started out playing T-ball, and then the following year, Little League. It's funny. My dad had always loved baseball so much, and all his sons went into other sports like soccer, golf, and football. When he was very sick, I remember him saying, "The only regret that I have is that I didn't get a baseball player out of the three of you." It always got to me that out of the whole family, Adam was the one who turned out to be the baseball player. It was just that my dad didn't live long enough to see it.

I think the best thing of all was traveling with Adam. Even when he was a baby, every now and then I would pack up all his gear and take him on business trips. People used to freak out that I had a little kid in my hotel room with me at night. It wasn't really the kind of thing that working fathers did in those days. But when I look back on things, it's one of the things that I'm most glad I did.

I had been a million places and done a million things. And it seemed that with Adam I was going to teach him everything. He was like a little sponge. I had spent hours as a beach boy swimming out on a little Sunfish with no sail. I would bring home big horse conch shells and sand dollars that I'd bleach. I couldn't wait for Adam to learn how to snorkel. I would tell him what all the plants and fish were that washed up on the beach.

When he was still really little, I took him down to the Bluff House, a beautiful thirty-six-room resort in the Bahamas owned by Les Davies, who became a good friend of ours. The Bluff House was all by itself on a small offshore island that I was marketing and sat right on top of the seventh-largest barrier reef in the world. The water was crystal clear and beautiful, and that's where Adam first learned to snorkel. I would put a mask on him, float him in the water, and lean down in his ear. "That's a sea urchin right there," I would say. "And this is a four-eyed butterfly fish. Here's a royal gurami. And that over there is a tiny moray eel."

I always say that the ocean is the best psychiatrist. No matter what's bothering you, if you go down and really study it, it will reveal to you the whole spectrum of life. It will put things in perspective and help you sort things out. Adam and I used to walk on the beach for hours, looking for lucky sea beans that come up from Brazil. During storms they make a long, incredible journey through the Gulf Stream into the waters of the north. And when you find them, you polish them and they're supposed to bring good luck.

As a cabana boy I would scour the beach really early in the morning, and again at sunset. That's when you can find the best things. I had a huge collection of shells that I had found during dives, mostly underwater on coral reefs. Some I found in Eleuthera a hundred feet down. Helmet shells and trumpet tritons, like the ones they blow in Polynesia—five that I found in one year alone.

One of my greatest joys in life was to walk with Adam along the beach and teach him all of it. Anything you showed him, he could learn. He would ask incredibly intricate marine-biology questions. Very scientific. Even at two and a half, he was learning about the ocean. That's how old he was when he pointed to a beautiful belt buckle that Les Davies was wearing and said, "Dolphin." Then shook his head, made a *tsk-tsk* sound like, "How could I have been so stupid?" and said, "I mean *porpoise.*"

When Adam was a little older, Jeff and I took him diving with us. Revé would say, "Oh, my God, you're out there spearing everything in sight and you're going to take him with you?"

I said, "We're not going to spear anything. We're going to take him over by a rock and maybe show him a nurse shark. Pull a little one out by the tail." I couldn't wait until he was old enough to use a tank, which you can do when you're about eight or nine years old. Until then, we would snorkel. I always held his hand in the beginning. And then he started to learn to swim by himself. We would be out there in a boat with a beautiful sunset and the water. Jeff loved Adam and was always so gentle with him. He was a big, tough, patient guy.

We'd be sitting around having dinner or a drink, and other people would come by with the kids screaming and yelling. Adam would sit there, wait until people had finished talking, and then ask whatever it was that he wanted to know. This is not an exaggeration: he would go into a restaurant and order escargot for an appetizer.

During a trip to the islands in the spring of 1981, we spent the afternoon on the beach, and Adam made friends with a little Bahamian boy. The little boy, like everybody on the island, didn't have much in the way of material things. He had come by, trying to make a little money selling trinkets to the tourists. Then he spotted Adam with all his trucks and toys, and the two of them started playing together.

I wasn't really paying much attention until later, when the little boy started heading for home. As he was leaving, I saw that he was hauling away all of Adam's toys. That didn't faze Adam at all. "I had to give him my things, Dad," he said. "He doesn't have any toys."

By that time, I had left Warren Binder and had taken a partnership position with the Hotel Management Associates, a Houston-based company that managed the Houston Grand. Then I was approached by a group of investors who were developing a new project on Paradise Island in the Bahamas called the Paradise Grand. It was going to be a $26-million resort hotel, and I eventually became its vice president and director of marketing. I had a beautiful office in the Harbor House right on the Intracoastal Waterway in Bal Harbour, which was our base of operations in Florida. My brother Joe was working for me, and John Monahan, who was a consultant to the project, had his office just across the hall.

I would take Adam to work with me, and I set up a little desk for him in my office so that he could come in and pretend. He had a list of things to do for the day and would buzz me from his desk. Whenever he called me from home, he would ask my secretary for "Mr. John Walsh."

Not "Daddy." And she would play along.

The new job meant that I was no longer working seven-day weeks, fifty-two weeks a year. I was spending a lot more time at home, and it was making a difference in the way things were with Revé. I didn't want to be like those couples who've been married forty-eight years, only it's really twenty-four because the guy wasn't home for half of it. I was feeling as if we were all a family together. For maybe the first time in my life, I was beginning to feel a little bit peaceful, as if things were really working out. Revé and I celebrated our tenth wedding anniversary on July 10, 1981.

I gave her an antique diamond ring, and we decided it was time to make a brother or sister for Adam.

About a week or so later, Les Davies came by the house to drop off some tour operator packages that I was going to submit. I was home from work, sick as a dog, and hadn't shaved in days. I looked like Serpico when I came to the door. But I invited Les in and we started talking. I told him about how the week before Monahan had set it up for Revé and me to go to St. John's Island, a really nice resort on the Florida coast. It was Monahan's tenth-anniversary present to us, and we took Adam along. We had pretty much decided to wait until he was all set in school before having another baby.

And now we were so happy that we had decided we weren't going to wait anymore.

We have home movies of one of the trips that we took to the Bahamas with Adam. I don't remember which. Of him with all his coloring books there in the Out Islands. Garfield and all my friends down there loved him, this little blond boy. He was so different from what they knew. I don't know how many islands we went to on that trip. Six or seven, maybe. We flew on little puddle jumpers.

One afternoon we were all out on a gorgeous

sailboat together. We had been diving all day, and the sun was starting to set. I still have a vivid memory of being at the ship's wheel that day.

Sitting with my little boy in my lap.

Steering that big, beautiful boat on a calm, lulling sea.

WHEN I GOT UP AROUND SEVEN O'CLOCK ON THE MORNing of Monday, July 27, 1981, Adam was still sleeping. Jimmy Campbell had taken him out to a movie the night before, and I was angry that Jimmy had kept him out so late, even if it was summer vacation. I had kissed Adam good-night and put him to bed. If it hadn't been so late, I would have read him a story.

Just a few days before, he had spent the night at Clifford Hofman's house, his first official sleep-over away from home. Gram said that he was just getting to the age where he was curious about what I was like as a little boy: what I did, how I acted, and where I went.

That morning over breakfast I skimmed the paper. Bill Casey, the CIA director, was trying to keep from getting fired. An eighty-year-old Dade County woman had been found slashed to death. There was a science story on how surgery was being performed on babies before they were born. Medflies were threatening to take over California. And England was getting ready

ʀ the wedding that week of Prince Charles and Lady
Di. The weather was typical Florida in July.

Highs in the nineties. Maybe rain. A scorcher.

Adam would always cry whenever I was leaving on
a trip without him. But that wasn't going to happen
today. Tonight I would be home with him, maybe too
late for dinner, but in plenty of time to play with him
before bed. Without waking him, I gave him a kiss
good-bye.

A couple of hours after I left, Jimmy Campbell
stopped by for a cup of coffee. I appreciated the way
he spent so much time with Adam and helped out
around the house when I was gone. But lately things
had been getting on my nerves. I told Revé that I
wanted my privacy, needed more one-on-one time
with just my family. It was time for Jimmy to stop
hanging around our place so much. Time for him to
start getting on with his life.

Revé had cleaned out the room that Jimmy slept in
when he stayed over and put some of Adam's things
in it instead. Later, Jimmy said that the last thing he
remembered about leaving the house that morning
was the sight of Adam lying on the couch, being
cuddled by his mother.

Revé had turned thirty just three days before and
was planning on getting her driver's license renewed.
But she would have to do another errand first. For the
past month or so we had been talking about getting a
pair of brass barrel lamps for the living room and had
just seen an ad saying they were on sale at Sears. I was
bugging her to run over and get them, and when I
called the house at around ten o'clock that morning,
she said she would do it, but it meant that she was
going to be rushed. She was planning on taking a
check for Adam's tuition over to St. Mark's, then
dropping him off at Gram's before she made her one-
o'clock workout appointment at the gym.

While she made the beds and was cleaning up after
breakfast, Adam sat in the den with an orange Popsi-

cle, watching *Sesame Street*. She gave him his clothes
for the day—green running shorts and a short-sleeved
Izod shirt. He put them on, and then his favorite hat,
one that I had picked out and given him. It was an off-
white captain's hat that was still way too big for him.
He loved to wear it pulled all the way down over his
ears.

When they left the house a little after eleven, Revé
noticed that instead of wearing the shoes she had told
him to—his sneakers—Adam had slipped on the
yellow flip-flops that we called his "slaps."

Since I wasn't actually there, it's probably best that
Revé and Gram tell about what happened next. This
is what Revé remembers:

*The first thing we did was to swing by St. Mark's. I
took Adam with me into the school office where a lady
was sitting at the desk, talking on the phone. It didn't
look like she was going to be hanging up anytime soon,
so after a few minutes of waiting, I laid the tuition
check on her desk, turned around, and left.*

*After that, we drove over to the mall, which was
about a mile away. I parked where I always did, on the
north side near the receiving dock. I held Adam's hand,
as usual, while we walked across the parking lot to the
entrance. We went into the store the same as always,
past Receiving and the catalog desk on the left. That
put us in the middle of the toy department. Beyond it,
way over on the right, was the garden section, where all
the pesticides and poisons were kept on the shelves. It
always made me mad that they would keep those
chemicals right next to the toys. "Great," I said to
myself whenever I passed it.*

*Right in the middle of the toy department was the
big attraction: a television monitor displaying computer video games. Still a big novelty factor. They were
brand-new back then.*

*I don't remember what the game was. Maybe Star
Wars or Pong. All I remember is that I was in a hurry,*

and the lamp department was on the other side of toys, just around the corner at the end of the aisle to the left. From the video game to the main counter in the lamp department was about seventy-five feet. Out of the line of sight. But not very far.

It was summer vacation and kids used to go back and forth between the mall and the park next door. Some of them were standing at the game, playing with the joystick, and Adam asked if he could stay and play, too.

That was our ritual: Going in the north door, by Receiving. And Adam begging me to let him play the video game.

I pointed to where I was going to be. "Okay. I'm going to the lamp department for a minute. Right over there. You stay here and I'll be right over there." I don't think I specifically said, "Don't go anywhere," because I never had to. Adam didn't wander off. He didn't go anywhere. He just wanted to stay with the other kids and play that damned game.

When I got back, we would go get him an ice cream.

"I'm going to be right over there. In the lamp department, Adam."

And he said, "Okay, Mommy. I know where that is."

I went into Lamps and asked a saleslady if she could get the brass barrel ones for me because I couldn't find them anywhere on the floor. Then I waited while she went into the back. There may have been one other woman in the department, but I didn't speak to her. Finally the saleslady came back out and told me they didn't have the lamps in stock. They would have to be ordered, but I didn't have time. I left my name and asked to have someone call me when the lamps came in. That was it. I was going to pick up Adam at the video game and swing back out the way we had come in.

I was gone a few minutes. Five. Maybe ten altogether.

But when I came around the corner, I didn't see Adam.

At first, I thought that maybe he had walked over to one of the other aisles. I called out his name, but he didn't answer. And then I started getting a strange feeling. Something odd. Almost eerie. It wasn't just that I didn't see Adam. It was that it seemed as if everyone had suddenly gone away. Just a minute ago there had been a bunch of kids around, jostling. Now even the video game wasn't making any noise. Everything seemed so suddenly silent. The first thought in my head was, "Hey, where did everybody go?"

I went up and down the aisles. It wasn't a big department, but I couldn't find Adam. And then I noticed a little boy with dark hair, wearing a captain's hat. A less expensive-looking, knock-off version of the one that Adam had on.

I went up to him and said, "Did you see a little boy wearing a hat like yours?"

He nodded, and I thought to myself, "Whew. Okay."

"So where is he?"

But the little boy didn't say anything. He just pointed to the door. Not the north door that we always went in and out of, but the west door over on the far side of Toys. It was then that I realized that he must be Spanish. Or at least that he didn't understand English very well.

Because it was ridiculous to think that Adam would have gone out the west door. We never did that. I even didn't bother to ask the little boy anything else—where Adam was, or why everyone had gone. There was no reason to. This little kid was probably just trying to be polite to a grown-up. I just assumed that he didn't understand what I'd said.

I went back into Toys and found a clerk. "Have you seen my son? He was here just a minute ago." She said that she hadn't.

So I started asking people, anyone I could find. But

they all said the same thing. "Oh, well, he probably just wandered off."

"I'll bet he went looking for you."

"He could be in the mall."

"He might be there."

"Have you tried over that way?"

I kept saying, "You don't understand. My son is a little boy who does not wander off."

And all the while, a horrible, cold fear was building. I knew something was wrong. Really wrong. I was absolutely convinced of it.

But no one seemed to understand or believe me.

"Oh, well, you know how kids are. Maybe he wandered off with the rest of the kids. He's gotta be around here someplace."

I kept saying, "No. My son would not do that. You don't understand. Something is wrong here but I'm not exactly sure what."

Cash registers kept ringing up sales. Clerks kept waiting on people as if nothing had happened. I was trying to think of the words to make them see that something was really out of whack. That something was going on that just wasn't right. I couldn't just go up to the counter and say, "I have a missing child," because in those days there was no such thing.

No one paid any attention to me. They were acting like I didn't exist. Invisible. Just some woman who had lost track of her kid. But he would come wandering back and it would all be okay. She just didn't know what she was talking about.

But it wasn't okay. That much I knew.

Finally they told me I could go to the service office and have him paged, but I couldn't do that because it would mean leaving this spot. If I went to customer service, he might come back and not see me. I had to stay right here in case he came back.

He was just a little boy.

The only thing they kept saying was, "I'm sorry."

I don't know if fifteen minutes went by or fifteen seconds, but nobody found him. I was standing in the middle of the store by myself, trying to figure out what to do. Sweeping the place with my eyes, every corner.

Then, as I was looking out past the garden shop, I saw, of all people, Gram. Thank God. Oh, thank God. Adam's with Gram.

I ran out to the sidewalk. "Gram, have you seen Adam?"

She looked surprised. "No . . . no . . . Isn't he with you?"

"Gram, I can't find him anywhere. He was right here with me and now I can't find him."

We started going through the whole mall. All the stores. I ran up and down, into every shop. Every place, as fast as I could. All of a sudden, though, I stopped.

"He would never come out here all by himself," I thought. "He's not out here in this mall. And I know it."

I could feel the panic growing, and I was fighting it. I had to stay in control. No one was listening to me, and no one was doing anything, but Adam was gone and I couldn't find him. I kept telling myself, "Don't get hysterical, because you've got to stay calm. Nobody else is doing anything, so it's all up to you. Screaming is only going to make them go, 'Oh boy. She's nuts.'"

"Take it easy, lady. He just wandered off."

"Now, hon, don't worry. Kids always come back."

I'm sure they meant well. Of course they didn't know. But after a while I started hearing the things they were saying under their breath. "Well, there was a guy who used to work in the auto department. Come to think of it, he was kind of strange . . ."

I was wearing a leotard, gym shorts, sneakers, and socks. Obviously the wrong thing to have been wearing that day. Too revealing. Not demure. I should have been wearing something conservative, a nice dress. Something that, had I worn it, might have made them listen. Something more appropriate for the day when you go to the mall and all of a sudden your little boy isn't there anymore.

Then I realized that at the bottom of my purse was my wallet, and in it a picture of Adam from his first-grade class. Wearing the same shirt that he had on that day—a short-sleeved Izod with red and white stripes. Oh, my God, the picture.

"Here. Here. This is his picture. He's got on the same shirt. See?"

A typical school picture. It didn't even look like him. But it had the shirt—red and white stripes with tiny bands of kelly green. "There. Take a look. Someone must have seen him."

"Sorry."

"Haven't seen him."

"Nope, not here."

A half hour had gone by, maybe more, I don't know. Finally I got somebody to go over and page him on the intercom. I made the request and ran back into the store to listen. An announcement that would say, "Wait, everybody. Stand still for a minute. Just stop what you're doing and look around. There's a little boy who's lost in the store. His name is Adam. He's six years old and three and a half feet tall. He weighs forty-five pounds and he's wearing a captain's hat. A nice one, not a cheap knock-off version. He's probably standing right next to you. Adam, come back to the toy department. Your mom's there, and she's looking for you. She's worried. But you don't need to be scared."

Instead, a blaring voice, full of static, boomed out over the intercom: "Adam Walsh, please come to customer service."

Come to customer service? How was he supposed to know where that was, or how to get there?

That was how much they were prepared for what was happening. That was how much immediate concern they were showing that my little boy was suddenly gone *and I knew that something was terribly wrong here. That was their response. That was the help they gave to me over their loudspeaker.*

I went back to the toy department and I looked everywhere. Through all the aisles again. There weren't very many people around. There were hardly any. He wasn't lost in a crowd. There weren't all kinds of mothers with shopping carts and mobs of people. There was just maybe one person here or there. I went up to anyone I saw. "I'm looking for my little boy. You must have seen him."

"Sorry."

So I went to Receiving, to the clerk with the intercom, and told them to page him again. Do it again, and do it the right way this time. I was not hysterical, but I was not going to put up with this. Twenty minutes after the first page, there was a second: "Adam Walsh, please meet your mother in the toy department."

Nothing.

How long, exactly, do you keep standing there like an idiot, saying, "My son's missing. He's not here . . ." Gram and I had been looking for almost two hours. By now, the whole store was aware. I was crying. I couldn't help it. I was so scared. We had looked everywhere, in the store and the mall. I had run out to the parking lot and checked the car, twice. I had asked everyone in sight if they had seen my little boy. I had had him paged over the loudspeaker and he hadn't come back. By now it was pretty obvious that we needed some help.

Finally, I don't know who—but someone—called the police.

The Hollywood Police Department (HPD) was right across the street from the mall. Just across Hollywood Boulevard, no more than a few hundred yards away. We could see it from where we were standing in the parking lot.

The whole police force didn't come. There were no sirens. A couple of squad cars slowly pulled in. The policemen asked a few questions about Adam and said they would run a "BOLO" on him. They told me it meant "be on the lookout for."

Be on the lookout for a little boy who is lost.

I heard that, but it was almost as if I had cotton in my ears. Things were distorted. I couldn't hear what people were saying to me. The wheels were turning so fast in my head. There was nothing going on anywhere around me. Everything was happening inside my brain. The cops were standing there with their hands on their hips. Crackling noises coming over their radios. Them shaking their heads. Trying to think what to do. Trying, above all, not to make eye contact with me. It seemed like they were trying to get out of doing anything. There was apparently nothing in the book, no page in the manual, for what to do in this emergency. What to do if a little boy went missing.

I kept saying, "Well, what do you do in a case like this?"

They said, "Well, we only handle runaways."

"But he isn't a runaway."

"Well, maybe he ran away."

What they wanted was to pacify me. Everyone just wanted me to go away. Maybe they all had plenty of kids who had been separated from their parents and it had always turned out fine. I don't know. All I knew was that this was not turning out fine.

They kept saying, "Maybe he walked home."

I said, "He doesn't know how to walk home from here. I am his mother and we live more than a mile away. Believe me, my son would not walk home from here."

Every now and then if some cops were driving by, they would pull in, check things out, and then go off on their routes again. They had put the word out over their radios. They were looking, supposedly, while they were driving around.

I called Clifford Hofman's house to see if Adam was there.

But he wasn't. And I knew that.

It felt like no one was doing anything. There was no game plan. So I went outside and looked in the Dumpsters. I walked all around the outside of the mall and looked in every car in the parking lot. Then I spotted a man who was loading things into a camper, bags of groceries, camping supplies. I started screaming that he must have taken my son. But it turned out that he was just some guy going on a camping trip.

By that point I was grasping at straws. I would try any suggestion at all now. Anything. Because by now everything was already so far from reality that nothing made sense. It was like a bad dream, one where you can't get there from here. It was like drowning in a pool and not being able to reach the ledge. I was trying to reach my child, but he couldn't hear me. I felt so helpless. My body was trying to process everything, to hang on, but it was like the life was being sucked right out of me.

I kept thinking that everything around me was moving so fast. The air and the traffic and the people walking. If I could just get everything to slow down for a minute, then I could get my bearings and catch hold of everything. And then I could reach out and pull Adam back.

It was like one of those horror movies where, out of the blackness, distorted, laughing faces come bubbling up. Everything was spinning and I wanted it to stop— for just a second. Until I could figure it out.

But it never quite stopped long enough. The clock refused to stop ticking, and I needed it to. For just a second. Because if I could catch what was being said just one more time, then I might be able, finally, to comprehend it.

Except that no matter what I did, I couldn't seem to stop time.

The voices kept coming at me.

"Oh, he hasn't shown up yet?"

"You haven't found your kid?"

"Hey, lady, you mean he's still not here?"

People tried to help, at least for a moment on their way out the door. People who had come in earlier, spent an hour or two, finished their shopping, and were heading for home. It began to dawn on me that time was passing. That people were leaving, but that I was still here. So my mind just began to turn all of the voices around. Now, on their way out the door, they were saying:

"Oh, I see that you've finally gotten your son back."

"Hey, that's great that you found him."

"Gee, lady, it's nice to see you with your little boy."

I don't remember exactly when it was that John got there. I think it must have been about three o'clock. I don't know if I finally called him or if someone else did. What I do remember was that at some point a girl came up to me in the store. She wasn't wearing a uniform, but she seemed to be a security guard. She was young, maybe seventeen, and she was upset. "Gee, Mrs. Walsh, I just don't know if that was your son or not. I don't know if he was one of the ones I put out of the store." It was as if she was trying to apologize for something.

I had no idea what she was talking about.

Gram says that she was the one who called me at the office, but the way I remember it is that Revé called me from a pay phone. People remember things in different ways. This is what my mother says about that day:

I had been out, and it was a boiling-hot day. I stopped at the Hollywood mall, which they called the Sears mall because that was its anchor store. It had a big Publix grocery store, too, where I ordinarily shopped. I had pulled into the mall parking lot, back behind Sears. And for some reason, I sat in my car for a few minutes before getting out. I don't remember exactly what I was doing. I think I had the paper with me and spent a few minutes glancing at it before I got out of the car.

Then I opened the car door and walked into the back door of Sears. Right in back, where the garden shop is. I had just walked into the store a few feet when I saw Revé. She was further inside, with her back to me. And then she turned around. She had been crying, and she was in such a state. Her words to me were, "Oh, I can't find Adam, Gram. I can't find Adam."

So I said, "Well, let's start looking. Tell me what happened."

She told me that they had been over at Adam's school, and that then they had come over to the mall. She had been looking at lamps, right down the aisle. Right where you could have come around the corner and seen him. Instead of making him come with her, she had let him stay right there at the video games.

And then she couldn't find him.

She and I started down the two sides of the stores in the center of the mall. She went into every store on one side, and I went into every one on the other. At any store that had an intercom, I asked if they would announce that we were looking for a little boy, Adam by name, and what he was wearing. And if Adam was in the store, would he please come up to the counter.

I can remember going into the Publix grocery store and asking them to announce it over the intercom and nobody would. They just said, "Nope, haven't seen him. No little boy alone in that shirt and those pants."

Adam was not a little boy who would run away. We knew him too well. We knew what to expect from him. We knew his behavior and what he had been taught. He would not have wandered away in the first place. We had never had the experience of him doing any such thing.

It was serious. You knew right away, from the first minute. You just knew. There was that heavy, terrible kind of fear. Like the kind when someone is dying, and you just know that things are bad.

The mall wasn't large. It was a self-contained area. You could see from one end of the mall to the other. Hear all the intercoms. Count all the stores. So after a while, everyone knew. When people started hearing Adam's name over and over, they began to get concerned.

"Have you seen this little boy, Adam Walsh?"

He had to be right around somewhere because he couldn't possibly be anywhere else. It was noon, the middle of the day. There were big parking lots on both sides of the mall, people walking around, a bus stop out front with some wooden benches.

And nobody saw anything, which was so hard to believe. He wasn't on the sidewalks. No one had seen him. It was like he had evaporated into the air. Bad news. A bad feeling. Bad right from the very first moment it happened.

The security people from the mall came over to us. Perhaps they were the ones who called the police. I don't remember calling them myself. When the police came over, Revé and I told what had happened.

One policeman said to me, "Mrs. Walsh, Adam probably just wandered off and he's on his way home. Why don't you get in your car, drive up the way that you always come to the mall, the regular route. And you'll probably see him along the street."

The police were so certain that he was just a lost child. That he would show up and be fine, and, you know, "Girls, don't you worry."

I thought, "No, I won't see him along the street." There was not a chance in the world that this little boy was out there on the street or hiding behind a tree or playing games, trying to worry us. But I had to do something, to keep on looking, so I wouldn't go crazy. So I got in my car and I did the very thing the policeman told me to. Wheeled out of that back parking lot and went right down Hollywood Boulevard. Then turned on a little side street toward their home on McKinley.

I think I started by going to every one of the neighbors, asking if they had seen Adam. John and Revé lived on a corner, and I went to the people next door, then across the road to the other corner where the lady who lived there would have had a good view of him at the playground.

"No, haven't seen Adam."

Then I went to the playground. It was summertime and there was a playground director and I asked her if she had seen a little boy. I looked in the group of children and asked them if they had seen Adam.

"Nobody . . . no. Hasn't been here."

I had a key to the house and I let myself in. I went from room to room. All the rooms, one at a time. And when I was done, I thought, "This little boy doesn't have a key to the house. This little boy isn't going to be here."

But I looked in every closet just the same. Under every bed. I called his name and went all through the house. But I knew he wasn't there and wasn't going to be. Then, as I was starting to lock up, the phone rang. It was John.

I told him that we had been up at the mall and had lost track of Adam.

I was at work in my office, on the first floor of the Harbour House, a high-rise on the ocean in Bal Harbour, about ten miles from Hollywood. It had been a pretty ordinary morning. Phone calls. Meetings. I don't remember the precise chain of events. I don't remember talking to Gram on the phone. I remember the call as having come from Revé.

She said, "John, something is wrong here. Really wrong. Adam is missing and I need you to get here." I could tell in her voice. That no matter what anyone had said to her, store security or the police, Revé knew from the minute it happened that something was seriously wrong. This was not normal behavior.

This was not anything Adam would do. Something was up. She wasn't buying what they were telling her.

Revé isn't ordinarily an aggressive person. But right now she wanted to know where her boy was. So this time she wasn't taking any excuses. This time she was in *everyone's* face. I knew something was terribly wrong.

Two seconds later I was in the car, speeding north on A1A. John Monahan knew people at the Florida Highway Patrol, so I had grabbed him on the way out of the office, and he took a separate car. Joe, who was working in my office at the time, rode with me. I drove as fast as I could over to the mall, and when I ripped into the parking lot, the first thing I saw was our car—a big, gray Checker cab—just where Revé had said it would be.

I walked in and saw the back of Revé and called her name. She turned around. Her face was white, absolutely ashen, and it was obvious that she had been crying. A terrible, desperate look was in her eyes that said, "You can fix this. Yes, you can. I've seen you do it a hundred times."

But the only words she spoke were, "It's Adam, John . . . I can't find Adam."

No one was listening to Revé. Why would they? She had on shorts, she was a woman, and she looked nineteen years old. She needed a man to show up to ask the questions. Pound the table. Demand the answers. No one was paying any attention to what she was telling them. At that point, she still looked relatively calm. She hadn't come unglued yet, but I could tell that it was coming.

The cavalry had just ridden in, and I was supposed to lead the charge. That was the hard part. Being the Lone Ranger. The businessman husband in a suit who's going to make the cops shape up and stop patronizing his wife. John Walsh, accompanied by John Monahan—a big, imposing guy, all puffed up, in a suit.

I went into crisis mode. Think calm. And then I started in. I told myself, "Let's just get right into the drill here." Who was in charge? They pointed me to a uniformed cop. I went right up to him, got in his face. Who saw what? Where have you checked? Who's doing what, and where and how are they doing it? This was what I had done during every emergency in my life. Stay in control. Keep a cool head. Get the answers.

If you're in a crisis situation like that, you expect to see some outward signs. A bunch of police cruisers parked outside with their lights flashing, television crews gathering, something. But there were only a few uniformed cops standing around. I expected detectives.

I wanted somebody bigger than a uniform cop.

All my life I had taken care of my family. I knew that if anything ever went wrong, I was the best possible person to fix it. But on Monday, July 27, 1981, at the Hollywood mall, for the first time in my life, I began to know what real fear was. I had never really been afraid before. People had told me about fear. I had seen it in the faces of people I had rescued from drowning. But now, for the first time, I was learning the feeling myself.

We gradually became aware that it had begun to get dark. They were starting to lock the doors and turn out the lights. It was getting obvious that there was no point in hanging around the mall. We could be more productive elsewhere. Someone, probably one of the uniformed cops, suggested that we move over to the Hollywood police station across the street. Just a short walk across the parking lot. Not even driving distance. Finally, there was nothing to do but leave. Walk out of the store and leave without Adam.

Revé, John Monahan, and I walked out into the parking lot to where the Checker was parked. The sun was going down. People were leaving. Soon, everyone would be gone. We didn't want to move the car in case

Adam found his way back to it. So we just left it there, unlocked. I don't know how long it stayed there in the parking lot. A few days maybe. But before we left, we opened the car door, and Revé made a little bed for Adam in the backseat. She stacked up all of his books and toys and made a pillow for him out of his favorite blue blanket.

We wrote a note and put it up on the dashboard so it would show through the windshield. So that he would be able to see it before he even climbed in.

Adam, it said. *Stay in the car. Mommy and Daddy are looking for you.*

Book Two

Book

Two

5

The Search — Part I

I KNEW THAT MY SON WAS OUT THERE. I WAS JUST HOPING
that he hadn't fallen into a canal. A lot of unfenced
waterways were near our house, and kids drowned in
them all the time. But Adam was a great swimmer. He
could dive down ten or twelve feet. My little boy
wasn't going to panic in a canal. What about all the
hours of drown-proofing that I'd done with him? If he
had fallen into a canal, he was going to be just fine.

Unless the banks were so steep and slippery from
the mud that he wouldn't be able to climb out . . .

We all knew that Adam had not simply wandered
off. He was not that kind of kid, not one to just take
off with some other little kids. He was shy, timid
even. He obeyed his elders. He respected authority.
He did what he was told to do. He was not a little
hellion who ran around unsupervised. There was a
thought, a fleeting thought, that was beginning to
work its way up . . . slowly . . . from my stomach
toward my brain. But I was doing my best not to pay
any attention to it.

"If he's not out wandering around, or trying to find

his way home, and he hasn't fallen into a canal," I told myself, "then maybe a woman who recently had a miscarriage, or someone who had lost a child hit by a car, or a set of grandparents whose little grandson has been tragically killed in an accident, someone like that must have him. And they're going to bring him back, because they're loving people."

That was the only way I could deal with the thought that was just now beginning to circle in my brain: the thought that somebody out there, somewhere, might have taken him.

Who would take a little kid? The only reason anyone could possibly do such a thing was to replace his or her own great loss. I could understand that. Someone had seen a beautiful child, our little blond, six-year-old boy, and she was trying to ease her own unbearable pain. I had read about things like that, about deranged women who took babies from a nursery or a maternity ward because they had had a miscarriage or a stillborn.

In my head, I was thinking, "He's trying to find his way home, but he's never walked home before, from anywhere. He doesn't know where he is. He thinks his mother's left him. And he can't understand why. Because no one has ever abandoned him before. Something must have happened to make his mother not come back."

I don't know what Revé was thinking. At that moment we did not know a lot of things. But Revé was sure of one thing—had been absolutely positive about it even by the time I arrived at the mall. I kept telling her that what she was saying made no sense, that it couldn't possibly be true. But no matter what I said, she was adamant. She kept insisting that a young girl, a security guard at Sears, had come up to her, crying, because she was afraid, according to Revé, that Adam might have been "one of the ones she had ordered out of the store."

We left the Checker and walked through the parking lot, out across Hollywood Boulevard to a pale brick building on the other side of it that had the words *Hollywood Police* on the front. Inside, we took an elevator to the detective bureau on the third floor, a big room where a lot of guys were sitting around with their feet up on the desks. Their sport coats were off, hanging on the backs of their chairs, so that you could see the holstered guns that they were wearing underneath. These were the detectives.

Almost immediately, I began to meet cops. All kinds of cops. "Mr. Walsh, I'd like to introduce Sergeant so-and-so. This is Detective such and such." These weren't investigators. Just the hodgepodge of the Hollywood police. They started asking us questions. And I was asking just as many questions back.

I think they were starting to get the idea that something was drastically wrong here. And I began to get the distinct impression that somehow they all knew something that I didn't: that this particular incident was going to be resolved before daybreak.

One way or the other.

After a while, Revé went back to the house, but I stayed at the police station that first night until long after the sun went down. Until it was finally time to go home. When I walked out into the night from the air-conditioning, it was still sticky and hot outside. Silent. Not even the faintest breeze. It was more than a mile back to our house from the Hollywood mall, but I didn't want to drive it. I wanted to walk. To retrace what might possibly have been Adam's steps.

John Monahan had called some of his business friends, and they had come over to the station. We all began to walk, slowly, shoulder to shoulder, in a human chain across the Hollywood Golf Course. Moving like an army. Like the infantry. No one talking. Just shining our flashlights, searching. And over and over calling out Adam's name.

I don't know how long it took us to make it back to McKinley Street. I only remember that the whole time there was only one thought in my head: That it was late at night. The stars were out. And that for the first time in her life, my son's mother did not know where her little boy was.

By the time we got back to the house, people had already started showing up—friends, relatives, people who had heard what was going on and wanted to help. Someone had called a radio station earlier in the day, and they had made some kind of announcement. That's how Michael Monahan heard about it, on his car radio when he was driving around with his girlfriend. He was already at the house by the time his dad and I got there. Jane was on tour in Europe, but Gram was there, and my brother Joe.

That afternoon, Les Davies, down in the islands, happened to be listening to WINZ, a radio station that broadcast from Miami, and heard a news flash about a missing little boy named Adam Walsh. Les got out on the first flight he could.

And then, I'm not sure who called him, but my best friend, Jeff O'Regan, arrived.

Truck drivers heard about it on their CBs, and people began to drive up and down the streets of our neighborhood. On bicycles, in cars, on foot. At seven-thirty that night, Jack Simons, the president of the local Citizens Crime Watch, received a call from the Hollywood police and sent out forty-seven members who started a walking search of the city that they kept up until 3 A.M.

People were looking for Adam in backyards and Dumpsters, under cars and in canals. The police went out with search dogs, a boat covered the waterways, and a rescue helicopter flew overhead with its spotlight trained on the ground. All over, everywhere, there was a weird commotion.

Revé rode around the neighborhood on her bicycle, down the side streets and in alleyways, calling Adam's name. She went back to the mall again and looked in the windows of every store. She got up onto the roof of the mall and called down the ventilator shafts. Most of that night, John Monahan was out looking for Adam, too. He and some friends went up to every door in the neighborhood and knocked. "We're looking for a six-year-old. We've lost a little boy."

All of the people were concerned. But not one of them had seen Adam.

Tips and leads started coming in from everywhere. The phones were ringing off the hook, both at the police station and our house. An employee at a convenience store told Joe that he had seen Adam climb into a white car. A woman who worked in the Hollywood mall bakery said she saw Adam wandering through the stores. A man reported that Adam had been at St. Matthew's Catholic Church in Hallandale. Three sanitation workers thought they had spotted him on the 4400 block of Van Buren Street. Another tip said that he was at the Fort Lauderdale airport boarding a domestic flight to the Midwest. One woman called the house saying that she had seen him at a stationery store in Fort Lauderdale with a Latino woman and another small child.

Reports of sightings were coming in from West Palm Beach to Miami. "We have fifty million people who thought they saw him," one police dispatcher said.

And not one of them really had.

Rather than go back to her house, Gram moved into the middle guest bedroom, between our room and Adam's. She remembers that as every hour went by, it just kept getting worse. She was trying not to picture anything. She couldn't allow herself to think about it. But on some level, she knew.

That he wasn't walking anymore. That he was in someone's car.

She kept remembering how she had always told Adam that she hoped she would live long enough to

77

see him as a grown man, to know what he decided to choose in life.

"Do you have any idea what you might like to be?" she once asked him.

"Oh, yes—a scientist," he said. "But only in the daytime, Gram. Because I'm so afraid of the dark."

In the house that first night, no one slept.

And the next morning, before dawn, it all started again. Revé and I went out to search for him in the car. Twenty-two HPD patrol officers asked for overtime duty at the end of their normal night shifts so that they could continue looking. Fifty people searched the West Broward gravel pits. That morning, there was a story in the *Hollywood Sun-Tattler:* "Massive search launched for boy, 6. Adam Walsh disappeared from Sears Monday afternoon."

The *Miami News* ran a story, too, a small item at the bottom of the local column. They got our address on McKinley wrong and said that Adam was seven, instead of six. Then they quoted a police aide who said, "The kid is probably lost somewhere, and we're searching the city for him.

"Kidnapping is not suspected."

At 10 A.M. that Tuesday morning, Revé and I went on local TV for the first time to plead for information about Adam. I don't remember exactly how we arranged it. Les may have set it up. We stood under some lights, in front of a camera, and said, "Look for landmarks, Adam. Look for landmarks, and you'll be able to find your way home."

Then, afterward, I went back to the detective bureau, where the most frightening thing started happening. I had gone over there expecting to hear some reports, to find out what the police were doing and what progress had been made overnight. But there wasn't any information like that. Instead, the police started asking *me* what I thought they should do.

"Do you have any ideas, John?"

"Anything we haven't tried?"

At the end of the day, Revé and I made another TV appeal. This time, there was no avoiding it: someone asked if I thought that Adam had been kidnapped. "I don't know what they would be looking for," I said. "But we're willing to negotiate."

Then we officially announced that we were offering a $5,000 reward for Adam's return.

By that point, a flyer had already been distributed to postmen, cabdrivers, and Florida Power and Light workers so that they could recognize Adam if they saw him. But it wasn't good enough. I knew that we had to circulate a poster that wasn't some piece of mimeographed, hand-lettered crap. At the police station, they had shown me a couple of missing-persons posters, and immediately I thought, "This is bullshit." My career was in the hotel-marketing business. I knew how to write ad copy for sales brochures, and I had friends who were in graphic design. So I started writing the copy myself. Simple and clear.

Missing Person, $5,000 REWARD
For information leading to the whereabouts of
    Adam Walsh.
Age: 6 years old.
Height: 3'6".
Weight: 45 lbs.
Eyes: Hazel.
Build: Slight.
Other: Missing one top tooth with second tooth
    coming in.
Clothing worn when last seen. Pants: Green
    shorts. Shirt: Short-sleeve pullover, predomi-
    nantly red & white striped. Shoes: yellow
    sandals. Hat: beige-colored captain's hat.

Then we designed the layout of the poster and went through a whole stack of pictures of Adam. Jeff picked out one that showed him in his T-ball uniform with his bat and red baseball cap because he thought it was the one that most looked like him.

But there was also another reason for choosing that particular photograph. I knew that the most important thing of all in a "missing" poster was to include mention of some identifying mark. But what identifying mark on our beautiful, blond little boy? He was young and perfect. He didn't have even the smallest scar on his body, let alone a tattoo.

So we chose the picture of him in his red baseball cap. Because it had been taken only the week before, and in it he was smiling. If you saw it, you couldn't help but notice that—right on top—he had a little missing tooth.

Joe took the pictures to a professional photo service that he knew. We put our home phone number and address on the posters, along with the local police number and a toll-free 800 number that we had installed. And at the bottom of the poster we included the message, "We are willling to negotiate ransom on ANY terms. Strict confidentiality. DO NOT FEAR REVENGE! We will not prosecute. We only want our son. If desired, contact any radio or TV station, newspaper, or any other media as a neutral party for negotiations or information. Do not fear revenge. We want Adam home."

We called a printing company and had them print up fifty thousand flyers. Someone donated the cost of the job, picked up the whole bill and had the printing done for us.

The community was starting to rally, which was great. But, even so, we still had a problem: now that we had designed and produced the posters of Adam, we had to figure out how to get people to see them.

Les Davies, using contacts that he had made as president of the Out Islands Promotion Board, got in touch with a guy named Jeff Niven, the vice president of Delta Airlines, who had called from Atlanta, offering to send down three-hundred people to join in the search. Niven said, "You know what we'll do? We'll come and pick up the posters and we can go to all the airports and give stacks of them to all the pilots. They'll take them on their planes and hand them out, and that way they'll be distributed in Atlanta and all around the country."

Both Eastern and Delta Airlines delivered Adam's poster to airports nationwide. We even had some of the posters printed in Spanish. I can remember Joe going to the Fort Lauderdale airport and putting them in every plane that took off. By the end of that first week, we had printed 150,000 flyers and 50,000 of them were distributed, free of charge, by a local postal delivery company.

While we were in the middle of all that, I started picking up on something over at the HPD that I could not quite bring myself to believe. Adam had been gone now, without word, overnight—for nearly twenty-four hours. And still, no matter what we told them to the contrary, the police were insisting on describing him as "missing." No mention of the fact that he might have been abducted. Not even that possibility. They were so sure, so absolutely certain that Adam had wandered off, or was playing a game, and somehow would just as easily meander back. As if he were a kid who was having a little life event, but it was all going to be okay.

Then, forty-eight hours into the search, on Wednesday, July 29, Fred Barbetta, the HPD spokesman, gave a quote to the papers: "I think it's time we hit the waterways hard. If he's in the water, this is when he'd come up."

It was not until the following day, on Thursday, that Jack Hoffman, the Hollywood detective who was in charge of the case, finally made a statement. He said that Adam's disappearance "appears to be an abduction. This is not the type of child to just walk off.

"But we don't have any clues whatsoever what the motive would be."

Even during the first twenty-four hours, Joe and Gram were right there with us. But by a few days later, the rest of our families still didn't know. Adam's story was a local one, so anyone far away wouldn't have known unless we told them. Jimmy was still living out in California, and my sister, Jane, was on her way back from a European tour. She remembers flying back into New York and calling our house from the airport to let someone from the family know that she was home. That's how she found out.

Eventually Revé realized that there was no more putting it off. She would have to call her family in upstate New York. She didn't want to do it. As bad as it was for her, she didn't want it to be bad for them.

Right away, they said they would come down. But she said that she needed them to stay where they were. That there were enough people with us already, and that we had made flyers, like the ones you see on telephone poles when a dog is lost. We had written down all the information about Adam. On one side of the poster he was in the shirt that he was wearing when he disappeared. On the other side was his baseball picture.

She told them that everything was going to be all right. That we were going to find Adam. And that they shouldn't worry. She tried in any small way to save them as much grief as she could. What else could she do?

Tell them that their grandson had not been seen now—by anyone—for three going on four days?

Gradually, even though things were happening so fast, it began to dawn on us that we weren't going to be able to really rely on the cops. I don't know that any one thing specifically sparked that feeling. Maybe it was when the two lead investigators, HPD detectives Jack Hoffman and Ron Hickman, came over to the house one day to question us. On his way out, Ron Hickman, who was a Baptist Sunday-school teacher, mentioned to me that religion would be a big help for us in getting through all of this.

I said, "Ron, with all due respect, you know, we're not born-again Christians. We're Catholics."

But he started telling me anyway about how someone in his family had gotten into trouble and prayed to Jesus and Jesus had helped them, and then he gave me a religious brochure.

I did not want to be hearing from a lead detective in charge of Adam's case that Jesus Christ was the one who would save me.

I wanted to know what the police were going to do to get out there and find my son.

All my life, I had always been successful at pretty much everything that mattered. I had never really screwed up on anything serious. And I was not going to fail at this. We, my family and friends, would be the ones to give Adam the very best shot. We would work day and night, travel to the ends of the earth, go anywhere, do anything, spend any amount of money to get my little boy back.

By now, press people had started camping out on our front lawn and on the sidewalk in front of our house. The coverage wasn't orchestrated by us. The media came on their own. Later, I learned that it was because they monitor scanners and police dispatch radios—all of them looking for that breaking story. At the time, I had no idea what police scanners were and how the press knew to rush to the scene of things. But they were there, and it was a good thing.

Except that they were making mistakes. About our address or Adam's age or what he had been wearing. Also, some of them were beginning to make it sound as if we had a lot of money; I was now a "marketing executive," and our Checker was "a custom car." I was afraid that someone might be holding Adam in hopes of getting a huge ransom. We hadn't received any ransom notes, but it was a possibility. So Les and

I tried to emphasize the truth: that I was a working person, and that Revé and I weren't rich people who had money to burn. That's how Les became our head of PR.

In the meantime, the Hollywood PD was being very cooperative about letting the press in for the sake of the Walshes. We needed the media, and for the moment at least, they needed us. I was white, and a businessman. They thought Revé and I were telegenic and "charismatic." Lucky for us that we weren't black or poor. Lucky for me that I wasn't Eddie Miles.

If I had been, we wouldn't have stood any kind of chance. We wouldn't have even gotten a mention in the papers.

I was pretty cynical about the press, but not all of its members were horrible. Some were genuinely concerned, trying to help in any way they could. One reporter even stopped by to ask if we wanted to borrow his search dog. But mostly, the press needed to sell newspapers, and I needed to get my son back. That was my deal with the devil. That was how we hit on the idea of jacking up the reward.

On the first of the missing posters, we had offered $5,000, made up of money that Monahan and Ray Mellette, one of my business partners, had put together with the help of friends. Then, a few days later, a TV reporter came up to me and said, "The story's old news, John. It's dying. Adam's been gone for days. Come on, increase the reward. Give us something to lead with tonight."

It was a new game that we had to learn to play. We knew that every time we upped the reward, more crackpots would call in with phony tips. It was unbelievable that people would try to extort money from us at a time like this, but a number of them did. So the idea was to raise the reward enough to keep the press interested, without making it high enough to bait the psychos.

Without anyone really setting it up, friends at the

house began gravitating to different roles. Les was handling the press. Gram's job was to answer the phones and keep a log, on a yellow legal pad, of every call that came in. My brother Joe was our legman, running to airports, being a presence at the police station, going everywhere to get the flyers out. Whenever I had been away from home, traveling, it was always Joe who had looked out for Adam. And now Joe—always more like Adam's big brother than his uncle—was doing everything he could to bring the little guy back.

And then there was Jeff O'Regan. A big, terrific, rough-tough guy with a huge mustache who emptied out his bank account and showed up at our door. A hundred dollars for this, a thousand dollars for that—whatever we needed to keep searching and manning the phones came out of Jeff O'Regan's pocket. He was the one who gave gas money to any searcher with a swamp buggy who needed it. Who was there, day and night, answering the two phones that he had paid to have installed. And by a day or two into the search, those phones were ringing off the hook. We had a recorder on one line in case anybody came up with a ransom demand. Nothing very sophisticated; the little suction cup kept popping off the receiver.

Our motto at the time was Money, Guns, and Lawyers. Ray Mellette was handling the business end of things. He was acting as go-between with my other partners—a group of potentially lethal, powerful management guys who knew how to pull strings and make things happen. They were the ones who put together the money we were offering for a reward. It started out at $5,000. Then we bumped it to $25,000, and before long, it was up to $100,000. All to keep the press interested. All from what Ray and the other partners were pulling together.

Of course we didn't actually have the money in hand, and we certainly didn't have it in the house. But the police were worried that some wacko, thinking that we did, might try to break in at night. So at one point, an HPD detective came over to the house and handed Jeff a wooden box that contained a .357 Magnum. His for the duration. Every night Jeff slept in the living room, draped over a little velvet settee, cradling his gun. And if anyone did try to break in, the first obstacle he was going to have to face was a fully armed six-foot-four O'Regan. That's how Jeff, in addition to everything else that he was, became our chief of security.

By the time Adam's story hit the papers, all kinds of people were showing up to search for him. The Florida Game and Fresh Water Fish Commission donated a helicopter, and seven of their wildlife officers conducted a ground search; Burger King donated three-hundred ham-and-cheese sandwiches and twenty gallons of orange drink for the three-hundred people who organized themselves to search the Florida Everglades; Jeff O'Regan jumped on a plane and flew up to both Orlando and Tampa on the same day to brief security guards at Disney World and Busch Gardens in case someone tried to take Adam there; the Broward County Airboat and Halftrack Conservation Club went out in swamp buggies to search desolate areas on the fringe of the Everglades.

There were a lot of creative people with ideas of their own, people from all walks of life who had nothing to do with law enforcement but were coming up with great ideas on how to look for Adam. I don't know—maybe it was just an excuse to get out there and be macho. But I believed they were doing it out of the goodness of their hearts. People who worked day jobs kept searching all night long; the ones who were on night shifts showed up at the door at dawn.

"What can I do?"

"Where can I go?"

"Where can I take my five kids to search?"

"I'll distribute posters on the turnpike. Can you loan me twenty dollars for gas?"

Rich people, poor people. Nice people. Humble people. It was because of them that this whole awful thing started to take on a life of its own.

People let us borrow their cars to check out the hundreds of phone tips that were coming in. A man was investigated after being seen on a city bus with a small boy. A woman said she saw Adam buying $68 worth of groceries at a local Publix grocery store.

And one night, a voice on the phone said, "We have the boy. We're going to put him out at The Falls," which was a shopping center not far away. Ron Hickman put on a suit, and they sent him out in an unmarked powder-blue Lincoln Continental that had been impounded in a drug deal. He stuck a New Testament up on the dashboard, like a Bible salesman, and sat there in an empty parking lot, waiting for hours.

People said, "Why don't you just take all of your information and feed it into a computer and see what it spits out?"

A woman called the HPD to say that she had had a dream that Adam was in a wheelchair being pushed by a black male down a long white corridor.

Another woman from Gulfport, Florida, sent a note saying that she would light a candle every night for Adam until he returned. "And by the way, I hate to bother you at a time like this, but do you think you could help me to dispose of some property that I own in the Bahamas?"

And that's the way it was. Tips . . . leads . . . garbage . . . nothing. Hour after hour. Day after day. Everyone had another idea.

And none of it was getting Adam back.

One morning Revé came into the living room and someone said, "Look at the beautiful flowers that came today."

"This isn't a funeral," she snapped. "What are they sending me flowers for?" It was a piece of potential reality that she had no interest in dealing with.

Then there were the psychics.

I don't know how they know when to descend from the sky, but they do. Maybe they hear it on the psychic grapevine. Maybe they've got a direct line to God.

Some called us themselves. Some went through the police. It was Jimmy Campbell's job to keep track of all their calls and predictions. "Go find a flag on a hill. That's where he is" or "He's going to be found near water." In Florida you can't get more than fifty feet from water. There's a pool in every backyard. Drainage canals, the inland waterway, the ocean. What the hell good was a psychic "vision" like that?

But that didn't stop any of them from trying to share our fifteen minutes of fame. My secretary later described the phenomenon as like going to Chappaquiddick and taking a piece of the bridge.

I remember Mickey Dahne, a forty-nine-year-old blonde from Miami Beach. She showed up two days into the search and told all the papers she would try to find Adam. At the time, she was doing a radio talk show and a weekly astrological forecast for a national tabloid. Her agent was advertising that she had a 98 percent success rate with psychic readings, and that she had solved two missing-person cases, including one involving two children in Texas who had been missing for three years. Unlike other psychics, Dahne, as her agent told the papers, was "a happy type of psychic. She likes to help people find romance and lost watches."

With Mickey Dahne on the case, everything became an even bigger media zoo. She and Revé and one of the police sergeants went back to Sears, accompanied by a whole gang of reporters and curious people. Dahne ran her hands over the computer video game, and the papers wrote that she "drifted into psychic space and retraced the last known steps taken by Adam."

Revé had brought along a bag of Adam's clothes

and toys, and Dahne rummaged through all of them with her hands. "He's scared and he's hurting, but I think he's all right," she said. "He got confused and didn't know where to go.

"I don't feel the person who has him owns a television or can afford one," she said as the TV lights shone down on her. "I feel a sandy-haired boy, about five foot eight inches, with shocking bright eyes."

All very impressive. All very dramatic.

That morning, when Revé had went over to pick Mickey Dahne up, she overheard her on the phone with one of her psychic friends in New Jersey.

Dahne was telling the friend to get on a plane. "The weather's a lot better down here than it is up there," she was saying. "Come on down to Florida with me and work the Adam Walsh case."

I don't think it dawned on me for a while, but finally, I began to understand: the authority running the command center in the search for Adam Walsh was not the government or even the Hollywood PD. What was happening was that a large-scale rescue effort was headquartered in my home, operating out of my living room, made up of my friends, business associates, and to some degree, the local police.

And that the guy who was running it was me.

I knew that my little boy stood the best chance of getting back alive if I ran the search myself. If I was the main coordinator of my own personal SWAT team. Because, I thought, the guys on my team were smarter, more sophisticated, and tougher than the cops.

The HPD basically turned over a conference room for our use, one on the third floor next to the detective bureau. A whole room for me and my boys. We had phones, people came in to see me, and I was there, running whatever I could whenever I wasn't talking to the press or having to do something else. Some days I'd go out to a little TV station or go places and try to talk to people or visit home for a little while to see how Jeff was doing. But any of us who could be were at the police station every day, so the cops would have to remind themselves, "Oh, boy, here comes trouble. The biters. Okay, boys, watch your toes."

I had always been an athlete, taken vitamins, worked out at the gym. I had always made it a point to take good care of myself. But now I couldn't sleep, and I couldn't eat. Someone would hand me some soup, and as soon as I swallowed it, I'd be puking in the sink. But I knew that I couldn't help my little boy if I wasn't healthy, if I folded. So, as hard as it was, I kept trying to eat.

At the house it was constant chaos, mayhem, twenty out of twenty-four hours a day. Thank God for the chaos. But even so, as the days wore on, a routine began to take shape. Everybody had a role to perform during the day. But then, before we called it quits for the night, which was usually at two or three in the morning, the last thing we would do was sit down for a strategy meeting. What had gone wrong today? What were we going to try next? Anybody have any new ideas?

We were trying to fill every possible vacuum, with work, with effort, and with strategic planning. One goal, for example, was to get on as many TV broadcasts as possible. At the time, south Florida had six local affiliates, so our job was to try to get eighteen placements every day—to appear on all the stations at noon, six, and eleven.

Every night, well after midnight, the last of the volunteers would stand by the front door, making small talk, as if they just couldn't bring themselves to leave. They'd go on and on, God bless 'em. Trying to be helpful. We hated having to hustle them out, but a lot of work was still to be done. As soon as the door closed, it was time to start the planning session. What were we going to do? What's the story going to be for the press the next day? We couldn't drop the ball. We couldn't let the momentum slow. The only time to get focused on the next thing was before you finished the last.

By now, everyone was getting a little frayed around the edges. They were exhausted, and even if they pretended not to be, they were worrying about Adam. One night I was heading into the kitchen to get a soda and happened to overhear a little bitchfest in progress. I don't even remember specifically who it was—just some of the volunteers, I guess, complaining about the greasy fast food, the no sleep, the hours, life. Les Davies says that he can still hear the sound of the Coke bottles rattling in the refrigerator door as I slammed it. I told everyone that if things were so bad, so goddamn tough, then they could get the hell out of my house. Because Adam wasn't going to be sleeping in his own bed this night, either. And that, wherever he was, he was crying for his mom and dad. I never heard anyone complain again.

The nights were the worst. By this time I was completely exhausted. I was spending most of my days over at the police station, trying to keep things moving. And then, when I finally came home to get some rest, there was no way I could sleep. I would try to lie down for a couple of hours, but that was about it. I wasn't having real nightmares about Adam—at least not sleeping nightmares. They were awakening nightmares. After an hour or so of restless sleep, I would wake up, lie there for a couple of seconds, and think to myself, "It isn't over. It's back."

Then I would get up and try to think of something else, because the only way I could deal with anything was to try to keep my mind as active as possible. If I let myself, even for a second, slip into that dark hole, then I couldn't make it stop: "What if somebody's got him . . . What if somebody's torturing him . . . What if somebody's molesting him . . ." Revé and I didn't talk a lot about it to each other. What was the point? We each knew what the other was thinking.

Revé would wake up in the middle of the night, not knowing if she was waking up or had fallen asleep. Was she asleep, dreaming a nightmare—or waking up into a nightmare that was real? Gradually, she would realize that she was waking into reality, and she would wonder how the human mind could be so cruel. Then there were the dreams she was having. The ones where she would see Adam from a distance, as if he were in the back of an open truck. He was calling her, reaching out his hands to her. But just as she got to him, just as their fingers were almost touching, his would slip away. In the dream, she was trying to reach him. But he was getting farther and farther away.

Going home at night was horrible. Of everything, it was the harshest. Sometimes I would try to lie down with Revé. Sometimes I would go into Adam's room by myself—never when Revé was there—and kneel down and press my face into his sheets and pillow. I would look at his toys, go into his closet, and touch his clothes. Think of him. Desperate. Praying that somehow he would come back alive. It was unbearable. I didn't want to go into his room, but I couldn't stay out of it. I would do anything to be close to things that had once been close to him. And through it all, I was beginning to get the sense that maybe we were never going to see him again.

I was also still believing, though, that if anybody could get him back, I could. I told everyone, "I'm going to do anything, anything it takes, anything to give this little boy the best chance, the best odds." I kept telling myself that, and Jeff and Ray kept saying, "We're gonna do it. You're giving him the best shot. What have we forgotten? Who can we call? Who do we know? What can we do? Let's give him the best odds ever of any little boy to get brought back alive."

I would wake up in the middle of the night thinking, "If somebody has him, if they are hurting him, whatever they're doing to him, maybe through a miracle I can somehow help him. If he's alive still, I can save him, no matter what they've done to him. And when he comes back, I will be able to make him better. No matter what they've done to him. We'll get by this, we'll get through it. He'll be all right. I'll spend every minute with him, and we'll make it."

But as each day went on, another voice was getting louder inside my head. One that was saying that the odds of getting my little boy back were not good. Not good to begin with. And now, getting worse.

The second day, the third day, the fourth day, the fifth. As the days wore on, it was getting harder and harder to talk to Revé. She was with the psychics, keeping index cards with their names and predictions. One called to say that she was sure that Adam was stuck in a box or a closet near the Sears store. Another called to say that he needed some unwashed pieces of Adam's clothing so that he could trace the "aura." The detectives would say to me, "It's probably good that Revé's off with these psychics, because it's keeping her mind off the reality of this."

I'd say, "Yeah, you know, I guess you're right. It's excellent that my wife is going out to a field in the middle of nowhere at three o'clock in the morning with two psychics because they think they've got a feeling that right here at this bench, or over there by that rock, or by this road or that parking lot, that Adam might have been pulled into a white car or a pink truck or a purple van."

Then I would go into Adam's room at night and find Revé crying her eyes out, lying on his bed with all of his toys and clothes and things around her. And I was the one who would have to get her out of there.

Fifty or sixty psychics had attached themselves to this case. And the minute those TV cameras would start rolling, they couldn't jump up fast enough to get next to Revé. All of them were talking about Adam's "aura." That was the big deal: everybody saw the aura. And the aura said that Adam was alive.

It was cruel to take that kind of advantage of Revé's desperate need to get her son back—of her tremendous vulnerability—for the sake of furthering their own careers, their psychic hot lines, their psychic this and their psychic that. I can still hear it:

"I worked the Walsh case."

"I worked with the Hollywood police."

"I aided the police in the Adam Walsh investigation."

Damn them. What good were they? How did they help? They didn't do anything but take a poor woman, one poor mother, and lead her on wild-goose chases in the middle of the night. Telling her that they had had a psychic vision that Adam was in a loving home with a beautiful pool. Or with a wonderful couple in North Carolina doing macramé. Get the fuck out of here. It was the most exploitative of all the exploitation—of all the vultures who swoop down when you're thrown into the melee of the media. The reporters know all the rules. The psychics know all the rules. The news directors know all the rules. The cops know all the rules. And you don't know shit.

Everyone was looking for what he or she could get out of this. Everybody except the simple, pure-of-heart, good people who came out to look for Adam. The people who came by the hundreds without being asked or paid, or sometimes even acknowledged. They were the ones who allowed me to keep my sanity: the good people who put up posters and searched all night. The people who cared, and believed. Not so that they could get their names in the paper. They didn't do it to plug their psychic hot lines. They did it to help a desperate, searching family. They did what they could to get our little boy back, and that was the one thing that kept me believing in humanity.

One afternoon a man knocked on the front door at the house. He was a veterinarian, he said, and he had something that he wanted to give us: a dog, a little black Scottish-terrier puppy. The dog had been born in Kansas, and we all kind of laughed about that and started calling him Toto. Later on, we just couldn't keep him anymore. But during the search he was there all the time. The man had said that he was giving the dog to us as a gesture.

So that the puppy could be Adam's dog when Adam got home.

Nothing stopped, and everything stopped. Revé was haggard, so desperate. It was horrible. So painful. When we talked, we pretended to be optimistic. We would tell each other, "We're going to get him back. Yes, everything is going to work out just fine." I was keeping up the ruse. Why see her destroyed unless I knew for sure that something had happened?

The things I was hoping for grew smaller and smaller.

I knew that there were people out there who had gone through what was happening to us, and who had never learned what finally happened to their children. I hoped that, no matter what, we wouldn't be cursed like that. Because even the thought of it was enough to make me go out of my mind.

After a while, I don't know how far along, what I was still hoping for most was that Adam would be returned to us. But if that was not going to be possible, then I was hoping that there would be a resolution. A definite knowing, one way or the other.

Adam's was the biggest case to hit south Florida in five years, since the search for a little girl named Lisa Lynn Berry. She had vanished from a Fort Lauderdale bowling alley, and her case was reported in all the papers, too. Five days after she disappeared, the police found her body in a vacant field.

I didn't want to tell Revé what the odds were, which is what I was learning from the cops. Revé is a woman, and women can handle it. They're stronger than men. They are the ones who have the children and bear the wounds and carry the scars. They are the ones who bury the dead.

But now her eyes were so huge and heartbroken that I couldn't bear to tell her.

I knew what she was thinking. So one night, in the dark, when we were both pretending to be asleep, I turned to her and said, "Revé, I'm going to say this once and never mention it again.

"Because I don't want you thinking it, even for a minute. Not once. Don't you dare think that this horrible thing that has happened is somehow, in any way, your fault.

"Because do you know what? Do you know what, Revé?"

She was listening to me. I could tell from the sound of her breathing.

I said, "But for the grace of God, it could have been me. I could have had him with me at the playground, turned my back for a second, and he could have been hit by a car. I could have been looking the other way for a split second and he could have slipped off and drowned in a canal.

"I know that you'll never talk to me about it. And I am never going to mention it to you again. But you had nothing to do with the disappearance of that little boy, Revé. And what we need to do now is to focus on staying together, and on staying healthy and strong, and on dealing with the media and looking for our son."

Revé understood what I was trying to say to her. I don't know if it helped. I know that it was true.

In bad situations, husbands and wives tend to blame each other. That's a common thing. It just happens. And I don't know why—maybe because we were so preoccupied in the search, so lost in the fear—but for some reason it didn't happen to us. Maybe it was because we both realized that we were each the only thing that the other one really had.

Revé said that she did not feel guilty, that she was not going to put that on herself on top of everything else. We didn't spend a lot of time talking about "What if" this or "What if" that. We would talk, but it was always about what we could do.

We would say things like, "Tomorrow we're going to do this." Or, "I can't sleep, so lie here right beside me."

It was excruciating to have to lie next to Revé and try to pretend that our life had some normalcy. She couldn't sleep, and I couldn't sleep. If she did drift off, she would start to thrash, and I would know how much she was suffering. She was tortured because she was his mother. I was tortured because I was the husband and father. The protector. The man. I was the one with the wordly business connections and the power. I was doing my job, which was to fight.

Revé was doing everything she could, but her job was different from mine. She was Adam's mother, and it was her job to stand there, not necessarily saying anything. Just, with her presence, asking the questions that needed to be asked. "Where is he? Why isn't he back? He's my son. Why haven't you found him? What is this? Why haven't they caught the person? Why isn't Adam here?"

The toughest thing was not letting her know how afraid I was. It was my job to go out and deal with the police every day, to demand to know what they were doing, and why they weren't doing it faster. Because they sure as hell weren't going to pay any attention to Revé. It was easy for them to turn their backs on a woman, a weeping mother.

But they *had* to listen to me. Me, they had to give an answer to: "How many more posters do we need? How is that going? I thought you were going to take care of those. Let's have another meeting."

During the search, I spent most of my days on the third floor of the Hollywood Police Department, with its beige walls and tile floor and smell of disinfectant coming up from the holding cells on the floor below. I had no sense of the passage of time, of whether it was day or night. The room was stuffy and completely airless. But being there was still better than being at home.

Going home was unbearable. I wanted to be in our house, but the only reason to be in it was if Adam was going to be there. That's what that house had always been about. Without him, it was just a place to go, only a lonely place to remind me of how hurt I was and how destroyed I was becoming. It was agonizing to be in it. The only real reason for going there would have been to welcome Adam home.

I kept thinking of that big news story from a few months before, the story of a little boy in Italy who had gotten stuck after falling down a well, and whom no one could seem to extricate. For a while the papers were full of the story, and Adam was concerned about it. He would say, "Don't worry, Dad. They can rescue him. Why don't they just drill in sideways? Then they could get him out."

Every day Adam would ask me what had happened to that little boy.

I never had the heart to tell him that he died.

It was all wearing on me. Everything was taking a terrible, physical toll. I was scared, tired, angry, and I couldn't keep anything down. It was agony. It was like being in hell for my whole life. For eternity.

And all the while, we never turned down an interview request from the press. Not one. No matter who wanted to talk with us, if it could help get Adam back, we would. We would let them into the house, cry for them on camera. We would take them into Adam's bedroom and let them take pictures of the wicker basket where he kept all the little clay figures of monsters that he had made.

But after a point, finally, Revé said that she had had enough. She would not cry in front of them anymore.

I don't know if that ultimately worked against her or not, because the news crews always loved it when they could get her crying on camera. I always imagined them going back to their bosses and saying, "Hey, I got a scoop. You wanna see Revé Walsh puking and crying on camera?"

Revé would stand there, trying to keep it together under the lights, with all of them watching her. And if she started to break, if she reached up once to wipe away a tear, all you could hear was the massive clicking of camera shutters. So at some point she made a vow to herself. And that was it. It probably hurt her in the end. People said she was cold and distant and wasn't acting the way they thought a grieving mother should.

The way she saw it, someone had already taken her son. The only thing she had left was her dignity. So she made up her mind. She wasn't going to let them see her cry anymore.

It was Revé's own personal "Screw you."

Within the first week, the search for Adam was being called the largest for a missing child that had ever taken place in south Florida. By the following Monday, August 3, our reward was up to $100,000, collected and donated by my business partners. A quarter of a million flyers had been distributed, and we had ordered three-hundred-thousand more. That morning, Revé and I went on television again, this time on a Miami station. Revé sat with one of Adam's stuffed animals in her lap. I told everyone, "I don't want to prosecute. I don't want revenge. I just want my boy back."

I remember being at Monahan's house with Les one night during the search. We were upstairs and started talking about Peggy's death. About how hard it had been, and about God and faith. That week, Monahan, who always described himself to reporters as Adam's uncle, told them that the search was "the only thing maintaining the Walshes sanity." Revé and I were "not the types to sit and cry," he said. We were "activists by nature."

At the time, hope was a precious commodity. We clung to it because it was all we had. Even in the physical world around us, things were deteriorating. Bills were going unpaid. No one was sleeping. Gram says that she doesn't remember getting undressed and going to bed once during that time. Instead, she would lie down with her clothes on at some point during the night and listen to everything that was going on in the house. Then, before dawn, it would all start again.

We were all trying so hard to keep up the front, at least to outsiders. On July 30, it was Joe's twenty-third birthday. "This will be a hell of a birthday present," he told the reporters, holding up the picture of Adam in his baseball hat. "To get this little guy back."

One night Jeff and Les got some kind of crazy phone tip and went to check it out. It turned out to be nothing, of course, but somewhere along the way they saw a big, red-brick building. Maybe an old Coca-Cola bottling plant. They looked around and realized they were in the middle of an abandoned, empty ware-house district and somehow got the idea that this would be a great place to stage the party we were going to have. It was the only kind of place that would be big enough to hold all the people who were going to be there to celebrate when we got Adam back.

We were not aware of it at the time. We couldn't be. We were wrapped up in our own nightmare trip, fighting for air. But around us, everywhere, there was a new kind of fear. In the Publix grocery store at the mall, mothers were holding their kids' hands so tight they turned blue. In the shopping mall, in the Sears store, you could hear parents screaming at their kids to stay close.

Up until now, there had been a kind of innocence, a

feeling that people were invulnerable, that their lives were safe. And now, somehow, because of what was happening to us, to Adam, they knew that they weren't.

It was hell. I didn't know the difference between day and night. There was nothing but anxiety and the feeling that my physical body was evaporating. By this point, I was running on adrenaline. On pure, scared, terrorized love for my child. But as each day went by, I kept up the brave front.

"I'm more optimistic than ever," I told a reporter. "The Hollywood police are following tips that they don't want me to get excited about. But I'm sure Adam will be coming home."

I was dealing with it, but I knew the odds were getting worse and worse. If you were even moderately sophisticated, you could see what was going on in the police department. They were sinking. They were getting the feeling, and I was getting the feeling, but I was still driving the train. I was the one pushing, the one trying to turn the little snowball into a great big avalanche.

By the middle of the second week of the search, I was still a long way from being able to face my wife and say the words, "Adam might be dead." But now I knew it was a possibility. More than anything now, I needed to know where he was. Dead or alive, I needed to know. I had to know. I was bound and determined that I could find my son, and that I would get him back alive. But then I started to lose that sureness, because no matter what I was doing, how much money I borrowed, how many friends I brought in, I still wasn't getting him back. So instead of being desperate just to get him back, I became desperate to find out what had happened to him. Hopefully, alive. But if dead, then I needed to know. Because I was starting to have the sinking feeling that he might be dead.

I began to say it to myself when I fell into my darkest fears. And I may have said it out loud, once, to Jeff O'Regan:

"Nobody keeps a six-and-a-half-year-old boy for ten days.

"Nobody does."

But we were keeping up the search. One man painted the side of his van with the slogan We Are Looking for Adam Walsh. A member of the Guardian Angels called to meet with us so that he could help them develop a strategy for searching in Dade County. A Miami woman whose teenage daughter had disappeared in 1984 sent us a check for $100 and told us not to lose faith.

Then, one day when I was up in the third-floor command center at the police station, they came in and took me off to the side, to a quiet place. I don't remember when it was. Day three or day seven, I don't know. A man came in and was introduced to me as Dr. Ronald Wright, the Broward County medical examiner. They sat me down at a table and brought out a big loose-leaf binder and said, "This is a book of sex offenders who have been released on parole into the community."

And I said, "Sex offenders? What do you mean? They release perverts?"

That was when Ronald Wright first spoke. "John, they do it all the time. These guys get a slap on the wrist. They don't do serious jail time."

"What do these guys do?"

"They rape little girls and they rape little boys. They're called pedophiles."

"What's a pedophile?"

"It's someone who enjoys having sex with children."

"Who could enjoy having sex with a child? How could a grown man have sex with a three-year-old girl? How would you even do it?"

"Oh, they do it, John. They do it. They hurt these

children, and they love doing it. It's their predilection. It's their preference."

Then they handed me the book and said, "You've gotta look at these pictures and tell us if any of these guys have been to your house. You've had people in to work on your house. You have gardeners. If anybody in this book looks familiar, if you've seen any of them in your neighborhood or hanging around Adam's school, then we might have a suspect. It might have been a pedophile who grabbed Adam."

I still wasn't quite getting it. Not yet. I said, "Why would they grab Adam?"

"To have sex with him. They're into having sex with children."

"With a six-year-old boy?"

"Absolutely."

"Don't they stay in prison a long time?"

"No, John, they don't. They do a year, maybe two years. There are guys in this book who have been arrested fourteen times, and released. Back out on parole. They live all over Hollywood."

And I said, "But that's not possible."

Then I looked at the book they had given me, and there were two-hundred photographs in it.

I had known that there were mug-shot books of guys who've been convicted of rape, and that when burglaries happen, they show victims the books of burglary suspects. But this I could not believe. I looked at the photographs of these scumbags, and a lot of them actually looked like regular guys. Like grandfathers. There was obviously no way to tell a child molester just by looks. Because the way they looked was like everybody else.

I studied every mug shot in that book, but I didn't see anyone I recognized. And finally, finally, I began to understand what they were trying to tell me.

"One of these monsters could have Adam?"

"Yes," they said. "That's probably who's got Adam."

Until that time, even though I had thoughts in my heart of hearts that I was not admitting, I was still trying to convince myself that some wonderful grandparents had Adam. That they had taken him up to Disney World because his favorite ride was Pirates of the Caribbean.

But now I knew that it was all bullshit. I was deluding myself. I was in denial. I wasn't facing facts. I knew it at the time. One side of me was saying, "No one could hurt this gentle, gentle, beautiful little boy. If they had him for even an hour, they'd know how special he is. If they talked to him for fifteen minutes, no matter what kind of monster they are, they couldn't hurt this little boy. This is one of God's children."

And then there was the other side of me. The other voice.

The next night, for some reason that I don't understand myself, I went back to talk to Ronald Wright again. I don't know why. I just needed to. And it was during that conversation that he first said to me, "You've got to accept the fact that Adam might be dead."

Of course Adam wasn't dead. He was with a wonderful, grieving mother whose child had been hit by a car, or a lovely pair of grandparents.

Ronald Wright said, "You have to accept the possibility, John. I've got four girls up in the Broward County morgue, all homicide victims. They range in age from thirteen to sixteen.

"I believe they were all runaways. A couple of them were tortured very, very badly. Florida law says that after six months I've got to bury them. And if I don't know who they are, they go in a Jane Doe grave. John, all over the country there are people buried who no one knows—six thousand of them in potter's field in New York alone.

"So what I do is I hold bodies up at the morgue on my own for a year, a year and a half. On the chance that a grandparent or a brother or sister of one of those runaway girls might somehow find their way to us.

"Somebody loves those four girls here in the morgue. Someone does. How can I bury them if no one knows who they are?"

And I said, "I'm certain that someone loves them. I know that somebody does."

He kept talking. "I'll tell you something, John. You've got to accept the reality that in the state of Florida, coroners exchange information about unidentified bodies only on a voluntary basis—by mail, once every six months. There is no system. It's all voluntary. And this is only within Florida. There are forty-nine other states."

"Do you mean to tell me that the same country that put a man on the moon, the same country in which I can go into my office and access the Japanese stock market in five seconds, that in this country there is no way to identify these dead children?"

"John, there is no such thing as a comprehensive 'Unidentified Dead' file. Anywhere. The FBI has a few cops who voluntarily track these kinds of things—if a coroner is mentioned in a file, for instance. They'll take the information, but they don't solicit it. They don't seek it out.

"There is no system. Nobody is really looking for Adam except you and your friends and the Hollywood police. If he's in a morgue in Tallahassee or Jacksonville, one in the Florida Panhandle, there is the chance that, at least for a while, you may not even hear about it. It is not inconceivable that he could be buried in an unmarked grave."

Ronald Wright told me that the only option I had was to expand the area of our search. I said, "But I have. I've been up in West Palm Beach on TV."

"West Palm Beach? What about Georgia, John? What about South Carolina? And New York?"

And he was right. People in those states wouldn't

have known that Adam Walsh was missing. The only people who had even heard about Adam's disappearance were ones living in south Florida. His story wasn't in the *Washington Post* or the *New York Times*. None of those papers' readers knew that Adam Walsh was missing.

That was when I realized something for the first time: that if Adam was dead, then there might be a way that I could at least get his body back. At least I might not have to wait six months to find out if he had been murdered. If his little body was in a morgue somewhere in Oklahoma or Texas or Louisiana.

Ronald Wright said, "If there's a system in other states, I don't know about it. I'm just a county coroner. If I want to find out the identities of these four girls in my morgue, who do I send flyers out to? To what agency? To every parent in the United States for nine zillion dollars?

"John, the electronic media is your best bet."

And that's when it dawned on me.

We would take the search national.

6

The Police

THE COPS MEANT WELL.

They were a tiny local police agency that had limited resources and had never manned a search anywhere near this size. It didn't seem to me that they really knew what they were doing. But they were caring and well-intentioned. At least in the beginning, we had no question about that.

We did have a gut intuition that mistakes were being made. Everything seemed so chaotic and disorganized, and certain guys in the press were sidling up to me on the sly, saying, "You know, John, this thing ain't going so good."

The rank-and-file cops were serious about looking for Adam. The vice-squad cops—undercover narcotics cops who looked like dirtbag hippies with pigtails and ponytails—were working straight twenty-four-hour shifts to find him. If a reporter walked in, they'd run out of the detective bureau so their cover wouldn't be blown. Then they'd come back in to finish talking with me when the press guys had gone.

These street-level cops were the ones telling me,

"Well, we've got an informant over here we're going to go out and talk to. And then there's that other guy we figure we can roust." They were out shaking down suspects and the lowlifes. They were the ones who knew about pedophiles and child molesters. They were street-smart guys, not shirt-and-tie detectives.

And privately, on the side, they were saying, "John, these detectives are taking down phone calls on matchbook covers. This is the most disorganized search we've ever seen."

It was not until Thursday, four days after Adam's disappearance, that the Sears security guard, a teen-aged girl named Kathy Shaffer, was finally interviewed. She told police that on the day of Adam's disappearance, four older boys, two white kids and two black, had been playing with the video game in the toy department. They had started causing a ruckus, and she separated the kids—putting the two white kids out the west door and the two black kids out the north door.

She wasn't sure, but she thought that the younger of the two white boys might have been Adam.

If Adam had been put out the west door, he would have been completely disoriented, because the only entrance he knew was the northside door that he always came through with Revé. If Adam had truly been forced out of the store, then it seemed pretty logical that whatever had happened to him had begun to happen then. The search should have followed that track. But with all the chaos that was going on, it didn't.

A week later, Dick Hynds, the HPD's supervisor of detectives, gave an interview to the *Hollywood Sun-Tattler*. He said that lots of calls and tips were coming in, but "we wouldn't know where to direct them to.

"Considering the time lapse involved, [Adam] could be anywhere in the world by now. We don't have proof that he's dead. We don't have proof that he's alive or been kidnapped. We just don't know."

The scariest thing of all was that it was completely true.

We soon learned firsthand what every cop investigating the disappearance of a child already knows: that until they are definitively cleared, all family members have to be considered possible suspects. During the second week of the search, the police broached the subject of giving me a polygraph. I immediately agreed. It was standard operating procedure, we understood why, and no one had a problem with it.

Joe Matthews, a detective from Miami Beach who was an expert in administering lie detector tests, was invited in by the HPD. He had worked hundreds, if not thousands, of homicide cases, and even though the HPD had a few guys on staff who knew how to give polygraphs, for a case this high profile, they wanted what Matthews was—the best.

On the morning of Friday, August 7, I went over to the detective bureau and did what Joe called the pretest interview. We sat down together, in a room by ourselves, and he started asking me everything about my family and my life. Everything.

I answered all the questions and volunteered anything I could think of, regardless of how irrelevant it seemed. The questioning went on all day and into the night—for more than seven hours. I told Joe everything—about my father, how much I loved him, how I was raised, about my relationship with Revé and our friends, my job. I even told him about how, back in college, I had smoked marijuana a few times and tried LSD. Joe filed his report, addressed to HPD captain Robert Mowers:

As per your request, on Friday, August 7, 1981, an extensive interview and specific polygraph examination was conducted on Mr. John Walsh. Said polygraph examination was conducted to determine, if in fact, he was criminally involved in or had guilty knowledge as to who was responsible for the abduction of his son, Adam Walsh, which occurred on or about July 27, 1981. The following are excerpts from this interview:

After his father passed away, he brought his mother, brother, who is 22 years old, and sister, who is 30 years of age, to south Florida. At this time during the interview, Mr. Walsh became emotional concerning the pressure that has been on him in reference to the caring for his family and the supporting of his mother. He stated that he feels personally obliged to help everyone, especially family members. He said at times he feels he is being taken for granted but after expressing this to this examiner, a feeling of guilt came over him and he said he really does not mean it; he loves his family very much and since this is the first time he has had a chance to express himself, he is letting everything out, even though he does not mean it.

He stated that for the past two years, since he has spent less time working, he found that his relationship with his wife has improved, and he became closer to his son, Adam. Mr. Walsh stated that he believes his wife has always been very loyal to him and his son. He reiterated the fact that she is very close to his son, Adam, and loves him very much, and both he and his wife, Revé, are very protective of him.

When Mr. Walsh was asked who resided in their house, he said that he, his wife, Revé, their son, Adam, and a close friend by the name of Jimmy Campbell. He described Mr. Campbell as being 25 years of age, and he has known him for over ten years. Subject recalled that they met when he worked as a beach boy at the Diplomat Hotel. Jimmy was 12 or 13 at the time, and used to spend his time at the Diplomat doing odd jobs, just to be near the ocean.

Jimmy liked to surf and was very much into diving. Subject stated that Jimmy always looked up to him and confided in him and he honestly feels that he is Jimmy's only true friend. Campbell also goes by the name of Dudley. The Walshes gave him that name because he was so helpful and always there when needed. He was their "Dudley Do-right."

Mr. Walsh realized that even though Jimmy Campbell's father did not kick him out of the house he was not really accepted and the father preferred that he did not live there. After he and Revé married, since the Monahans were mutual friends of both Jimmy Campbell and Mr. Walsh, Jimmy would come by their house and visit.

After his son, Adam, was born, the visits were more frequent, and Mr. Walsh did not mind this for he felt that his wife and son were left alone, at home, unprotected, during the night, and if Jimmy Campbell stayed there, he would feel that his family was being protected. At first, he would occasionally pay Campbell for some of the time he spent there baby-sitting and doing minor repair work around the house. As time went on, Mr. Campbell spent more and more time there each day, and before anyone knew it, it was taken for granted that he was living there.

Mr. Walsh stated that not only did he like and respect Mr. Campbell, he and his wife decided that he would be their child's godfather, for they realized the sincere love he had for Adam.

Mr. Walsh stated that "Dudley is Adam's godfather and is totally distraught." Mr. Walsh stated that he knew Adam was alive and well and that he would get him back. He stated, "Whatever you want me to do, I will do." Dudley stated to Mr. Walsh that the police probably think he is distraught running around with psychics. He would say to me, "John, tell me what to do." Mr. Walsh stated that he has seen Dudley by himself crying and he has told me not to give up hope. Dudley has done everything everyone has asked him to do.

In the beginning, Walsh stated, he and his brother Joe thought they would find [Adam]. Dudley was not living with them at the time. . . .

It was an exhausting, draining, difficult interview. What most struck Joe about it, as he later said, was that I had been willing to lay bare my soul like that, expose even my most private thoughts and feelings, for one reason and one reason only: because I was willing to do anything in my power—anything—to help get my son back.

After the pre-interview came the actual polygraph exam. Joe hooked me up to some electrodes and arm cuffs and asked me a series of questions: Did I intend to answer truthfully? Did I know who took Adam? Did I conspire with anyone to cause his disappearance? Was I withholding information from the police?

Then Joe read the polygraph charts, compared my answers to the baseline interview, and concluded that he could say with certainty that I had played no role in Adam's disappearance.

A few days later, Revé was interrogated, too.

The cops were looking at clues, which there were none of, and the facts, which there were not very many of, and basically trying to get the caseload off their desks: "Who can we put this on? If we can't find out who did it, if there are no concrete clues or physical evidence, where do we go next? What's the next best thing?"

They were fighting criticism and panic from the community, trying to keep everything calm and under control. Revé went over to the HPD and the cops took her into the back. The first few times she was in a fighting mode, but after a while she went in slumped over. Beaten up, broken down. For her, it was like having salt poured in the wound.

The cops would ask her, "Well, what did you do on that day?" And she would tell them. Again and again. They were grabbing at straws.

They told her that the lady in the office at St. Marks had said that Adam wasn't with her when she went in to drop off his tuition check. "She remembers you, but she doesn't remember seeing Adam," they said. Then they said that no one in the store remembered seeing him with her, either.

So all of a sudden there were no witnesses at all who had seen Adam with Revé. Revé knew full well that Adam had been standing behind her in the office at St. Mark's, and the woman hadn't noticed him because she was busy talking on the phone. Revé finally put the check on the desk and left. And in the Sears store, why would anyone have noticed him? He wasn't loud. He wasn't doing anything to draw attention to himself. He didn't sass the security guard. He wouldn't have made a fuss when she told him to leave.

Revé knew what the truth was, even if no one believed her. She and I didn't have lawyers or a PR firm. All we knew was that whatever time the cops spent investigating us was wasted time—because it could have been spent looking for Adam.

We knew that the cops were looking at James Campbell, too.

In those days, Jimmy was running the sailboat rental concession at the Golden Strand Motel in Miami Beach, and we considered him a friend. What I couldn't understand was why the cops were leaning on him so hard. Rumors were even circulating that the cops had beaten him up in the interrogation room. Actually, what Dick Hynds had told the papers was that they were being so rough on him that they were *on the verge* of violating his constitutional rights.

I was defending Jimmy Campbell to the cops,

telling them that he would never have done anything to hurt Adam. But they didn't care. They just kept pounding away at him. I couldn't understand why they just kept after him, why they kept calling him in and leaning on him. Why they wouldn't just leave him alone.

Then I found out why.

It was because, at the time, they all knew something I didn't.

What they knew was that Jimmy Campbell had been having an affair with my wife.

During the time that Revé was pregnant with Adam, there was a dresser that needed painting. She wanted to stick some flower decals on it and put a pad on top, so that she could use it as a changing table for the baby. I was working enough hours at the time that when the weekends came, I just couldn't seem to get around to helping her with it, and I guess I was that way about doing a lot of things. So one day Jimmy said, "You know, Revé, I'll do it for you."

He painted the dresser and they put the decals on, and the changing pad. Revé thought it was really nice of him. She said, "Jeez, thanks a lot."

Pretty soon she wouldn't even ask me to help her with things anymore. She'd just ask Jimmy, or Johnny or Michael Monahan. They were "the kids." We all hung around together—them, me, Revé, and the Monahans.

After we had Adam, Jimmy came around even more. Not by himself. Usually with the Monahan boys. They would come over to see the baby or just stop by to say hello. Then, when Revé and I moved out to Miami Shores, Jimmy started coming all the way over by himself. I would ask him to do things in the yard and I paid him a little bit on the side. By then we were calling Jimmy "Dudley," because just like Dudley Doright, he was always there to help out. Dudley was always happy to help out and so patient with the baby. He really loved Adam.

I was traveling all the time.

Revé was home alone a lot.

I don't know how or when, exactly, but years later somehow the line got crossed.

Revé says that she has now grown to the point where she knows that I love her. I guess she didn't know it then. She says that I am the man she always loved. The strong man she looks to as her husband and the father of her children. But at the time, she had somehow believed that, for certain emotional things, she would just have to look outside our marriage.

She says that it was warped thinking. Really sick thinking. And that, finally, she couldn't stand it anymore. She told Jimmy that it was over. That she and I loved each other, and that we had decided to have another baby.

It wasn't an easy thing for her to get out of. She told Jimmy that she and I cared for him. But that whatever was between them wasn't going to go any further. That she had made the decision to get her life back on track.

And then, two weeks after that conversation, her little boy disappeared.

Soon, things that were already awful got even worse. I had always been the person that Revé confided in, and now there was something important that she couldn't tell me about.

She took the blame for it. That she had done this thing, and now, even though it had nothing to do with Adam being missing, it was getting all mixed up with the investigation. It began to derail the search. Because it gave the cops a ready-made motive. They thought that because James Campbell was jealous of me, he had taken Adam. Which might have seemed possible. Plausible, even. Except that it wasn't true.

I kept defending Jimmy to the cops. Telling them that they'd better get off Jimmy Campbell and onto something relevant to the case, or else I was going to hire a lawyer and do God knows what. I made some pretty serious statements in Jimmy's defense. I really went to the wall for him.

The cops kept insisting to Revé that she was going to have to tell me. She kept saying that she couldn't. That she just couldn't do it.

"Well, you know, it's not like you broke the laws or anything," they said. "You can't get arrested for having an affair."

In the end, someone else finally told me. Not Revé. By then, she wasn't doing anything except waiting for the ax to fall. Totally submissive. Completely resigned. Ready to accept whatever I felt she needed to do. She knew there was no justification. No explanation, no cop-out, no excuse. She had known it was wrong. She had done it anyway. And now there was nothing that could be done except to live with whatever I decided to do.

I came to a decision, that some of this was probably my fault too. I told Revé that I would not leave her. And that was the truth.

The important thing was that our little boy was definitely missing, probably kidnapped, and maybe dead. That was more important than anything else, even this. I am not going to spend a lot of time discussing this. It isn't anyone else's business. It was private. It became an issue later because the press made it an issue, and Revé had to answer for it the best she could. I don't know if she spent nights torturing herself about it. Somehow, she dealt with it.

It wasn't that this thing was small. It was not a small thing.

But compared with Adam's being missing, it didn't even register. If it hadn't been for Adam's being missing in the first place, I might never even have known about it. Who would have told me? Not Revé. But after all, there were some things in my life that I wasn't exactly proud of either. By the time I found out about it, it was already over. She had ended it. She had already come to the decision, by herself, that it was over. James Campbell had moved out of our house before Adam disappeared, and that was when Revé said she had ended it.

That squared with what she had told me.

It was awful.

But it did not mean that we deserved what happened to our son.

What mattered was Adam. The only thing that mattered to me or Revé then, or ever, was Adam. James Campbell was relevant to the case because he gave the cops an easy out, the perfect solution: Jimmy Campbell is jealous of John Walsh, so he kidnaps the kid. A big movie ending. Now they had a suspect, someone with a perfect rationale for hurting Adam to get back at me. Once I had this information, everything was a lot clearer. Now I knew why the cops were leaning so hard on Jimmy Campbell. And I knew that it was bullshit.

I didn't know to what lengths the police would go to force the issue. It was their first big mistake, wasting so much time on such a dead-end lead. They thought they had the case solved. It would have made a great crime story, a great ending to a movie. But it wasn't true. It wasted time and resources and energy. And by that point, all of those things were in pretty short supply.

Every day when I went into the station, I would say, "You guys, you're only local police. Who's looking for him in Broward County?"

"Oh, everybody in Broward is looking for him."

"But who's looking for him in Jacksonville? What if he's a hundred miles away?"

They didn't have an answer for me.

Four days into the case, I knew how much trouble we were in. I remember looking at what they all called "the wire," a big Teletype that sat in the middle of the floor. It would say, "Two Hispanic suspects wanted for a double murder in Arizona believed to be heading south. Be on the lookout for a 1956 Chevy . . ." I said to some captain, "You know, I've been over here watching this Teletype for two hours to see if there's anything on it. And all that time, nobody else has even looked at it."

He said, "Well, we've got our own local problems, you know." In other words, he wasn't really concerned with what was happening in Arizona or Denver, Colorado.

"Well, if you're not watching the wire here, who exactly *is* looking for Adam everyplace else? Just how many law enforcement people know that Adam is missing?"

"Well, we do. We're looking. And Fort Lauderdale knows. And so does Pembroke Pines."

I thought to myself, *"Pembroke Pines?* My son could be in Alaska by now, and these clowns are talking about Pembroke Pines?"

My son was missing. Seriously missing. And I was realizing that my very best law enforcement allies were a bunch of underpaid cops. As well-intentioned as they may have been, this was not something that gave me a whole lot of confidence. Or a lot of hope. My friends and I had, on our own, already spent three days calling every police and sheriff's department in the state of Florida. We had mailed five of Adam's missing posters to each and every one of those offices. If we had had the authority to call out the National Guard, we would have. But we didn't. So instead, we turned to the FBI.

On Thursday, July 30, the fourth day that Adam was gone, John Monahan called a friend in Washington who was in the Reagan administration. He asked this guy if we could get some help from the federal government. We didn't even know what kind. Just any kind of help. Monahan's friend immediately placed a call to William French Smith, who was the U.S. attorney general at the time, and who gave assurances that the FBI would become involved in the case.

I don't know exactly who called them or when or precisely what made them show up. Maybe it was because there was starting to be so much publicity. But one day in the HPD detective bureau, all of a sudden a couple of FBI guys walked in. They were wearing suits, always suits. I think they came from Miami or Fort Lauderdale. You could always tell who they were. They didn't look anything like the Hollywood police.

"Mr. Walsh, I'd like you to meet Special Agent so-and-so."

"How do you do. What are you guys doing to help find my boy?"

"We are monitoring the case, Mr. Walsh, and we are making resources available to the local authorities who are becoming—"

"Why are you not involved in this case? Why aren't you really in it? Why aren't you assisting the Hollywood police?"

"Our forensics labs are available, Mr. Walsh, and any resource we have is available to the Hollywood police for their use, but our internal policy is such that we do not routinely become involved in local matters."

I said, "If Adam is outside of Broward County, it's not a local matter. And what if he's outside of Florida?"

"Well, here's the policy, Mr. Walsh. We can quote it to you again. You must understand . . ."

I must *understand?* They said that there had to be either a ransom note or proof that Adam had been taken across the state line in order for them to become officially involved.

I said, "Don't *you* understand? This is 1981. When was the last big ransom case of a kidnapped child that you can remember? The Lindbergh kindapping?

"Today, people don't kidnap kids for money. And

I'll tell you something else. I will bet my life that whoever has Adam Walsh isn't going to pull off the highway to a pay phone just so they can call you to let you know that they're taking him across the state line. Of that, I can assure you."

And they said, "We're monitoring the situation, Mr. Walsh. The Hollywood police have the situation well in hand."

Screaming was not going to help. All I could do was demand that the FBI get involved, which I did. Repeatedly. And they assured me that they would. As soon as they were convinced that something more was involved.

"More than *what?* More than that a little boy's been missing for seven days? *What?"*

In retrospect, I think what they were trying to tell me, between the lines, was that for them to become involved in Adam's case, the Hollywood police would have to officially invite them.

Top CEOs of corporations know enough to ask for outside help when they are outmanned or outgunned. But the Hollywood police didn't behave like savvy businessmen who know when it's time to bring in a top-notch consultant or a ruthless, hired-gun attorney.

At one point, even though I never acted on it, I was actually so desperate that it crossed my mind to forge a ransom note myself to bring in the FBI. Instead, I kept on playing the game. Pushy, but not too insistent. Demanding, but not outrageous.

When you're not the professional yourself, when you're put in the position of begging for help, then you cannot alienate the people in charge who are looking for your son. I knew one thing. That as much as I wanted to scream and yell, as much as I wanted to hit somebody or throw them out of a third-floor window, that if I did any of those things, they would never let me back into the police department again. I was walking a tightrope.

In truth, the HPD was already bending the rules, making concessions for us. They did things on our behalf that would ordinarily never have been allowed. My team and I would just walk right in and go straight on up to the third floor, past the holding cells on the second floor, and wave to whoever was manning the window so they could buzz us in. They allowed food and beer to be brought in for those of us who worked all night. And they let the press in for media interviews whenever we wanted.

Meanwhile, Dick Hynds and Bob Mowers, the captain, spent hours over at the house, just kind of hanging around. Later on, Hynds admitted to a reporter that that was definitely not normal procedure.

"We could see early on that this thing was building, and the department could end up with a lot of egg on its face," said Hynds. Which is why the HPD operating procedure, as Hynds himself put it, was closer to "CYA." Which stood then, as it does now, for "cover your ass."

The Hollywood Police Department was the investigative agency that I had to work with. I understood that this was their jurisdiction, and they were in charge of the case. And if I saw things I didn't like, or things that scared me about how they were doing their job, I had to bite my tongue. I had to swallow my pride. They could have shut me out in one minute. If I had thrown a fit, or said something in the press that they didn't like, they could have thrown me right out.

On Thursday, July 30, someone gave the cops a tip about a late-model, dark blue van. Someone said they had seen this van, with mag wheels, dark-tinted windows, and a chrome ladder in the back, cruising the Sears parking lot the afternoon that Adam was abducted. They described the driver as a white male about six feet tall, with a muscular build and curly, dark hair, and said that for a time the blue van had been parked near Revé's car. Two kids with their grandmother, who was partially blind, said that they had seen the driver pull Adam into the van and speed out of the parking lot.

At first, the police tried to track the lead on their own, keeping it out of the press. Then, two days later, they decided to go public with it in case anyone else had seen something. At the time, it was huge news. Dick Hynds, the HPD's chief of detectives, told the papers that it was the first solid lead the police had, and that he was now certain that Adam had been kidnapped.

Then a twelve-year-old boy said that he had seen the same thing—a shiny blue van pulling up near Adam on the sidewalk outside the Sears garden section. And after the van pulled out, the little boy said, he didn't see Adam anymore.

A BOLO on the blue van was sent out by the FDLE, the Florida Department of Law Enforcement. In the first two days alone, police searched fifty blue vans. A few days later, it was hundreds. The Crime Stoppers were out looking for blue vans. Florida State troopers were stopping blue vans on all the highways.

By August 4, the police didn't seem so sure about the tip anymore. Hynds mentioned in the press that he had "some misgivings" about the tip. "We checked hundreds of blue vans," he said. "Some of them have been stopped twice. It's hardly safe to drive a blue van in south Florida these days."

A month later, the police confirmed that the actual time that the blue van had been seen in the mall parking lot was at around 1:25 P.M.—nearly an hour after Adam disappeared—and therefore could not have been involved.

The blue van thus became a false lead. A bum steer. A dead end. An error. But no one, let alone anyone in an official position, ever made that clear enough. Instead, anybody in the general public who was following the case simply assumed that Adam had been picked up by somebody in a blue van. On the turnpike, blue vans were still getting pulled over. Newspapers kept mentioning stories about blue vans. People never stopped calling the detective bureau with tips about their creepy neighbor who drove a blue van. By the time, years later, that the paperwork on Adam's case had grown to a 10,000-page file, 2,247 of them—nearly a quarter of those pages—was nothing but bulletins and Teletype traffic on blue vans.

It wouldn't be hard to understand how, if anyone did see a little boy matching Adam's description in anything other than a blue van, they might conclude that it couldn't be Adam. No one could have known it at the time, of course. But it was the HPD's Big Mistake Number Two.

Meanwhile, hundreds of tips were still pouring in, even if no one was cataloging or coordinating them. Ray Mellette spent a lot of time on the third floor DB with me. He kept his eyes open. "John, we're watching detectives on the phone," he said to me one afternoon. "And they are writing phone tips down on matchbooks and scraps of paper."

"Well, maybe they collate them after a while," I said. "Maybe they organize them later."

"No way, John. No way."

After that, Les Davies actually went out to a drugstore and bought yellow legal pads for the cops. "Here," he said to them. "Here's some more paper."

One day, the police came in and out of the blue asked me what Adam would want to drink at an amusement park.

"A Slurpee, probably," I said.

"Well, supposing they were out of Slurpees. What would he ask for then?"

"Oh, I don't know. A root beer maybe. Why?"

The next day there was a huge story on the front page with a police sketch of a woman with her hair sticking out, in huge, white glasses. "A lead we have got to follow," said HPD spokesman Fred Barbetta.

All because a woman who worked at a Fort Lauderdale amusement park had seen a woman with a little boy at the refreshment stand who had asked for a Slurpee and, when they didn't have one, then asked for a root beer instead.

So that was the HPD's hot lead for the week.

I was asked by reporters for my reaction.

"Hopeful," I said. "Enthused."

During those days in the police station, I learned an interesting fact. It was not the kind of thing I would ever have known before or anything that I would ever have cared to know. But now I realized how incredibly important it was in the search for Adam.

The fact was that in almost all cases, the bodies of children who had been abducted and murdered were generally found either within five miles of where they were abducted or else hundreds of miles away. No in between.

Still, in our case, there had been no official, mapped searches of the many empty fields around Hollywood. Volunteers—groups of police cadets, or two-hundred truck drivers who had taken a day off work—were going out to search one field or another. But that was it. No one at the Hollywood Police department was saying, "There's a big, abandoned, overgrown field between Fourteenth and Eighteenth Streets. Let's get over there and walk it."

The tips were coming in like crazy, but no one was coordinating them. These were the days before computers, and since no one was in charge of logging all the information, there was no way to look up all the leads on, say, a blue van. Or a white car. Or anything else, for that matter. At night a detective who had been working all day at something else might take a phone tip, which he then might—or might not—give to someone else the next day.

Everything was so disorganized and chaotic that it was driving me nuts. And I wasn't the only one noticing. Reporters were watching things, too. The *Miami Herald* was interested because they wanted to know if someone in the family might be responsible for Adam's disappearance. But they were also interested in keeping an eye on how the Hollywood police were doing. So, at least to the media, I became the great public defender of the Hollywood police.

Privately, we were in trouble, and we knew it. The law enforcement response to the search for our little boy, who had clearly been kidnapped and was probably scared and possibly hurt or worse, should have been a coordinated effort by as many law enforcement agencies as possible. But this small-town police department didn't seem to want to ask for the help that was so obviously needed.

The one exception to the whole depressing situation were the troopers of the Florida State Highway Patrol. Ordinarily, police can't stop a car unless they have reason to believe that there are drugs or a gun inside. But when the tip about the blue van first came up, the state troopers found excuses to stop vans all over the state. Hundreds of people who drove blue vans complained about being pulled over by Florida State troopers.

The troopers were one police agency that really, really looked for Adam. They basically said, "Screw it. Wouldn't it be great if that little boy is in this van, and we get him back alive?"

Every now and then Revé would go over to the police station just to see what was up. Just to sit there and project her famous attitude: "Don't tell me how sorry you are for me. Do something."

John Monahan was there a lot because he knew the chief of police, and whenever the chief would start talking about anything else, or laugh at something, Revé would think to herself, "You stupid buffoon. How can you sit there laughing? How can you even think of anything but Adam?"

It was late at night, three or four days into the search, back when the cops were still scrutinizing everything she did, probably wondering if she had anything to do with Adam's disappearance, when she noticed a machine, like a Teletype, in the auto theft section. It was running on and on. A big pile of paper from it was forming on the floor, and every so often someone would come by and rip the paper out of the machine and take it who knows where. Then another pile would form, and they'd rip that one off and take it away, too.

Finally, she couldn't stand it anymore. "What is this thing?" she asked.

"Oh, that's the NCIC. The National Crime Information Center computer."

"What does it do?"

"Oh, it tells about things that are going on in other areas."

"What happens to the printout? Is anybody looking at it?"

"Well, ordinarily they do. But with everyone being so tied up with your case, we haven't had the time."

They didn't even bother answering her last question, which was, "Well, what if there's something on there about Adam?"

So that was the big revelation. That the cops could tell you where your stolen car was, but not your stolen child. The idea that it was a pretty big country out there, and that police agencies all through it didn't necessarily share their information. And even if they did, who knew if anyone else was reading it?

That was the first time that I remember feeling that we didn't have a chance. That we might as well just go on home. Because there was no system. What there was, was nothing.

I remember saying to myself, "Maybe they should just go ahead and bomb this building and turn all the criminals loose. Because we're definitely out in the weeds on this one. We're so far out behind the eight ball here that it's nothing but a big, sick joke."

7

The Search — Part II

ONLY A FEW WEEKS BEFORE, A MONTH MAYBE, I HAD HAD to tell Adam that, because I was so busy at work, I probably wasn't going to be able to take him to see the dinosaurs at the Smithsonian, as promised. At least not anytime soon. So, if he and his mom and me couldn't go as far away as Washington, was there someplace closer he might like? "Yup, Dad," he had said. "Disney World."

That's why we were thinking that if anyone had taken Adam, they might end up in Orlando.

Ever since Adam went missing, the pressure to keep getting media coverage never let up. We fought for airtime, headlines, column inches. We cursed the royal family for scheduling their wedding that week. My only child, my little boy, was missing. And the location of Charles and Di's honeymoon was bigger news.

I found out that there were guys called news directors, and I tried to get them on the phone. I called NBC, CBS—all of them. People were so rude to me. A friend of ours had gone to Atlanta to talk to one of

Ted Turner's reps, and I taped an interview that we were hoping to get on CNN. Les was calling, I was calling, I was pleading as the father of a missing child. But it was always the same old thing: "It's a great story, Mr. Walsh. But it's a local one."

No one outside of Florida even knew about Adam's disappearance. No one else cared. Why would some big-time news director for a network give a damn about one little boy from south Florida who was missing?

Les and I were a couple of pretty sharp marketing guys from south Florida who had contacts all over the Bahamas. But we didn't know whom to call in New York to get on the nightly news. All we knew was that Adam could be anywhere in the country by now. And that south-Florida TV wasn't big enough.

On Sunday, August 2, six days after Adam's disappearance, we got a call at the police station from a guy by the name of Bill Frederick, the mayor of Orlando, who was also a good friend of Les's. In Orlando, the managers of Busch Gardens, Circus World, and Disney World had already put three-hundred security guards and twenty detectives on alert, and local volunteers were sweeping the theme parks for Adam.

Bill was calling to let us know that he had gotten himself booked onto a radio talk show so that he could go on and publicize Adam's case. And now, he was asking if there was anything else he could do.

Les got an idea. That same week, a case had broken about a missing boy north of us, in Tampa, and Les said, "John, why don't we take Bill Frederick up on his offer, go up to Orlando, and then shoot over to Tampa and draw some attention to that case, too. We could put it all together and do a little barnstormer of the state."

What we were hoping was that our statewide swing would kick up a little dust. Generate some interest, create domino-effect publicity.

On Wednesday, August 5, six of us, the pilot, Revé, me, Les Davies, my brother Joe, and Charlie Brennan, a reporter from the *Hollywood Sun-Tattler*—boarded a Piper Navajo en route to Orlando. It was my company's private plane, and it had seven seats. One, we held open for Adam.

On the flight, Revé read news clips. We talked a little, but mostly everyone just looked out the windows at the sun-scorched earth below. We landed at Herndon airport in Orlando at 9:45 A.M. A sign read, Welcome to Orlando—The City Beautiful. As soon as we got off the plane, a reporter hollered, "Why do you think Adam might be in this area?"

"He loves the attractions in the area," I said. "He loves Disney World. But we'll go anywhere people will listen to us, anywhere where we can talk about Adam."

One of the first people we called when we got in was Bill Frederick, who in addition to everything else just happened to be an old college roommate of David Hartman's, then the host of ABC's *Good Morning America,* which at the time was the top-rated network morning show. Earlier that year, there had been a lot of local press about a woman with amnesia in South Florida State Hospital. After trying for weeks to identify her, the authorities were at a dead end. Then in February, they arranged to get her story on *GMA*. Within days, she was reunited with her parents, who had not seen her in seven years.

Bill's press guy set up a conference call with the *GMA* guy in New York, and we all got on the phone together. The *GMA* flack basically didn't want to be bothered, and Les was swimming hard upstream. The flack kept asking Les if the story was "genuinely newsworthy," and the mayor's press guy kept assuring him that it was.

Finally, after much back-and-forthing, the *GMA* guy agreed to take a look at a big book of press clippings that Jane had been working to compile.

"Well, okay, why don't you send it up? I guess we can take a look at it."

A limousine picked us up from the airport and took us to a motel called the Court of Flags. Revé told Charlie Brennan how hard it was for her to get in front of TV cameras, but that she did it because "it's the only way we'll get him back."

At the motel we hooked up with a guy named Chad Martin, an old friend of mine from our days in Eleuthera who was now the motel's VP of sales and marketing. Chad was the one who, over the past week, had been coordinating the search for Adam at all the theme parks in Orlando.

In the old days, Chad and I used to have a great time, hanging out together at the hotel-marketing trade shows. Now, it seemed as if all that had happened in a former lifetime. Over breakfast, Chad was shocked at how bad I looked. I wasn't really sleeping, and I had lost about thirty pounds.

Revé was telling Chad about her progress with one of the psychics, a retiree from Lauderdale named Schermerhorn. He claimed that when he looked at photographs, he saw a black aura around anyone in the picture who had died. Before he read Adam's aura, he wanted to know if Revé was ready for the outcome, either way. She had told him that she was. So he went ahead and read the picture.

And in it, he said that Adam's aura showed he was alive.

Maybe to spare Revé's feelings, Schermerhorn did not tell her that when he had first walked into the Hollywood police station, the cops had shown him a picture of Adam, too.

And that time, as soon as he saw it, he had blurted out, "That boy's dead."

We had an 11 A.M. press conference scheduled in one of the motel's conference rooms, and this was a big break for us. The chance to get some attention statewide, which could snowball to who knows what.

I was nervous beforehand, talking nonstop. The day after Adam disappeared, during my first appearance on TV, I had stammered when a reporter fired a question at me. Revé had had to finish my sentence for me. After that, I considered it my duty to be better prepared. I needed to be coherent, concise, and making the best possible appeal for Adam's return whenever we were lucky enough to get coverage from the electronic media. From then on, I never stumbled again.

At that first press conference in Orlando, only one newspaper reporter, three radio newscasters, and one TV cameraman showed up. I didn't care. It was better than nothing. I talked about all the help we were getting from law enforcement and all the average, ordinary citizens. I said again what I had been saying a million times in the previous ten days. That we would go anywhere to find Adam. That we would negotiate with anyone if it would help bring him home. "He's our only child. He's our little boy and we want to get him back. We'll never stop looking for him. We'll never give up."

We had lunch at the motel, met with some people, and afterward, as the room was emptying out, Charlie Brennan saw Revé looking at a menu. "I know what Adam would have," she said. "A hot dog, chips and a soft drink."

"Yeah," said my brother Joe. "He's definitely a hot dog kind of guy."

Just before three o'clock, we left on the short flight to Tampa. We had to wait for a while because there was a nationwide air traffic controllers' strike. But the airline people really tried to help us out. When we got into the Tampa airport, they took us right into the VIP lounge for another press conference. This time, we met with newspaper, TV, and radio reporters one-on-one. And this time, there were media people not just from Tampa and Orlando, but from St. Petersburg and the Panhandle, too. Revé said that anyone who thought they were seeing Adam should call out his name. I kept talking about the reward.

Later on, we were sitting with some reporters inside the airport and Revé all of a sudden came out with what was in her head. "I just can't wait until Adam comes home," she said to no one in particular. "You know how it feels the night before Christmas? This is like that. Except a hundred times more."

Charlie Brennan asked her what the first thing was that she was going to do when Adam got home. "We're going to have the biggest party south Florida has ever seen," she said. "I don't care if it takes two years. I'm going to invite everyone who's helped. We're going to have it in a big hotel, and I know Adam is going to want to shake everybody's hand."

As we were getting ready to leave, Revé walked across the room to where someone had put up a whole display of Adam's missing posters. She reached up and touched his face, gently, with her hand. At that point, I think, just as some reporter asked me one last question, Charlie Brennan finally lost it. Later, he said that it was all he could handle. He just broke down and cried.

That single, one-day barnstormer across Florida changed everything. The focus of the search was getting wider, more people were hearing about the case, and it began to feel as if national news organizations were going to take some interest. When we left Hollywood that Wednesday morning, there had been one TV camera present. By the time we got back, there was a whole raft of them.

Even more important was that it looked like Adam's case might actually get on *Good Morning America*. That it might finally be on television nationwide.

In addition, because of the publicity that we were generating, it also now seemed as if we might actually start to get a little help from the FBI. In Tampa we had been filmed for a segment on the local CBS affiliate, and one of the people who saw it was a woman named Ivana DiNova. She was the president of something called the Dee Schofield Awareness Program, a Brandon, Florida–based group that tried to help families of missing children. Dee, Ivana's twelve-year-old niece, had been missing since 1976.

After the CBS segment aired, DiNova called us to say that she was working on something called the Missing Children Act, a law that would require the FBI to get more involved in the cases of missing children. She said that she would contact Florida's Republican senator, Paula Hawkins, cosponsor of the bill, and Florida's other senator, Lawton Chiles, to urge them both to put some pressure on the FBI.

It didn't take long to get a response from Washington.

"There is nothing that Paula Hawkins can do to push the FBI into this," a Bureau spokesman told the *Sun-Tattler* on August 7.

Then the HPD's Captain Mowers got into the fray. He told the papers that the HPD had "made [the FBI] aware of [Adam's case] from the first day. I would welcome anyone who would want to come in and help. But I don't think they're going to dedicate street people to come in and start investigating. Realistically, there's nothing that can be done on our level that hasn't already been done in this case. We've even done a lot of things we normally wouldn't do.

"If the federal government has jurisdiction, it just comes in. And we certainly can't keep them out if they want to come in. I would call them in a second if I felt we needed help. We would utilize the services of the Royal Canadian Mounties if we had some direction to go in. It's not a matter of who does it, it's just that it gets done."

Everyone, including the cops, knew that we weren't asking for the FBI to invade Hollywood. It was that police in neighboring counties didn't really know anything about Adam's case, at least not officially. All we were hoping for was to get a little help outside of Broward County.

A little boy's life was at stake here, for God's sake. What the hell was the matter with them?

It was all making me crazy. That week, for a story he was writing, Charlie Brennan asked me if, once Adam was home, I would be willing to get involved politically in the issue of missing children. "Absolutely," I said. "Once you've been through this thing, you can certainly empathize with anybody who's going through it. A lot of people don't have the friends and the community support that we have. We would do anything to help."

As things went, our main contact at HPD became, and continued to be, Jack Hoffman. Whenever anyone called to say that they knew where Adam was, or that they had some kind of tip, Les would turn it over to him. Things had kind of reached status quo. The leads would always turn out to be nothing. It would have been a lot for an entire police department to follow up on, let alone one man. Les later said that he always imagined Hoffman taking down the information and then just throwing it into a wastebasket under his desk.

By the second week of the search, while no one wanted to say it out loud, especially in front of Revé or me, it was becoming obvious to the people closest to us that the search might go on for some time. Jeff O'Regan and Les Davies had already had a critical, private conversation. At the time, they thought that the best thing was to try to get Revé's and my life back to some sort of normalcy. It wasn't really possible under the circumstances, but even so, they decided to move the whole search operation out of the house.

Up until that point, 2801 McKinley and the third floor of the Hollywood Police Department had been Search Central. It wasn't a good idea anymore. Things at the house were getting too overwhelming. And the HPD would be just as happy to see us move out, too.

So they gave us some space in the old HPD building on Hollywood Circle.

The building was on a rotary in the center of downtown Hollywood, not far from the library and the court and all the government buildings. Upstairs there were jail cells, still being used as part of a holding facility. And our space, on the first floor, was one big, cavernous room. Dark, with a low counter that ran the whole length of it.

At first, we only had one telephone line, the one we had transferred over from the house. But by Sunday night, there were five phone lines, all installed to handle the expected deluge of calls from our appearance Tuesday morning on *GMA*.

It was late on the night of Monday, August 10. Les was in the office alone, getting ready to close up for the night. Revé and I were already in New York. Jane had flown up, too, as had Charlie Brennan. Things were quiet. It was hot. No air-conditioning. Just the hum of a ceiling fan. That and the sound from upstairs of the inmates in their cells, playing Ping-Pong and watching TV.

Then, just as Les was getting ready to turn out the lights, the phone rang.

A reporter from Orlando was on the line. She told Les that she had just heard a report over her police scanner. That two fishermen in Indian River County, near the town of Vero Beach about 120 miles north of Hollywood, had found something in one of the canals that ran past the citrus groves along the Florida Turnpike. There were reports that it might be the remains of a young, maybe ten-year-old, boy.

This obviously had nothing to do with Adam's case, Les said. It must be that missing boy from Tampa. He was older than Adam. It couldn't be Adam. Because if it was, Les said, he would have heard something by now.

No sooner did he put down the phone than it rang again. This time, it was Dick Hynds, who gave Les the same information that the reporter just had. As Les remembers it, Hynds may even have said something like, "We're getting ready to go up to Vero."

Hynds wanted Les to know about it, he said, in case he got any calls from the press.

He told Les that they needed dental records, and that they were trying to locate Adam's dentist. So Les sat there by the phone until about eleven o'clock.

But there were no more updates, and no more phone calls.

He was by himself, and there was nothing more that he could do. So he eventually checked everything that was supposed to be checked. He turned off the lights, locked up the office, and headed out the door for home.

We had been battling for fifteen days to get any kind of law enforcement agency outside of the Hollywood police to investigate Adam's disappearance.

None of them would. No one would help us.

In spite of that, we had launched what was now being called the largest hunt for a child in the history of south Florida. At last count, we had printed and delivered nearly 1 million posters throughout the United States. We had learned to use the power of the media. We were no longer innocents.

And now it was obvious, at least to Les, that our efforts had paid off. That, against all odds, we *had* accomplished what we had set out to do: we had gotten the word out.

Because the call that came over the police scanner that night, more than a hundred miles away, was not "We believe we've found something out here" or "We have the remains of a young male."

What the voice on the radio, full of static, had said, was:

"I think we've found the Walsh boy."

8

The Day

I HAD BEEN TO MANHATTAN A MILLION TIMES BEFORE ON business, and it had always been a whirlwind—hustle and bustle and restaurants and meetings and phone calls. This time, it was as if the whole city had stopped. Like time was standing still. Like moving around inside of a dream that I couldn't wake up and get out of. I wanted to do the morning show, get it over with, get back to Florida, and keep going with the search.

The only thing in the world that I wanted more than that was to get a phone call from Ohio and hear a voice saying that they had spotted him and that he had been taken into protective custody and was a little shaken up, but was safe and hadn't been hurt. Or that somebody knew who had taken him and could describe where he was being held. Or that someone was really almost sure that they had seen him that morning. Or anything at all.

Revé and I went to our hotel room at the St. Moritz on Central Park South. A small room, up high. Right over the park. We didn't sightsee. We didn't go for a ride. We sat there. Prisoners of time. Suffering. We decided to try to go for a walk. There was no press. Nobody knew who we were. Nobody cared—just two ants on the streets of New York.

We walked down Fifth Avenue for a few blocks, until we came to St. Patrick's Cathedral. I felt like going inside, and Revé said that she did, too. We walked through the doors of that magnificent cathedral, over to one of the side altars. The one, I think, to St. Jude, the patron saint of lost causes.

In my heart of hearts was the deadening feeling that we were never going to see our little boy again. But it was cool and dark inside, and so we prayed. We lit a candle for him and prayed to God that somebody would find Adam and bring him back to us. That God in his infinite wisdom would make it so that this thing would have the miracle of a happy ending.

Revé and I held each other's hand as we walked up the aisle. Other people were in the church, but nobody noticed us. It was the first time that we had really been alone together since Adam was missing.

We told each other that somewhere, somebody had to know something. That maybe, even now, someone would come forward to help us. Revé believed that Adam was with a person who would never hurt him. That Adam was so beautiful and so gentle and so handsome that no one could possibly harm him.

After a while, we went back up Fifth Avenue to the hotel, but Revé said that she couldn't go upstairs. For two weeks now we had been doing something every second of every day. So while I went in to use the phone, Revé went to sit at the little sidewalk café outside the hotel, because it was New York, and you never knew. He might be anywhere in the whole wide world. Who could say that if she was standing on this corner, that he might not come walking by? Hadn't things been strange enough already?

I had a different opinion. I had seen the pedophile book. I had listened to all the cop stuff. I wasn't telling her anything. What right did I have to tell her? What right did I have to take any bit of her hope away? I kept saying, "We're gonna get him back. Someone's going to come to their senses and we'll find him. Whoever has him, now that we're going national, people will see him."

To myself I was saying, "Two weeks. It's just too long. It's been way too long."

One day was too long.

Two weeks was an eternity.

That night, we met for a drink with the two women who were going to appear with us on *GMA* the next morning. One was Julie Patz, the mother of a little boy, Etan Patz, who had disappeared on his way to the school bus in New York two years before and had never been found. Julie was working, she said, for some kind of change in the system. With her was Kristin Cole Brown, the information director for an organization called Child Find, based in New Paltz, New York, and founded by a woman whose daughter had been missing for seven years.

Julie and Kristin had picked us up at La Guardia, and it was obvious from the start that, finally, we had found someone who was going to help us.

And then the oddest thing happened. Just after we sat down for drinks, Julie said, "On the show tomorrow, do you think you could hold up Etan's picture, or pictures of some other missing kids? Could you do that, please?"

Right after that Kristin Cole Brown told us that she was running Child Find—this big, sophisticated East Coast organization—out of a little room in her house.

All of a sudden, it was so obvious. They were asking *us* for help. These were women. Mothers. No one was listening to them. And I was a man, wearing a suit.

It was another of those horrible realizations.

We had been following a trail of crumbs in the hope that it would lead us into the house with the dining room that had the table loaded with all of the food.

And now we knew that it wasn't going to be that way after all. Because there was no food, no table, or even any house. There was just the trail of crumbs.

Julie Patz and Kristin Cole Brown said, "John, this is the first time that a man has come forward on this issue. We just feel that, with your involvement, we can start to make some serious headway."

They were quoting all kinds of reports and statistics. And the whole time, Revé and I were pulling back, sinking down farther into our chairs. It was as if the lid had suddenly been yanked off the whole can of worms.

"My God," I said to myself. "This thing is snowballing."

Our *GMA* appearance was scheduled for the next morning, Tuesday, August 11, at 8 A.M. They were going to send a car to take us for the short ride to the studio. For most of that night, I didn't sleep. Revé was asleep but I was lying in bed, staring up at the ceiling. I didn't trust the wake-up call, and we would have to be showered by six o'clock. Then, at five, the phone rang.

I don't remember who it was. I honestly don't.

They wanted to know who our dentist was.

Because a severed head had been found in a canal.

They were couching it. Saying everything in a way so as not to panic me. They didn't really think it was Adam's remains. Another boy was missing, a boy a little older. And they thought it might be him.

I told them that Adam's dentist was Dr. Marshall Berger and that his office was in Hollywood. Then they told me that John Monahan would be going up to Indian River.

The next call was from a *Good Morning America* segment producer. "John, we've heard that there have been some remains found north of Hollywood that might possibly be Adam's.

"It's up to you, John. It's your call. You can go ahead with the appearance, or you can certainly feel free to cancel. If you'd like to be flown home immediately, we can arrange that. Because this may be too painful for you. You have to consider what might happen if these remains turn out to be Adam's."

I told them that no one was sure that this had anything to do with Adam. And that no matter what was going to happen, we wouldn't know anything for some time.

"We have to go ahead with the appearance," I said. "You're our only hope. This is the only chance we have to get Adam's picture on national television. And you know what? I want to bring pictures of other missing kids. Because whatever else happens, at least we'll be able to get some publicity for other people's children."

They said, "Okay, then, that's what we'll do. We'll send the car over to pick you up."

I was in the bathroom, shaving, when the third call came. I picked up the extension and it was Charlie Brennan. "Charlie," I said, "I don't know anything. They're getting the dental records."

And he said, "John, the location is one hundred and twenty miles north of Hollywood. We aren't going to know anything for a long time."

It was just a short phone call.

I didn't tell Revé. I didn't tell her anything. I was scared to death, hoping against hope. I had a horrible, paralyzing feeling. But I wasn't going to let anybody know. I was the guy with the stiff upper lip.

I knew what I had to do. I was prepared to go on television to plead for my son. I had his picture. I knew exactly what I was going to say. I had it all memorized: first, a description of what he looks like; then, where he was last seen. If they gave me thirty seconds, I was going to cram it all into thirty seconds. If they gave me five minutes, I could go on longer, about how he acted and what his favorite games were, everything about him.

I knew that Revé wasn't going to say much. It was

my job to do the talking and to get in everything that I could in that short time, and then to still cover Etan Patz's case, show his picture, and talk about other children, too. But I had it down. I was going to do it all.

The call almost threw me off the track. "Stay focused," I told myself. "You've got to stay focused."

Revé and I had finished getting dressed, and when we arrived at the studio, everyone was so gracious to us. When we were on the air, David Hartman covered everything. He got it all in—Adam's description, Adam's picture. They got the other pictures of children on, too, and I talked about other parents' cases.

Like any good interviewer, David Hartman had to deal with all the information that he had, and I understood that. "John," he said, "this morning there has been information that some remains have been found in a canal near Vero Beach."

"You know, I don't think it's Adam," I said, "but no matter what happens we wanted to come on the show anyway. Because of all these other children." The whole time, Revé was sitting there next to me. Not saying a word. Looking like a bomb had gone off in her head.

Afterward, everyone said, "Good luck. We're praying for you." They were gentle with us.

We thanked everyone and left the studio, and I remembered thinking that Revé seemed buoyed by it. Because after all that we had been through in those past two weeks, we had finally done the impossible. We had badgered our way through, we had persevered, we had gotten Adam's face and his story on national television when hundreds and hundreds of other parents—even Julie Patz in New York City— had been turned down. We had gotten further than the parents of any other missing child had ever gotten before.

My sister Jane, Revé, Kristin, and Julie all decided to go over to the Plaza for something to eat. They wanted to talk, to strategize. Jane had traveled all over the world, she was sophisticated, and when she said she'd look out for Revé, I felt safe in letting her go off with them.

"Tell me exactly where you're going to be," I said.

She pointed up the street.

"Okay," I told her. "I'm going to go back up to the room to make some calls."

I walked back to the hotel, went upstairs, and waited. Just waited.

I sat on the bed, by myself, saying, "It can't be. Nobody could do this. Nobody. Nobody could kill this little boy. There is no creature on the planet who could do that."

By that point, I knew that there *were* people out there who did that. But not to this little boy. Not to this one—ours. He was too gentle and gracious and beautiful a child.

And then the phone rang.

"Is this Mr. John Walsh?"

"Yes, it is."

"Mr. Walsh, we are so very sorry to have to tell you this. But the remains that were found last night in Vero Beach have been positively identified as Adam's."

I went down.

Right onto the floor. It felt like somebody took a huge, wooden stake and shoved it into the wall of my chest.

Like somebody killed me right there on the floor.

I couldn't breathe. I thought I was having a heart attack. It felt like I was dying.

"Please let me trade places with him . . ."

Death would have hurt me so much less.

I thrashed and I screamed. I yelled and pushed over

143

the mattresses and smashed things. I broke glass and a picture frame and tore off the sheets and threw lamps and kicked the table over.

I was like a wounded animal. Dying the way a wounded animal dies. I could not deal with it. It was unbearable, unbearable. I thought that my heart was going to explode.

I had known what it's like to be beaten to a bloody pulp, what it feels like to have your ribs broken and to be scared for your life. None of it, none of it even came close. If someone had walked in with a rusted knife and said, "I'm going to spend two days killing you slowly with this blade. But after I do that, I will let your boy go," I would have begged them.

"Please . . ."

The little boy I had waited all my life to have was dead.

Someone must have heard me screaming because two security guys came to the door. They knew by then. Someone had let the management know. Everyone was hearing about it. There were the faces of the security people saying, "Mr. Walsh, can we get a doctor for you?"

I don't think I answered them. I was saying, "How am I going to tell my wife? How am I ever going to tell Revé? How can I tell her? She's his mother. I can't tell her this."

But there was no one else to tell her. I had to get her back to the hotel. I called the Plaza and asked for my sister. They paged Jane and she came to the phone and I said, "It's over."

"You must not tell Revé. Don't you tell her. I will tell her. Bring her back to me at the hotel. Do it right now.

"Because I have to tell her."

Revé was sitting at the bar. Waiting. Someone came over to say something to Jane, and then she told Revé that they had to leave because I was waiting for her back in the hotel room.

She remembers walking back. Knowing that she was going to get bad news. But hadn't quite gotten it yet. Jane was saying, "It's okay. It's okay."

The whole way back, all the way up in the elevator, Revé kept patting Jane's hand, telling her, "It's all right. It's going to be all right."

Then they came to the door of our hotel room and I opened it.

And I said, "Our baby's dead."

And Revé said, "I know."

I don't know how she knew.

I had already watched her for two weeks, suffering. It was like seeing somebody being tortured slowly . . . slowly . . . in front of you. And then watching them let out a last sigh and die.

At first, she turned from me and started putting her clothes into a suitcase. Like a robot.

Then Jane left, and the door was closed. And as I watched, the spirit that had made her who she was slowly collapsed into her. As if her whole being was caving in on itself.

She was still my wife. But she went from being a girl to an old woman right before my eyes.

I didn't know what to do for her except hold her.

Hug her and hold her. I couldn't say, "We're going to live through this. We're going to make it." I could not say those useless things. There was nothing to be said except "I love you."

So that's what I said. Over and over. I hung on to her. I tried to console her, and she tried to comfort me. We were like two wounded, dying animals.

I had watched my father die of the most painful cancer. I had been in a car accident where a man died in my arms. It is not a huge, earth-shattering event to see someone die. I don't think it is.

Unless it is your child.

Children are supposed to outlive us. They are immortality and legacy and the special, special part of

life. They are to be revered and loved with an unconditional love.

It's not about partnership or a merger. It has
nothing to do with money. It is not about the bond of
being a brother or a stepbrother.

Your child is part of you.

The phone rang again. This time it was a *GMA*
producer. "John, I've got some really great news.
Every talk show wants you. Every radio station. We'll
find Adam. We'll get his name all over the place."

And I said, "He's dead."

While we were in New York, Gram had stayed at
our house on McKinley Street, with Jeff and Les and
Joe. It was Jeff who told her that the sheriff had called
to say that they had found a body up in Indian River.
But that they didn't know if it was Adam, because this
boy might be a little older.

My mother remembers sitting there all night, waiting for the sun to come up. And then, toward morning, in the semidarkness, Jeff came into her room. He
was gentle, and as big as the doorway. He sat down at
the foot of her bed and said, "Gram, we found
Adam."

Then my mother got a terrible pain in her chest that
went up one arm, across her throat, and down the
other arm. They had to call for a doctor, who came
right over and gave her something. He sat there with
her and held her hand until she could absorb all of it.
Until she understood that it was finally over.

My mother didn't learn until a few days later, when
she overheard it in the house, that we had only found
part of Adam's body. But even worse than that, she
says, was the one thought that she could not get out of
her mind. Of how frightened Adam must have been
when he finally realized what was happening to him.

They took us in a car from our hotel to the airport.
We didn't know where to go or what to do. We only
knew that we had to go home. We were like two

helpless children. We were reduced to being children. The security people took us right out to the runway, and I thought of all the help that the airline people had given us. How pilots had put stacks of Adam's missing posters under their seats and taken them all over the country. How they had flown us places and been so wonderful to us.

They put us on a plane for Florida and we waited for two hours to take off because of the air traffic controllers' strike. It was the longest plane ride of my life. When we landed at the Fort Lauderdale airport, it was late Tuesday night, and when we got off the airplane, all of a sudden a million lights and cameras were in our faces.

I couldn't understand. What did these people want to see, exactly? Two destroyed human beings on the six-o'clock news?

It was chaos. We lost Jane in the crowd. Got swept away from her. Someone ushered us into a VIP lounge to give us some breathing room. Revé went into the bathroom and, in the middle of everything, suddenly found herself alone. Later, she told me that she had stood there for a long time, looking at herself in the mirror and trying to make herself believe it.

"Your little boy is dead. They cut his head off," she said, looking right into her own eyes.

When we got home, we could barely get up the driveway to our front door. Reporters were all over the lawn, camped out on our street. Cops were there to try to protect us, and they had to push people back just so we could get into the house. Like we were going to the Oscars.

Then, without our little boy, we walked across the threshold. It wasn't a home anymore. It was a building. It meant nothing now. Without Adam in it, it was nothing. A place to keep your clothes. It was now the area that we were forced to return to at night to be reminded that we were never going to take him on another trip. That he was never going to play with his toys again. That we would never again put him to bed in his room.

And then, gradually, after a few hours, the press finally went away. Some out of common decency. Others because they gave up. Then, it was only Revé and me. We didn't sleep. We were lying on the floor, crying. Hanging on to each other. Weeping.

And then, at four o'clock in the morning, there was a knock on the door. I thought it was the Hollywood police telling us that a suspect had been picked up.

But when I answered the door, it was a woman staring at me. "Mr. Walsh, I'm a reporter, and I need to get a comment about Adam's murder tonight because my editor said that if I don't get a quote from you tonight for tomorrow's editions, I'm going to be fired."

At first I just stood there. I wasn't sure of what I had heard. I was trying to catch it again.

"What? What did you just say to me? Who are you?"

And then, it sank in, and I finally lost it completely.

"You tell that fucking coward son-of-a-*bitch* to come over here right now! Because I am going to pound his ass to a bleeding *pulp!* You take your notebook and you get the hell off my lawn, do you hear me? You get out of here and leave us the hell alone!"

And that was just the beginning. That was just my baptism.

The next morning it was in all the papers: "Adam Walsh Found Dead: Discovered in Vero Canal." "Adam's Body Found. Sixteen Days of Agony Grow Into Horrid, Tragic Climax." "As Parents Pleaded, Police Suspected Worst."

Talking to them, Les Davies let fly: "The FBI got involved in looking for a mare that was impregnated by Secretariat. They looked for a goddam horse because the foal would be worth five hundred thousand dollars.

"I guess a child's life isn't worth that much."

On Thursday, we had a wake for Adam at a local funeral home, and then—on Saturday, August 15, 1981, at St. Maurice's Catholic Church in Hollywood, Florida—his funeral.

Catholics believe that children who die before the age of seven—the "age of reason"—aren't capable of making a moral choice to sin. So when they die, they enter immediately into the presence of God. That's why the funeral service for a child is called a Mass of the Angels.

More than a thousand people attended Adam's funeral. My cousin Father Michael Conboy, a pastor in upstate New York, gave the eulogy and ended with the words, "We'll see you again, Cooter. We promise."

I remember asking him, "Is this the benevolent God that we have worshiped our whole lives? Is this an all-powerful, benevolent, gentle God who allowed this to happen? Tell me about that one, would you, Father Mike? Explain to me how it is that I'm supposed to deal with this."

He didn't have any answers.

Nobody had any answers.

So many people came to the funeral that most of them had to stand outside the church. We put a picture of Adam on top of his small, white casket. There was nothing inside it. We were not given anything to bury. They told me that the casket was only a symbolic thing.

They had to keep the remains for evidence, in case anyone ever came forward and confessed. Then they could see if the confession matched the evidence.

The children's choir sang a hymn:

> Children of the heavenly father
> Safely in his bosom gather.
> Nestling birds nor star in heaven
> Such a refuge 'ere was given.

Then the children gave us a banner that they had made. In gold lettering on white cloth, it read: "If His song is to continue, then we must do the singing." We knew that the word *His* was supposed to mean the Lord. But to us, it meant Adam.

Because it was Adam's testament. This was Adam's song.

Book
Three

9

Upstate

PEOPLE COULDN'T STAND US.

They loved us, they were concerned for us, and we knew it. It was just that this was new territory for all of us. Revé and I were in a place that they didn't know anything about, and they weren't sure how even to be around us. No one knew what to do or say, and we couldn't tell them because we didn't know, either. Everyone was doing the best he or she could. But no one could look us in the eye. That's how bad it was. So bad that people couldn't handle the fact of us.

I was worried about Revé. I was really afraid that she was going to do something. If she didn't actually die of grief, which I now knew was possible, I was afraid that she might do something crazy. So we stayed together, day and night.

And I was having a hard time even looking at my mother. She had just lived through the death of my father, and now there was this. All my life, I had always been her capable, handsome, charismatic son. Now I was just a brokenhearted shadow of that.

One day, Revé answered the door and it was Adam's little buddy Jeremy, asking if Adam could come out to play. Jeremy had been away at summer camp, and I guess no one had had the chance to tell him. So Revé explained to him as best she could that Adam had died, and that he wouldn't be here to play with anymore.

"Jeremy," she said, "would you like to have Adam's bicycle?"

He said that he would. So Revé went back out to the garage and found Adam's bike. The police had dusted everything for prints, apparently with a firehose. There wasn't anything that wasn't completely covered with a sooty black powder. So she got some rags and cleaned the bike off and wheeled it out to the driveway.

People always wonder about what Revé did with Adam's things. Well, now at least they'll know what she did with his bicycle. She gave it to Jeremy.

By this time, Jeff O'Regan and I had been through everything together. Everything. He had seen me almost die, and now he saw what was happening—that I was slipping away. I don't know how he knew what to do, but he came by one day and invited me up to the beautiful house that he and his wife, Karen, had in upstate New York.

"You've got to get out of here for a while," he said. "And if no one else can be with you now, then you can come with me." At the time, Jeff had started his own business as a construction contractor, and this was his busiest season. Without saying it, he let me know that he was willing to take time off, completely interrupt his life, and bring Revé and me into the middle of his and his wife's lives so that he could be with us, day and night.

"Come on, come on. Let's get you out of here," he said. "You need some time to relax. I'm going to take you up to the house."

So, after Adam's funeral, we gave one last press conference to thank the Hollywood police and the media for all their help, and to try to express our appreciation to the thousands of people who had taken the time to look for Adam, and all the people from around the country who had wished the best for us and prayed for us and for our little boy. Then we flew up to Ithaca, to my friend Jeff O'Regan's house.

The house itself was in the Finger Lakes in upstate New York, right on a lake and surrounded by woods. It was where Jeff and Karen spent part of every year, and he had boats and skis and all kinds of water toys there. We didn't know how long we would stay. We didn't plan anything. We just lived from day to day.

In the mornings, Jeff knocked on our door and came in and said, "You look terrible. You're losing weight. You can't eat. You're going to get up and we're going to get into the canoe and we're going to go out and paddle."

And I would say, "I can't. I can't do it. I cannot get out of bed."

He ignored me. "We're going to get in that canoe and we're going to paddle across the lake and you're going to talk to me, and I'm dragging you out of this bedroom. You're going to get up. Come on, come on, come on . . ."

Then, in the afternoons, he found me wherever I was and said, "I'm going to sit here with you, and I'm going to listen to you. I'm not going to pontificate, not going to tell you any bullshit. I'm going to sit here and listen to you."

And that's what he did. For hours and hours.

I wasn't sleeping. Couldn't get out of bed, couldn't function. All the classic symptoms, although I didn't know it at the time, of someone who is suffering from profound grief. Day and night, the only thing I thought about was Adam. Everything about Adam.

It took every bit of mental power that I had not to dwell on what his last hours were like. I tried desperately not to think about it or to discuss it or to wonder about it. Not to speculate, not to let Revé talk about it. Because I knew that kind of thinking could destroy me.

Anytime I lay down, the thoughts would start: "What did he go through? How painful? How long? Why?"

Nope. No way. None of that. I kept telling myself, "If you let them, those thoughts will kill you."

Revé and I had brought along a picture of Adam with us. We put it on the mirror in the bedroom, and that's what we did for a lot of the time: we would lie in bed together and look at him.

But there would always be a knock on the door— Jeff again, making sure that we were okay in there, and telling us that it was time to get out of bed, even when we thought we couldn't. There was always something for us to do, because Jeff always invented it. He forced us to eat, to go places, to do things.

He saved my life.

Jeff had a huge hang glider that he used to tow behind his powerboat out on the lake, and one afternoon he and I went hang gliding. I suppose it's a dangerous thing to do, because if anything goes wrong, you dive into the water at about ninety miles an hour, from way high up. But I was doing lots of dangerous things at the time. Riding motorcycles, being the daredevil.

On this day, I was strapped into the glider, being pulled behind the boat, really soaring out at the end of the tether. And then, all of a sudden, I crashed. I didn't lose consciousness, because I remember hitting the surface of the water, hard, and then the sensation of sinking. Settling down toward the bottom of the lake. I was all tied up in the towline and the glider's harness, hanging upside down, maybe twenty feet below the surface, tangled and drifting. Most people would probably have panicked. All I felt was suspended in time.

Throughout my life, I had survived so many close calls, so many brushes with death. Every time, I had struggled and fought against it. But now, this time, as I looked down at my chest to where the clasps and fasteners were, there didn't seem to be any point in unbuckling myself. I was calm. I felt no urgency about lifting my arm up to free myself. That far down in the ice-cold water, drowning didn't seem like such a terrible thing.

And then, I don't know why, but just as I was beginning to run out of air, I watched my hand come up and unfasten the harness. I held my breath, unbuckled the belt, and slipped out of the rigging. It was me who did it: I swam to the surface.

At some point after that, Jeff and Joe came up to me one day in the driveway and Jeff said, "I know what you're trying to do. You're not fooling us. I can see right through you, and if you do it, you'll break my heart. You'll break everybody's heart, and you're not going to do it. You're not going to get away with it.

"We know you. You are thinking that you can't deal with this. I've seen you in a lot of bad situations, and this time you want to leave the world because it's just too painful.

"But if you do that, you'll be a coward, John. That would be a coward's way out. And I won't let you do that to me, to your mom, to your brothers and sister. That would be the most selfish thing of all. And you're not like that. You're not selfish. You never have been. You've always looked out for everyone else.

"I've seen you beaten to a pulp and washed away in the ocean when everyone thought you had drowned. But you never gave up. Your dad was a fighter, and you're a fighter, too. You can't give up now. I'm not going to let you."

Then Joe said, "You're my brother, and my whole life I've always looked up to you. And if you do this to yourself, you'll destroy all of us. We can barely deal with losing Adam as it is. And if, in your own sneaky, stupid way, you figure out how to kill yourself, then there will be nothing left.

"Dad is watching you, and Adam is, too. We all know what it is that you're trying to do."

It was stupid. Very, very stupid. But I was hurting so much that I wanted to take the easy way out. I now believe that, at the time, what I was thinking was that I could kill myself and make it look like an accident. I could fool them so that they would never know. That way, Revé and my family wouldn't be destroyed, and I could go on to the next life and see Adam and my father and be out of my horrible pain.

Because I was already dying. Absolutely dying of a broken heart.

I thought that I could find a way to get rid of my pain so that no one would ever know. No one except Jeff and my brother Joe. But they caught on pretty quick.

It was Jeff who said, "I won't let you leave us."

And my brother Joe—so young—who said, "You cannot do this to yourself."

And Revé, who kept telling me, over and over, "John, we were not the victims here. Adam was."

And all of them were right.

Jeff had graduated from Cornell, and the campus wasn't far from his house. I needed to keep my mind occupied, and I decided that this would be a good time to find out about some things. I asked Jeff about it, and he said that he was sure that Cornell would let me use their library.

One morning I went over and said, "I'm the father of a little boy who was murdered. I don't go to classes here or anything and I don't have a card. But I was wondering if I could use the library?"

Ithaca wasn't that far from Auburn, and I guess there had been some coverage in the local press. Because they said, "Sure. Absolutely. We know who you are. Come on in."

I spent hours in the library in the microfilm collection, looking at newspapers, magazines, and statistical reports. I wanted to find out about the kidnapping of children, how often it happened and what had been done to prevent it. One of the things I pulled was the FBI's annual uniform crime report. In it, I was amazed to see that there were no official statistics on child abuse, missing children, or even kidnapping.

I found some magazine articles about the case that Les Davies had mentioned to the press. About how the FBI had gone in to investigate the disappearance of a $500,000 horse from a breeding farm in Kentucky. The Bureau assumed it had jurisdiction, said a spokesman, "because of the value of the horse."

Then I looked up the actual law that covered kidnapping, something called the Federal Kidnapping Act, which authorized the FBI to enter a case if someone was unlawfully abducted and held for ransom—"or *otherwise.*"

So what I had suspected all along was true: the Bureau *could* investigate a kidnapping case—even of an animal—without a ransom note or proof that state lines had been crossed. They could basically get into a case if and when they felt like it.

Next, I tried to find out how the FBI had gotten jurisdiction over kidnappings to begin with. That was when I found an article from the *New York Times,* dated July 30, 1933: "J. Edgar Hoover heads new crime bureau. A division created by President Roosevelt will war on kidnappers." And another article from the following year: "The Lindbergh Law and the activity of federal agents threaten to kill kidnapping."

As it turned out, the Federal Kidnapping Act was also known as the Lindbergh Law because it was passed by Congress—as a result of sheer public outrage—not long after the Lindbergh kidnapping in 1932. The statute made it a federal crime to send a ransom demand through the mail. And it did something else, too.

From the time it was first founded, the FBI had

basically been just a small, do-nothing agency that could investigate only crimes committed on federal land. But the Lindbergh Law gave it power outside those jurisdictions; it was this law that gave Eliot Ness and his G-men the green light to hunt down all the mobsters and crime gangs who were abducting people and then fleeing across state lines. In other words, the federal kidnapping statute was what had put the FBI on the map.

What all of this meant to me was that the FBI—whose agents had stood in the Hollywood Police Department and told me to my face that they had no authority to search for my son—was only in business in the first place because on a cool spring night fifty years before, someone had broken in through the second-floor window of an isolated house in the New Jersey countryside and kidnapped Charles Lindbergh's baby right out of his crib.

We stayed at Jeff's place for a few weeks and finally decided that it was time to go home. We got back to Hollywood at the beginning of September. Maybe that was too soon. We didn't know what the right time would be. There was no one to ask.

During the time that we were gone upstate, Gram had stayed at our house to keep an eye on things. And when we got back, Revé asked her not to leave. Not for Gram's sake, but because Revé was so used to Adam and all the activity of his life—his school, swimming, baseball practice—that she just couldn't stand the thought of the two of us being left together, alone. Things were too quiet without Adam.

So Gram stayed. She never asked why or said, "I've got to get back to my house." That was Gram: unconditional. If you didn't want to talk about it, she didn't want to know. She was there. Solid as a rock. Gram stayed with us for almost a year. She says that we went to Ithaca to try to save our souls, and when we came back, she was afraid that neither one of us was going to make it.

We both were getting thinner by the minute, and she was genuinely afraid that Revé was going to have a nervous breakdown. Some days, I might be able to function when Revé couldn't, and then if Revé came around and had a fairly decent day, it was my turn not to be able to do anything at all.

Gram understood how deep our grief was. In the middle of the night, Revé and I would get up and go into Adam's room to sit on his bed. And through the wall, Gram would hear us crying.

At first, I went to different religious people for help. But ministers couldn't help me, and neither could rabbis. "It's God's plan." What kind of bullshit is that? Even my cousin Father Mike, who had delivered Adam's eulogy and later became a monsignor, had his faith shaken to the roots by Adam's death, to the point that he started to question both God and his religion.

Priests don't have children. They've never been married. Most of them have never had sex with a woman. They don't know that intimacy. They certainly don't know how it changes your life to have a child. The clergy had no answers for me—and they were supposed to be the experts.

So I tried it: I went to this well-known therapist down in Miami whose son had been murdered. Everyone I knew recommended this guy—a psychiatrist whose specialty was grief counseling. At the beginning of the first session he set the clock and said, "You're a very special patient. I don't even think I'm going to charge you."

I said, "Well, you know, I certainly don't expect you to do this for free."

"Tell me about it. I know that your pain is unbearable."

By the second session he was sitting there, tears in his eyes, talking about his son's death. About how it had destroyed him and cost him his marriage. Across the desk from me, crying.

I was thinking, "I am not supposed to be the counselor here. *You're* the psychiatrist."

I never went back.

I knew what had helped me: it was Jeff O'Regan saying, "I'll sit with you for hours and I won't say one word."

And my brother Joe saying, "We love you."

As for Revé, she was always so afraid to do anything that might reflect badly on me or tarnish my image. But she went to a therapist, too, and in typical Revé fashion cut right to the chase. She went in and sat down and said, "You know, I was having an affair, and then my son was murdered."

"My God," the woman said. And then she put her hand on Revé's arm to comfort her.

We were searching. Completely desperate.

People said that we should give his things away. Start our lives over. But we didn't know how. One of the things we needed to know was whether we would be allowed to have Adam's remains cremated. We wanted to scatter his ashes out over the ocean because he loved it so much.

During the two weeks that Adam was missing, Dr. Ronald Wright, the Broward County medical examiner, was the one who had reached out to me and said, "You must come to grips with the fact that Adam may be dead."

He was the first person I trusted. He understood what it means to have a child. And now, he was the one who had official custody of Adam's remains. So that was where I went one night: to the morgue to see Ronald Wright.

The first thing he said to me was, "You look terrible. You look like a ghost. You're not dealing with this well, are you?"

I had been trying so hard to keep the stiff upper lip after finding out about the FBI. I was so bitter and so angry. Mad at everyone. My days were filled with crying. I couldn't stop throwing up. No one was giving me any advice. No one knew what it was like. I was an intelligent person. But I felt that no one had walked in my shoes. I was so desperate for someone to tell me, "You will survive this."

By this point, I had learned about reality. I knew about death. I knew all about what men do to children and to women. So I asked him, "How do you perform autopsies on twelve-year-old girls who have been tortured by drug dealers and pimps, who've been disemboweled and had their nipples cut off?

"How do you deal with it? I've got to know. *How?*"

Dr. Wright was a lawyer, a doctor, and an expert witness highly regarded by the judicial system. He took a breath and said, "Well, then, I'll tell you.

"I'm not a deeply religious man, John. At least not in the traditional sense. But there is something that I've come to learn firsthand over the past fifteen years, and it is this. I believe that there is such a thing as true goodness in this world.

"And also, that there is true evil.

"People who don't believe that the Devil walks this earth have not seen the things I've seen. I know through experience that there are people out there who believe that they have the right to do whatever they like to whomever they choose. If they want to have sex with a woman or a dog, or to rip, beat, and torture anyone at all, they do. These people are not insane. They're as sane as you or me. But they don't live by the rules of any moral code, at least not one within human society. They are so incredibly selfish that they live only by their own rules. And these people are horribly, horribly evil.

"But I also know that if there is one thing about the Creator—whatever that higher power is—it's that we as human beings are given the choice between doing good and doing evil. Because I'm equally certain that there are people who are good.

"John, there's an old saying which says that all evil

needs to succeed is for good men to do nothing. And you are one of the ones who has the ability to do good. I know that, because I've never seen anyone do what you did during those two weeks that your son was missing. The way you used every facet of yourself to mount that search.

"What you are living through now will not destroy you. It will not kill you, in and of itself. But if you let it, it will take you down, and then the evil will have victimized you twice. You will become the second victim of this killer. If you allow him to, he will destroy you as well.

"Do you know what? At night in here, when I do these autopsies, and when I'm called on to testify as an expert witness at trial, I love it when my testimony helps put someone who deserves it onto death row, or behind bars. Because I do believe that I'm on the side of the good—and that there are others who are on the side of evil.

"And that's how I deal with it, John. Because that's my mission. And that's what I know."

Ronald Wright was the one who focused me. He was the one who said to me, "It's just that simple, John. There is evil. And there is good."

My mother says that when I came back from Jeff's house, I was different. I was still the same person, but something about me had changed.

She says that she can still see me pacing in the hallway on McKinley Street, saying, "I don't know what I'm gonna do, Mom, but I've got to do something."

I had this anger, she remembers. Suddenly, I was furious.

One ruthless, heinous act by a remorseless individual.

It could have destroyed us.

Instead, we became a movement.

10

Politics

When we got back home to Hollywood, twenty-thousand letters were waiting for us—prayers and condolences, Mass cards, and notices that trees in Adam's name had been planted in Israel. We stored them in boxes and garbage bags in the garage and, eventually, rented a mini-storage space. At first, while Adam was still missing, the letters hadn't asked for anything. But now, there were others, the ones that said things like "I am the parent of a murdered child" or "Ten years ago, my ex-husband took our kids to Guatemala and I haven't seen them since" or "My child's been missing since last April and I could never get the police to do anything."

And then there were the envelopes, more by the day, that said, "I can relate to what happened to you, because this is what happened to me. I don't know what to do to help, but here's some money. Here's a check. Use it any way you see fit."

Then, sometime in the middle of September, right after we got back from Jeff's place, I got a call from the Washington office of Paula Hawkins, the Florida senator who, a month or so earlier, had tried to get the FBI involved in the search for Adam. The call was from a guy named Jay Howell, the chief counsel of the Senate investigations subcommittee that Paula chaired, a committee that was beginning to look into the issue of missing kids—runaways, stranger abductions, and parental kidnappings. Jay said that he wanted to talk to me about a piece of legislation that we had first heard about back when Adam was missing. It was called the Missing Children Act.

As Jay explained it, about five months before, Paul Simon, a Democratic congressman from Illinois who was interested in children's issues and was trying to help Julie Patz, wrote a guest editorial in the *Washington Star,* saying how it was outrageous that the FBI would look for stolen automobiles, but not for missing children. Almost immediately, the FBI fired back a response. There was no need for any national legislation on the issue, it said. That's when Paul Simon introduced a bill in the House that would require the government to keep a file on missing children and the unidentified dead. A week later, Paula Hawkins introduced a similar version of the bill in the Senate.

Together the two versions were known as the Missing Children Act, and in Washington, they hadn't even made it to first base. They were dying on the vine. Still, they were the only legislative initiatives going. Nothing else was even on the table. Jay had lined up Julie Patz and Camille Bell—the mother of one of the twenty-nine young black boys who had been found murdered in Atlanta—to testify on the Hill for a hearing on the bill. He asked Revé and me to testify, too.

I knew nothing about Washington. I had never been involved in the political process except to vote, and I knew nothing about how legislation is enacted. But I knew what we were up against. It seemed to me that most legislation and lobbying on the Hill dealt with big business and powerful interest groups that had money behind them. But no pressing economic incentives were attached to children's issues. Children can't vote.

Still, Jay's gut feeling was that, in spite of all that, if we worked at it, we could get this bill passed. And I agreed with him.

So Revé and I said yes.

The first week in October, we flew up to Washington, and got into a taxi for a little tour around town. The driver was showing us the sights—the White House, the Washington Monument, saying things like, "This is the National Rifle Association and this is the ASPCA building, and this is the Organization of American States." We were interested in doing some research into the issue of missing children, and Revé thought it would be a cakewalk. She was matter-of-fact about it. "Could you just take us to where they do all the business on children's issues?" she said. "To the children's building, please?"

He said, "Well, there really is no such thing as a children's building. There is no building that's specifically for children."

We couldn't believe it. There were big, beautiful buildings for guns and dogs and cats and the Red Cross and the U.S. Mint. And nothing for children? Revé thought to herself, "Well, somebody'd better get the bricks and mortar, then, because we're coming in. And it's going to be a skyscraper."

On the morning of October 6, 1981, eight weeks after Adam's death, Revé and I appeared for a hearing before the Senate Subcommittee on Investigations and General Oversight of the Committee on Labor and Human Resources of the ninety-seventh Congress, "to explore the cause and effect of missing children, focusing on home environment, local law enforcement agencies, and citizen action groups."

Ted Kennedy was there, Paula Hawkins, and also a horde of press, which we were really grateful for—at least until they all suddenly went running out of the room. We had no idea what all the commotion was about, until somebody finally told us. Which was when we realized we probably wouldn't be getting so much coverage after all: Anwar Sadat, the president of Egypt, had just been assassinated.

The hearing went on as scheduled, and at the start of it, Julie Patz told the committee how, on the morning of May 25, 1979, she had taken her six-year-old son, Etan, out to the sidewalk in front of her home in New York City on what would have been the first morning that he ever walked the block and a half to the school bus by himself. She could see the bus, and lots of other children and parents were around. She watched Etan walk for half a block, then turned around and went inside. That was the last time she ever saw her son.

At the time, of course, no one knew that no trace of Etan would ever be found. One of the news photographers had asked Julie's husband, Stan, to cry for a picture, because that way "when they find the body, I won't have to come back."

Camille Bell testified that on October 21, 1979, an elderly neighbor asked her nine-year-old son, Yusuf, to go to the store, because he was the only kid in the neighborhood who would go for her without asking to be paid. Yusuf left for the store at four o'clock in the afternoon and never came back. A few weeks later, his body was found in an abandoned school.

"We did not have the influence, the money, the power, the things that are necessary to get a story told," Mrs. Bell said. "Finally, when he was found, the community did rally. That was a little late. Yusuf had been strangled, and things went on. And things go on now."

When it was our turn to speak, Revé and I placed a

picture of Adam in front of us on the witness table. I told the committee about Adam, about how much his life had meant to us, and about how hard it was to lose him. We told the committee firsthand that we had learned how little help there is for parents in our situation.

I testified about how, since Adam's death, we had contacted nearly twenty small missing-children agencies throughout the country, and that there were estimates of over 150,000 missing children each year—100,000 runaways and victims of parental abduction—and perhaps as many as 50,000 stranger abductions. I told them that as a result of our one seven-minute appearance on *Good Morning America,* three of the missing children whose pictures we showed had been found.

"Apparently, people believe what they see on television," I said. "That when a small child is missing, the FBI comes in immediately with an individual similar to Robert Stack in the role of Eliot Ness and that a SWAT team swoops down on the villains and the child is found. The grim reality is that of what happened to Adam. In most cases the individuals get no support or help whatsoever and return to their homes emotionally and financially devastated."

The next day, under a picture of Julie Patz wiping away her tears, the *New York Times* ran an article about the hearing. "It is certainly evident the priorities of this great country are in some disorder," my quote read, "when a country that can launch a space shuttle that can return to the earth and take off again, a country that can allocate millions of dollars to save a small fish—the snail darter in the Tennessee Valley river, threatened with extinction—does not have a centralized reporting system or a nationwide search system for missing children."

We had no idea where we were heading. Not a clue. The house was ready to go into foreclosure. We had gone through our life savings, at that time something like $13,000. We still had all our bills to pay, and I was trying to hang on to my marketing job, with not much more than adrenaline and drive. But Revé kept saying, "John, what are we going to do with all of this knowledge that we have? About the terrible state of things that no one seems to know about?"

We were angry for a lot of reasons, but mostly because when we had most needed help—any kind of help—nothing had been there for us. It didn't exist. But we also had enough faith in human nature to think that if people knew about the problem, they'd do something to stop it. "It's just that they have no idea," we told ourselves. "It's just that they don't know."

We now had tens of thousands of letters offering help, and a few thousand dollars in contributions. It began to dawn on us that maybe we weren't so alone after all. So we decided to take things to the next level.

We decided to get organized.

We didn't know the first thing about starting a nonprofit organization. We barely knew what one was. But that didn't stop Revé. In a statement to the local papers, she announced that she was going to open an office to work full-time on the issue of missing children. "Now I have a cause," she said. "It's like something that's been determined."

Its name was the Adam Walsh Outreach Center for Missing Children.

We had to move out of the old Hollywood police station, so we ran ads in the local paper asking for available office space. The mayor of Pembroke Pines, right next to Hollywood, called us and said that he would donate a little police station in his town that wasn't being used. It was pretty grim—one big room with a partition in it and three spaces with bars that had been used as holding cells. Revé moved file cabinets into the cells and used them as storage space. Her office had a door and a two-way mirror that looked out into the main room. She figured that in the old days, it must have been an interrogation room.

People donated a lot of things—office furniture and couches, typewriters and office supplies. The first volunteers were many of the same people who had been searching for Adam. Joe and Jane and Gram volunteered, too. And pretty soon even more people started showing up to help. John Monahan told a reporter from the *Sun-Tattler* that we could still use stationery and some business equipment, and that he had an old IBM typewriter "which would do fine if it were repaired."

At the very beginning, the Center had three goals: doing whatever we could to help Paula Hawkins get the Missing Children Act passed; helping police agencies to recover abducted or missing children; and offering a $100,000 reward for information leading to the arrest and conviction of Adam's killer.

One day, while Revé was still getting things set up, a woman came into the office and seemed really upset. She asked if she could talk to Adam Walsh's mother, so Revé told the woman to come into her office and sit down. The woman told Revé that she needed someone to help her find her missing baby.

The woman and her husband had been camping down in the Keys along with a friend, a guy who was staying with them in their camper. One night, the guy had started doing drugs, then everyone went to bed. The next morning, when the woman and her husband woke up, both the guy and the baby were gone.

Later on, the guy came back, but he seemed strange and wouldn't tell them anything. The woman was scared and she did go to the police, but they didn't seem particularly alarmed. So she had come to the Center.

That was when it hit Revé. What could she do? She wasn't a professional. She wasn't a social worker with a big case file or anything. She had only started doing this work the week before.

The little boy's name was Thomas Perry, but everyone called him Boo. He was two and a half years old. And as it turned out, Revé wouldn't have had time to do much of anything to help find him anyway. Because pretty soon the cops did.

Little Boo Perry's body was found in a Key West swamp.

This guy who was supposed to be the couple's friend had taken the baby out and drowned him.

We had some money from donations to get the Center going, but even before we left to testify in Washington, we knew that it would take a lot more to keep it running and really get it established. So we had scheduled our first fund-raiser, the Adam Walsh Memorial Benefit, to be held in the parking lot of the Hollywood mall on October 17 and 18, right after we got back from D.C., and at the start of what President Reagan had declared as National Missing Children Week. One of the people helping Revé was Ada Wolff. She had been working the phones, going door-to-door, publicizing the benefit to reporters, and before long she told us that she had collected $21,000 and lots of raffle prizes for the benefit.

Then, on the morning of the benefit, Revé got a call from Ada Wolff. She was in hysterics. Revé asked her what was wrong, and she finally broke down and told her. Ada Wolff had not actually collected any money after all, and there were no raffle prizes. She had just felt so sorry for us and wanted to help us so much that she had made the whole thing up. All along, everything that she had told us about getting the benefit together was a lie.

Revé hung up the phone and didn't even slow down. "Okay, everybody, we've got to get this thing together in a hurry. Let's get going. We've got to get some prizes." It was less than an hour before the benefit was supposed to start, but Les and Jeff ran out and with their own money bought bicycles and kids' watches and whatever else they could find.

That's how things were in those days. There was no time to catch your breath.

That same weekend, a TV crew from NBC's *Real People* came down to film us. Then we went back for a second interview on *Good Morning America* to push for the Missing Children bill. And we also went to Chicago to be on the *Donahue* show. Jesse Jackson was supposed to go on ahead of us, because he was the most important guest. But he told me to go on first instead. "You've got a story to tell, John," he said. "So you get out there and tell it."

In the meantime, Jay was prepping me for a parallel hearing scheduled for November 18 before a subcommittee in the House of Representatives. Jay told me, "Paul Simon is sponsoring the Missing Children bill in the House, and he's on the subcommittee, so he's going to be a very sympathetic ear. But Don Edwards is the committee chairman, and he's got a lot of power. He's a former FBI agent and he's siding with the Bureau on this one, against us. He thinks this legislation would interfere with local police jurisdictions and make more paperwork for the FBI. So he's going to try to keep the bill from ever getting to the floor of the House for a vote. What you've got to understand is that other members of the committee are going to bow to his wishes. They're going to knuckle under to him and vote against us, too."

Jay kept it up. He was prepping me in cars, on elevators, in offices—everywhere. I'd say, "Tell me this. What about that?" and he would. We were like the coach and the boxer getting ready for a fight. Jay was my source, giving me all the background. He knew all the staffers on both sides, knew who was for the bill and who was against it. He did his homework. He knew the scuttlebutt. "John, take a look at this, but stay away from that. Focus on this. Don't pay any attention to that . . ."

Jay Howell had worked on the Hill with legislators and had a lot of respect, even reverence, for the process. I didn't. To me, none of it was particularly impressive. I wasn't arrogant about it, but I had come from the business world. I was used to having a staff, running meetings, being responsible for budgets, making presentations, talking to bankers and CEOs about financing and development. Going to Washington wasn't a big, intimidating step for me. The only reason I was going in the first place was to get some things done. I had no time for pleasantries, for all of the BS that's part of the political world.

True, the buildings were beautiful, and the Capitol was impressive. But that's not where the congressmen's offices were. They were in buildings across the street that looked pretty much like any other big, white marble building in Washington. When someone refers to a person who's testifying before Congress, most people picture it happening in the House or Senate chambers—those big rooms that you sometimes see on TV. But that isn't the way it really happens. You actually give your testimony in much smaller hearing rooms that are in buildings across the street from the Capitol—such as the Russell or Dirksen Senate office buildings.

Even Paula Hawkins's office looked pretty much like any other office. There was a big, official seal of the great state of Florida, but otherwise it was a room with desks and chairs and cabinets in it. Paula Hawkins was my senator, but she was also a good human being and a caring grandmother. That's the way she treated people, and that's what impressed me. Paul Simon over in the House was the same way—a bright, gentle, humble man. He and Paula were the kinds of people that I had enormous respect for.

The House hearings opened on the morning of November 18. Revé and I were already up there with our name tags on, waiting to be called to testify. Don Edwards was going through all the usual stuff about how today this august body is holding hearings, and I would like to recognize my distinguished colleagues, and is there anyone who would like to enter a statement for the record? Two people who did were two Democrats, Harold Washington from Illinois and Pat Schroeder from Colorado. Both of them said that they wanted to have their prepared statements entered into the record—and then they stood up and walked out of the room.

I couldn't believe it. I had come all the way from Florida to Washington, paid for my own flight and hotel room, and now these elected officials could not even be bothered to give us, the parents of a murdered child, the dignity of five minutes of their time to hear what we had to say. Revé was shaking. She was practically in tears.

I leaned back to Jay Howell and said, "Jay, can they do this? Do they have the right to just get up and walk out like that?"

Jay said, "Of course they do, John. They do it all the time. It's perfectly routine. They have other things to do, other hearings, other votes. They can't stay in this hearing room the whole time. They enter their statements for the record, and then they excuse themselves. You have to stick with protocol."

My response was, "The hell with protocol." I had been invited to take time off from my work to come, at my own expense, to Washington. And no matter what anybody said, it looked to me as if these people were making a statement by leaving—in effect saying that they couldn't be bothered to sit there and listen to witnesses who were testifying for a bill that they had no intention of supporting.

I don't know if they were busy. I don't know if they had other things to do. All I knew was that I thought they were being extremely insensitive to the parents of murdered children.

So when it came my turn to testify and I was introduced, I made a point of saying, "Chairman Edwards, I want to make sure that it's entered in the record that I am specifically addressing the absent

Harold Washington and Pat Schroeder, who have left the hearing room."

That set the tone right off the bat. Adversarial. No one had ever had the balls to address the committee that way.

That afternoon, I decided to pay a visit to Harold Washington. Jay knew a sympathetic staffer who was able to get us a fast appointment, and Jay explained to me that Washington was important because he was going to be a swing vote on the committee. We waited and waited in the reception area and were finally ushered in to see him.

Now that we were inside, I didn't waste any time. I got right to it: "Congressman Washington, how could you even consider voting against this bill? As a black congressman, you must know that there were seventeen murders of black children committed in Atlanta before the police even called the FBI in to start investigating. It was a travesty down there. And the reason the investigation was such a mess is because everyone just assumed that it was the Ku Klux Klan who was killing those kids.

"You know, sir, you should have stayed in that hearing room to listen to Camille Bell today. You should have paid attention to what was going on. I wish she could come here herself, right into your office, to tell you these things herself."

The whole time, Washington's staff guy was sitting there thinking, "Good Lord. This guy is giving the congressman holy hell."

Washington finally said, "Well, Mr. Walsh, we have to weigh these things and take the prudent course," and all this pompous hot air. I was looking straight through him, thinking to myself, "You know, John, this is pointless. This guy isn't hearing you. No matter *what* you tell him, he's going to do whatever Don Edwards, the committee chairman, tells him to do."

Finally, Jay and I got out of there, and in the hallway outside the office I turned to him and said,

"That guy has survived political scandals, an IRS investigation, and disbarment from practicing law. He wasn't listening to me any more than the man in the moon. The whole time he was looking right past me. All he was waiting for was his next appointment to come walking through the door."

Then, something happened that would take place many more times over the years. Washington's staff guy, who had been sitting in the room with us the whole time, came up to us out in the hallway and said, "You know, you guys did a good thing in there. I've never heard anyone talk to a congressman like that. And you know what? You're right. He *is* one pompous son of a bitch."

While I was doing the Washington end of things, Revé was learning about running a nonprofit by the seat of her pants.

One day a guy showed up at the Center and asked to speak with her. She had no idea who he was. She looked out her two-way mirror at him thinking, "Who is this guy and what does he want?"

At the same time, she was on the phone with a detective down in Virginia somewhere who was telling her about a pilot program that some people were trying to start. Something that would put the most dangerous criminals—killers and rapists and really bad people—into a computerized profiling system.

It all sounded pretty important to Revé, like really serious law enforcement stuff, and she was understanding everything that this guy was saying. The problem, he said, was that they couldn't seem to get this program off the ground.

"You mean, we don't have anything like this now?" she said. "You mean the FBI isn't already doing anything like that?"

"No, ma'am. We've been trying to get it going for a few years now, but no one is really interested." What this guy really wanted to know was if the Center could help him with some political and financial support.

By the time Revé finished with the call, the guy waiting outside was gone, but he had left a packet of materials with his card. His name was Denny Abbott.

At the end of November, three months after Adam was killed, Revé and I went to a four-day conference in Louisville that turned out to be one of the first national gatherings of people who were looking into the issues of missing children, runaways, and child prostitution. Some years before, a guy named John Rabun, a Baptist minister and social worker who ran a half dozen shelters for runaways in Jefferson County, Kentucky, began to wonder why as many as twelve hundred kids a year from that area were running away from home. Since a lot of the kids wound up working for pimps as street prostitutes, he asked the police for help. And they basically told him to buzz off.

"We decided to bring them facts they couldn't ignore," Rabun later said. So for nearly a year, he spent his nights on the streets, taking down license plate numbers, learning the names of pimps, mapping out how and where Louisville's sex industry operated. After talking to Rabun, a Jefferson County judge by the name of Mitch McConnell decided to organize a task force to look into the problem. And that task force found out that what was happening in Louisville was also happening in Chicago and in a lot of other places: kids hanging out on sidewalks. and cars of customers cruising by to pick them up.

McConnell's task force eventually grew statewide, and pretty soon the cops couldn't ignore the problem anymore. They started making major arrests, and within three years there were twenty-eight major prosecutions, including ones of a couple of guys who had been prostituting at truck stops two thirteen- and fourteen-year-old girls who had been missing for two years from a foster home. Another case involved a minister who ran a Louisville mission and was caught trying to sell a young boy for $6,000 worth of food stamps and $1,000 in cash.

The city of Louisville had made a lot of changes. It cut way back on its child prostitution problem, created and funded "body safety" education programs in the schools, set up a statewide missing-child clearinghouse, eliminated parole for certain sex offenses against children, and started allowing courts to videotape testimony of children under twelve in sexual abuse cases so they wouldn't have to go through the trauma of testifying in open court. And now, the conference made a list of twenty-one recommendations for other work that still needed to be done.

We learned a lot at that Louisville conference, and it also brought us together with a group of pioneer child advocates who would become important to us—Ernie Allen, chairman of the Jefferson County task force, Ken Wooden, director of the National Coalition for Children's Justice, Howard Davidson, director of the American Bar Association's Center on Children and the Law, Dr. Dan Broughton, pediatric consultant at the Mayo Clinic, John Rabun, Mitch McConnell—as well as people we already knew: Paul Simon, Paula Hawkins, Kristin Cole Brown, Jay Howell, Julie Patz, and Camille Bell.

Another person who was there was Denny Abbott.

By that point, Revé knew very well who Denny was. A few years before, he had started a group in Florida called Child Advocacy, Inc., which did education and training on children's issues. Denny had been a representative for children in court, acting as an advocate for them if their parents were trying to do something that wasn't in their best interest.

Revé went up and introduced herself, saying how sorry she was that she hadn't been able to talk to him that day at the Center. Denny told her that he had come in to talk to her about how his group was losing its government grant. He wanted to know whether, with all the publicity about Adam's case, Revé might be able to help him get some funding.

At the time, Revé hadn't been running the Center

for long. She had used some of Adam's drawings to make Christmas cards for fund-raising and had done some mass mailings. But even at that point, it was beginning to dawn on her that things were getting too big for her to handle by herself.

Revé understood that to get anything going, you need a "poster person" to get people interested in an issue, and that's what she and I were. But she also knew that to really get things off the ground, it would take a whole staff of professionals who knew about legislation, law enforcement, and program implementation. It was time to get the pros to move in and take over.

Denny Abbott was a terrific guy, and he had a lot of knowledge. His organization had been around for a while, and he had done a lot of work with runaways. So he and Revé talked it over and decided that the smartest thing for everybody concerned was to merge our two groups.

We each had things to contribute. Denny's group had structure, a board in place, and leased office space. We had a high profile, publicity, and our logo: the picture of Adam in his red baseball cap. We agreed on our goals, pooled all of our resources, and the organization that came out of it was the Adam Walsh Child Resource Center, located in Plantation, Florida.

Not long after that, we went to another conference, this time in Covington, Kentucky. One of the child advocates who was there remembers that it was the very first time he ever saw Revé. She was sitting in the back of the room, by herself, watching one of the speakers, and the whole time was rubbing a small piece of paper between her fingers. Not even looking at it, but just kind of stroking it, like you would some prayer beads. He looked a little closer, and saw that the paper was actually a little picture of Adam.

That guy's name was Robbie Callaway.

At the time, Robbie was working in Washington

with the Boys and Girls Clubs of America, chairing a coalition of about forty organizations—the American Bar Association, National PTAs, the Boy Scouts, the YMCAs—all the big players in the juvenile-justice arena. He was working for the reauthorization of something called the Juvenile Justice and Delinquency Prevention Act, and the Missing Children Act was part of that bill.

Not long after that conference, he had gotten a call from a friend on the Hill who said that she had a constituent who was trying to get some things done in Congress and wasn't being very well treated. He asked her what the guy's name was, and she said, "John Walsh."

Robbie had certainly heard about the Adam Walsh case, so he agreed to meet with me and Jay Howell one morning. Jay was very knowledgeable and knew what he was doing. And me? As Robbie tells it, I was "angry, angry, angry." I was ready to come and tear the capital apart. Every chance I got, I would go through my whole rap—how if my car was stolen, the FBI would have taken a report, but they wouldn't take a report on my missing son. It's true: I was angry at everybody, completely wired, and not very focused. If anyone asked me a question, it would take me thirty minutes to answer it. It all made sense in the end, but if you tried to cut me off midstream, you couldn't tell where I was going with it.

Jay and I knew that Robbie could help get us meetings with key people on the Hill, and that's what we wanted. So he said, "All right. I'll help you. But you have to take things one step at a time." That, of course, didn't appeal to me. What I didn't know about the Hill would fill a book, but I didn't care.

During one of my very first meetings with Robbie, I said, "I've gotta meet with Strom Thurmond. He's the chairman of the Senate Judiciary Committee, and I've really got to talk to him."

Robbie said, "John, listen to me. Senator Thurmond is not going to meet with you, just like that. We've got to do it the right way: first, I'll set up a meeting with a member of his staff, and once the staff member does the right thing, then we'll try for a meeting with the senator. I'm sorry, but that's the way things work in Washington. You've got to go through channels."

Let's just say that I didn't fully appreciate that, and that if Robbie had been in my position, he would have felt the same way. I argued with him a lot back in those days. But he still says that I was the most results-oriented person he ever met, and also one of the most impassioned. So that became our little working group: me, the bereaved parent; Jay, the staffer from the Hill; and Robbie, the facilitator.

I remember the first meeting that I ever had in Strom Thurmond's office with one his staffers. The guy was being such an obnoxious, unbelievably arrogant Washington bureaucrat. He was saying things like, "Gentlemen, we are simply not going to take up this issue. I can assure you that the FBI knows what it's doing, and we are not going to put ourselves in a position of challenging them. And, no, the senator is not going to take an interest in this."

Robbie, of course, happened to know Thurmond personally and knew he *would* be interested in it, but this guy didn't care. He was totally blowing us off.

I was getting angrier and angrier. Robbie was trying to talk to this staffer, and all the time he was doing it, he was also leaning really hard on my knee, trying to push me back down into my seat. Because he could tell that I was getting ready to hit this guy. But Robbie just kept talking, trying to calm things down. In his head, he was saying, "Please, John. Do not slug this guy. He works for a United States senator, and that would not be a good thing."

I can still see that staffer's smug face. Nondescript, like all of them: blue suit, red tie, white shirt. So impressed with their own importance. "And, Mr.

Walsh, you probably don't understand how we do things here on Capitol Hill. You have to understand the complexities and nuances of the legislative process."

I said, "I understand them very well. What I understand is that you are the guy keeping me from seeing Strom Thurmond to explain to him why we need more hearings on the Missing Children Act. And if you don't let me see him, I will have my friend Paula Hawkins call him personally and your ass will be in a sling because I *am* going to see the senator personally, and when he finds out what a pompous asshole you've been, you are going to be history."

"Now, Mr. Walsh, there's really no need to resort to those types of intimidation tactics."

"It's not about intimidation. It's about doing the right thing."

I was getting right up there in this guy's face. I wanted to punch him. I was so frustrated and so heartbroken and had been jerked around so much by people who were putting me off or patronizing me or using me for their own manipulative games. People would make commitments, then blow me off because they got a better deal somewhere else. Or because all of a sudden it seemed like too much work. Sometimes I would just break down and lose it, totally. Those were such hard times.

To this day that guy does not have any idea how close I was to popping him. It would have gotten me arrested. But it would have felt good.

At the same time, the FBI was being brutal to us. I had been trying to get some help from them, and they totally turned their backs on us, totally. All during that period there was a lot of press coverage about the Missing Children Act, and all the opposition to it, including the FBI's. One day we got a phone call from a reporter who let us know just exactly what the FBI was saying about it. When she had asked a high-ranking Bureau official for comment, he said that missing children are domestic matters, that they should be reported to local police, and that if we kept pushing for the Missing Children bill, the Bureau would fight for its defeat.

As for Revé and me, he added, "That couple down in Florida can go pound salt."

I guess I was really starting to annoy some people.

There was, for example, the day that I went over to the Justice Department with Jay and John Rabun for a press conference to hear what Justice's position was on the Missing Children's Act. I hadn't been officially notified. Somebody had slipped me the word. The idea was that a lot of press would be there, and if they saw me, they'd probably try to ask me some questions, too. So I showed up, and sure enough, the pressroom was packed. The first thing I did was step right over to where the bank of microphones had been set up for all the officials who were going to speak. I got right up there where all the cameras were pointed. Really close. A real transgression.

As soon as they started taking questions, I asked one. I don't remember exactly what I said. Just dropped one of my famous bombshells. Immediately, I got grabbed firmly by the arm. The guy said, "Mr. Walsh, as far as you're concerned, that's the end of the press conference. Why don't you come with me."

Then all hell broke loose. Reporters were jumping up trying to talk to me. A woman from the Justice Department was trying to help the guy hustle me out: "No, Mr. Walsh doesn't have anything more to say. This is Justice Department property. Keep moving, keep moving."

The guy, firm grip on my arm, was saying, "You're going outside, buddy." And the woman was saying, "You've really crossed the line here, Mr. Walsh. You've really got a lot of nerve pulling a stunt like that."

And I was saying, "I thought this was the *Justice*

Department. Isn't this about justice? Isn't this whole thing about justice for children? Are you guys working for the KGB or something?"

The next thing I knew I was out the door, right out onto the street. Not handcuffed or anything, but definitely the bum's rush. Jay and John Rabun had no idea where I was. Nobody knew where I was.

That was the day I got thrown out of the Justice Department.

Revé had always wanted to have two kids. Not so close together that she'd be tearing her hair out. But far enough apart so that she could enjoy each one separately.

Just before Adam died, she and I had decided that we were ready again. Adam was going to be in second grade, and it seemed like the right time. Back then, we figured that the baby would just kind of come along when it did. But now, things were different. Now, we didn't want to wait. And then, around Thanksgiving, about four months after Adam died, we found out that Revé was pregnant.

After Adam died, we understood that he wasn't coming back, and we never made his room into a shrine. Still, Revé didn't want to use his room for the nursery, so she set it up in the middle bedroom instead.

All of her buddies gave her a baby shower at her friend Nancy Zakoor's house, and they all had a great time, picking through all the presents and doing girl stuff. The next day, they got the nursery all set up, and when they finished, everybody just stood around looking at Revé, like, "Well, kid, now the ball's in your court."

On the night of July 15, 1982, when she was eight months pregnant, I took Revé to her first Lamaze class. The teacher told us all to sit on the floor to practice breathing. But Revé couldn't seem to sit on the floor. She kept saying how weird she felt. During the break, she told the instructor about it, and the woman told her that what she was having was false labor.

And that's what she kept telling herself all night while she was tossing and turning in bed. "What the hell's going on?" I said. "You got ants or something?"

Revé says that everyone had told her that each baby is different, but she knew this was a little too different. "What the hell am I doing?" she finally said. "I'm in labor here, and there isn't anything false about it."

Fortunately, the hospital wasn't far away.

This time I was there in the delivery room, and my feelings about it have not changed. If men gave birth, the species would have died out with the first generation. I don't care if you're Pope John Paul. At a time like this, you're shrinking to the back of the room and, like every other male in the world, saying only one thing to yourself: "I'm glad it's not me."

I was there with the ice chips, checking Revé's breathing, holding her hand. For a while, everything was okay. But then, pretty soon Revé was screaming in horrible pain, and I was at the other end of the room, thinking, "This Lamaze stuff is just a cult. If I went over there with some ice chips right now, she'd take one look at me and say, 'You get those goddamn ice chips out of here!'"

So Revé was screaming, the doctor was shouting, "Push!" and I was basically cowering on the side.

And then the most amazing thing happened.

Meghan popped out.

The delivery was wonderful. Unbelievable. She looked like such a little girl. She was a whole new person, and she was like nothing we had known. We didn't compare. There was no reason to. We looked at her and felt nothing but joy.

Revé was so ecstatic. Everyone was rolling out the red carpets—real hometown stuff. The radiator, the countertops, every rolling food cart was covered with flower arrangements and Mylar balloons. You couldn't see the walls for all the flowers. Revé started sending them down to the kids' wing because no one could get into the room.

Reporters came in to interview her and wrote things like, "Speaking from her hospital room, Revé Walsh, with her brightly painted toenails sticking out from underneath her sheets . . ."

It was as if the whole country were celebrating our happiness. Letters poured in from people who wanted pictures of the baby, who were so glad to know that Revé and I were still together. It was like Adam's sister had been born. That's exactly what it was like. It was as if everything was finally okay again. And everybody needed to know that. Not just us.

I think the greatest blessing was that she wasn't a little boy. Of course we would have loved that child, too, but people would have said, "Oh, you have another son. Now it's okay." And that would not have been true.

Instead, by the grace of God, she was a beautiful, beautiful little girl. I remember standing there in the delivery room thinking, "Now I'll be able to take a baby in our bed again and cuddle her. I can tell bedtime stories again." It felt like a miracle.

After losing Adam, everything had been so tough. For what seemed like forever, I hadn't smiled or cracked a joke. There was nothing to smile about. But now that Meghan was born, for the first time since losing Adam we began to think, "Maybe we aren't going to die after all. Maybe we are going to survive."

Having Meghan was what saved our lives.

And then, for Revé, came the hard part—leaving the hospital. She was terrified. She was so afraid to put Meghan in the car and take her home. She remembers being wheeled out of the hospital and thinking that something could happen to Meghan, and that when she leaned down to strap the baby into her car seat, she said, "Well, here we go, baby girl.

Good luck, Meghan, I hope we make it." Like crossing your fingers and saying, "Hope, hope, hope . . ."

Then, after we got home, Revé never took her hands off the baby. Not out of fear, but because we just could not get over the wonder of her. Meghan was with us day and night, and when Revé was sleeping, I would get up and take her out of her bassinet and bring her into our bed.

We knew that this little girl should not have to live in Adam's shadow, in the sadness. But sometimes it was hard to prevent that. It wasn't until later that it finally happened. We were at the opening of the Paradise Grand in the Bahamas and a woman came up to Revé to admire Meghan in her stroller. She said, "What a gorgeous little girl. How many children do you have?"

Revé started to stammer, trying to get something out. She doesn't remember if she said "Two, but one died" or "I had two, but one was murdered." She finally just fell to pieces in front of that poor woman, who had no idea what she had asked.

Two months later, on Monday, September 20, 1982, the House of Representatives approved a version of the Missing Children Act. Four days later, the Senate followed suit. The only thing left was for the bill to go to what's called a conference committee, where the final differences between the two versions are hammered out. Ordinarily, those meetings are closed. But we got in, and saw a real fight.

Politics is usually the most boring, tedious process, but this meeting was different. Henry Hyde, the Rebublican congressman from Illinois, was there, gracious and courtly and white-haired, joining forces with little Paul Simon, the earnest Democrat from Illinois with his horn-rimmed glasses and bow tie. Strom Thurmond was throwing his two cents in. Don Edwards was still arguing against the bill, and at one point Arlen Specter, the Republican senator from

Pennsylvania, leaned across the table and said with such conviction, "Don, for the life of me, I cannot understand why you are opposed to this."

Paula Hawkins—the lone woman among all these men, more responsible than anyone else for getting this bill through, who had actually got the head of the FBI out of his swimming pool one night to lobby him—was right up in Edwards's face.

It was so passionate. It was great. All these odd bedfellows united in a fight to get the FBI involved on behalf of missing children.

When the time finally came to take the vote, I stood there counting under my breath each yea vote around the table. I was remembering how my father had always said, "I'm training you guys for the fourth quarter, when the other team is as tired as you are. Everybody's got bloody noses and broken fingers, but what wins in overtime is guts. Victory belongs to the person who stays calmest and coolest, who hangs in and toughs it out and goes the distance."

When the final vote was cast, we knew we had a majority. I held up a fist and pulled my arm down in a victory salute. "Yes," I said out loud. "Yes."

Of course, not everyone was as jubilant as we were. Afterward, an FBI official walked up to Jay and shook his hand. "Congratulations, boys," he said with as much sarcasm as possible. "Next year, why don't you try doing something that might make a difference."

In October 1982, just fifteen months after we lost Adam, Congress passed the Missing Children Act. By the time it passed, it had gone through a lot of drafts and redrafts. And in the end, it wasn't really earth-shattering. All it did was set up a separate category for missing children—and the unidentified dead—within the FBI's existing NCIC's computer base, and to allow parents to enter information about a missing child themselves if a local police agency refused to.

Not much, really, in the grand scheme of things.

But to us, it seemed like everything. Because when we needed it, it hadn't been there. And now, other parents would have something that we had not.

The day the bill passed in Congress was unbelievable enough. But the topper was when we heard that the signing ceremony was going to take place in the Rose Garden. One day, we got a call from the White House to let us know. I probably wasn't as excited as most people would be because I was so exhausted from trying to hold down my job and get all of this political work done besides. Ray Mellette was ecstatic and thrilled, proud to know me. But the other business partners were thinking, "Oh, great. Now he's going to Washington."

That day, we all got dressed up, even beautiful Meghan in her tiny pink sweater, and got in the car and drove to the White House. We went through all the security at the gate and then they took us into the Garden and seated us right in front. Tons of press were there. Revé remembers hearing Sam Donaldson bossing everybody around. And then, after everyone was seated, President Reagan came out, looking so regal, like such a statesman. It was a beautiful sunny day, and Reagan made a speech mentioning "John and Revé Walsh of Hollywood, Florida." He even got Revé's name right. He didn't mispronounce it as "Reeve" or "Reeva." And afterward he came up to us and spoke with us and said that Meghan had a good Irish name.

It was just a glorious day. A special acknowledgment of all of our efforts and pain. Meghan was beaming, and all our friends were there: Jay Howell, Robbie Callaway, Paula Hawkins, Howard Davidson—all the child-advocate guerrilla fighters. A ragtag little army of people who cared. That was the frosting on the cake, the first real moment of the win.

And throughout the ceremony, Adam was right there with us. I kept thinking of how proud he must be of all of us. He and my father, too. The two Adams.

That's when I realized that a heartbroken couple from Florida with no money and no lobby and no resources and nobody behind them except a bunch of caring, passionate people with no real power had actually helped get a federal bill passed.

We weren't General Motors or the NRA. But we had really, really done something. And maybe it could be the beginning of something else.

Once, after the bill had passed, Jay asked one of Don Edwards's staffers why the congressman had been so adamantly opposed to it. "Because it was sponsored by the other party," the guy said. That was the only reason. For sheer spite. But that was politics, and we got that kind of thing a lot. In a book that she wrote in 1989, Pat Schroeder referred to those early hearings about missing children on Capitol Hill as an example of "public hysteria-in-the-making." And whenever something like that was said, I never forgave or forgot. To me, children's issues were not politics as usual. After losing his congressional seat, Harold Washington was elected mayor of Chicago, which is where, in 1984, Gen. William Westmoreland and I were given a big citizenship award by the VFW at its national convention.

Harold Washington was on the stage that day, and he was supposed to introduce me. I said that I didn't want him to. And when he came up to me and tried to shake my hand, I refused.

Fuck him.

He voted no on the Missing Children Act.

During the 1981 Louisville conference, one of the people we had met, Carole Fleishman, was a field producer for a documentary maker who was interested in meeting with some parents of murdered children. She had introduced herself, and we spent some time talking to her about Adam and what we had been through.

Not long after that, the filmmaker herself, Linda

Otto, called us up and asked if we minded if a film crew followed us around for a while for a profile that ABC's *20/20* wanted to run on us. I didn't think it was a great idea necessarily, but we needed the publicity for the Center and the legislation, so we said okay. Over the next year or so, Linda actually ended up spending quite a bit of time with us; she was even in the room during that last crucial conference-committee meeting on the children's bill. Later on, she said that at one point she ran out of film but went on pretending to shoot anyway—just to keep the politicians honest.

Not long after the Missing Children Act passed, Linda's *20/20* piece ran. It opened up with file footage of the Sears store at the Hollywood mall during the search for Adam, and with me standing on the hood of a car in the parking lot during those first few days, coordinating the search with volunteers. There were clips of the first press conference that Revé and I gave, of us printing Adam's missing posters, and cops walking around on the little wooden dock in Vero on the night that Adam's remains were found.

Hugh Downs interviewed me for the show, and he read aloud the famous FBI quote telling us to "go pound salt." Then he asked me why I was doing what I was doing. "You don't owe anybody anything," he said.

"I owe it to the children," I said. "I owe it to Adam."

After the *20/20* segment aired, there was a lot of positive feedback, and Linda, who as it turns out was a respected documentary filmmaker in her own right, went to her husband, a big-time television producer named Alan Landsburg. "Alan," she told him, "I've met this Walsh couple, and I don't think I've ever met anybody quite like them." She said that she wanted to do a documentary about our story, and Alan agreed with her.

In fact, he said, "Let's try for a movie of the week."

I had already talked to Linda and Alan and told them that we would do the movie. But I wasn't giving them any information. I figured they could embellish the story and expand it themselves. Revé's initial reaction to that was, "Oh, great. Floating heads. Terrorized parents. This is going to be a nightmare." I told her that my strategy was the same as when I was dealing with the press: that if you say no to them, they'll just change the names and write whatever they want to anyway. But if you cooperate with them, then at least you'll have some control over what they write.

What no one seemed to understand was what private people Revé and I really were. We had been forced into the public eye by something completely beyond our control and had learned that you were crazy to automatically trust people. On top of that, I didn't know anything about Hollywood. I didn't know that Linda's heart was in the right place, that she was so tremendously well-intentioned, and that she would do the movie with such dignity.

So I put her through holy hell.

In those days, made-for-TV movies were still kind of a novelty, nowhere near as common as they are today. Anyone who signed up to have his or her story told generally got in the neighborhood of $25,000. We were broke, but that wasn't what we were most concerned about. The Center, which by then was getting some government funding, had lost most of that money in federal budget cutbacks, and we had no idea how we were going to make up the shortfall.

So in the end, Alan's production company paid us $100,000, and Daniel J. Travanti, an actor well-known for his role as Captain Furillo on the NBC series *Hill Street Blues,* who had signed on to play me, chipped in $50,000 of his salary. There was a little presentation ceremony, and we were handed a huge, oversize check for $150,000, made out to the Adam Walsh Center.

I was on the set in Houston when we started filming

in June of 1983. Dan Travanti was playing me, and Jobeth Williams was Revé. It was a pretty emotional experience for everyone. The little boy who played Adam was five years old, and I took him swimming in the hotel pool and spent some time with him. But it was hard for me to be around him, especially that first day on the set. Because he looked so much like Adam.

In the old days, I had earned a good living for my family, and we were always used to living comfortably. Now, we were completely broke. I hadn't been able to buy a present for anybody in such a long time. I will never forget how, at a time when the subjects of TV movies sometimes didn't get a dime for their stories, Linda arranged to have me hired as a consultant on the movie. It meant so much to me. At the end of the shoot, I took the money and went out and bought a set of pearls for Revé and little pearl earrings for Meghan.

After the movie was finished, Linda invited me to go with her to New York to see Grant Tinker, who was then the head of NBC. She said, "You've got to go with me, John. They're talking about not letting us show the pictures of missing children at the end of the movie, and if they don't, I'm not going to let them have it."

I asked her what she was talking about.

"No one's ever had interactive television before. There's never been an 800 number shown at the end of a program, and now nobody wants to pay for it."

So we went to Manhattan, right into the hallowed halls of 30 Rockefeller Center, for the meeting. We waited twenty minutes to get into Tinker's huge office, overlooking Manhattan. There sat Mr. Tinker with all of his people—all of these guys in suits.

First, one of the lawyers said, "Well, if we show these missing kid pictures and run an 800 number, then we'll have to do it for Save the Whales people and everybody else. It will set a precedent and we can't have that."

And then one of the marketing guys said, "You know, those are precious minutes of advertising time that we're going to waste by showing pictures of missing kids. We could use the airtime to make hundreds of thousands of dollars instead."

I was getting angrier and angrier, and Linda was getting more and more furious. Finally, she couldn't take it anymore. Right in front of all those powerful, condescending men, she sat up and said, "Enough!"

I had no idea what was going to happen. But then, much to my amazement, Grant Tinker agreed with her. "That's right," he said. "This is bullshit. The parents of these children are desperate, and we're going to show their pictures and we'll fund the 800 number. I'm not sure how we're going to do it, but we'll figure it out. We'll get the money. We'll staff it. You're lobbying for a law in Washington, aren't you, John? Okay, then we'll have the premiere in Washington, and we'll invite Congress."

I almost couldn't believe what I was hearing. It was amazing. But it was true: there were people in the media who had a conscience, who were saying, "We'll help you," who *did* care.

All of a sudden, we were a SWAT team again.

Adam had its prebroadcast premiere at a little movie theater in Washington on October 4, 1983. Our friends came, and senators and congressmen. That was the night that I first met Al Regnery, who headed the Justice Department's Office of Juvenile Justice and Delinquency Prevention (OJJDP)—which was the key governmental agency for anybody interested in law enforcement and kids. The one who introduced us was Robbie Callaway.

The made-for-TV movie *Adam* debuted on NBC on the night of October 10, 1983. "People who cover television never run out of bad things to write about, and never will. But it's gratifying that now and then there are some good things, too," the *Washington Post* TV critic, Tom Shales, wrote in the next morning's paper. The project, he said, "can only have come about because a substantial number of hearts were conspicuously in the right place."

That night, the Florida Department of Law Enforcement organized the hot line, manning a bank of fifty phones in a state office building in Tallahassee. Revé and I were there, and so was the governor, Bob Graham. At the end of the show, a roll call of fifty-five missing children's names and pictures was played, and those faces reached 40 million TV screens around the country. The toll-free number appeared for ten seconds and the calls started flooding in. For three days, over one hundred calls per hour came in to that number. Of the fifty-five missing children whose faces were shown, thirteen were located and reunited with their families.

Adam, which became one of the highest-rated made for television movies ever and was also one of the first examples of interactive TV, was later rebroadcast twice, and each time more children were recovered. In 1986, a second movie, *Adam: His Song Continues,* was aired, followed by another roll call. In all, sixty-five children were located as a result of the broadcasts of those two movies. That was the most rewarding thing for us, even if there were a few bad moments.

The night of that first airing, Revé and I went up to Tallahassee to help staff the hot line. A call came in from a young, frightened-sounding girl who said that she was one of the missing whose pictures we had shown. Revé was really worried, and she spent more than an hour on the phone with the girl, trying to calm her down and see what we could do to bring her home. But as it turned out, the girl wasn't really missing. She had been trying to pull off some kind of hoax.

So much of what we had done had been encouraging. The Missing Children Act, and the Center, which was starting all kinds of things related to children's issues: pilot programs to fingerprint schoolchildren as a form of ID; running educational programs in the schools; starting something called the Cracked Gavel Award, which Denny Abbott gave to judges who had handed down light or suspended sentences to child molesters.

But even those things couldn't change what had happened to Adam. And as far as Revé was concerned, there was still an unfinished piece of business on that score that she wanted settled. She had never let go of the memory of that young Sears security guard who had come up to her in the store that day, and of the idea that no matter how well-intentioned it was, she was the one who had put Adam out of the store, without trying to get Revé's permission, or even letting her know about it. We never knew if she had been told to keep quiet about it or not. We never knew anything. The only thing we were sure of was that no one had ever apologized for it or even really acknowledged it. And in Revé's mind, that was unacceptable.

On July 22, 1983, just before the two-year statute of limitations ran out, we filed a lawsuit asking for an unspecified sum in damages from Sears and the Hollywood mall for their negligence in contributing to Adam's death. We weren't trying to get the money for ourselves. As it was, the Center was getting some funding from the government, but each year we had to go back and ask for that budget money to be granted again. We knew that the funding could dry up, suddenly, at any time. So the whole idea was to use the lawsuit award to make sure that the Center would be able to keep on running, and also to finance the push for more legislation on children's issues, in other states, and also at the federal level.

But things never got that far. Sears and the Hollywood mall hired two lawyers, Rex Conrad and Richard Gordon. One of the first things they did was to depose Jimmy Campbell—in great detail—about his relationship with Revé.

They also interrogated Revé and my mother, who,

by the time they got done with her, was in tears. They saved me for last. Finally, when I went in to be questioned, they started asking me about everything that had happened the day Adam was abducted. I made it as difficult for them as I could. If they asked what I did when I got into the parking lot, I told them I parked my car. If they asked what I did next, I said that I had turned off the ignition.

Finally, one of them looked at me and said, "You know, you're a real wiseass."

I said, "And you know what you are? You're mercenary bastards. Worse than that, you're chicken-shits. My wife and I are trying to get a second missing-children's bill passed, and we're trying to fund the Adam Walsh Center so that it can survive for a long time. This isn't about money for us. It's about accountability."

At that point, Gordon told the legal stenographer to quit taking notes. Then Rex Conrad looked right at me and said, "I don't care about your legislation. I don't care about your Center." He didn't even care that my son had been decapitated. He said that we were in this for the money, and that it was his job to destroy us.

That was it for me. Something finally snapped, and I started screaming, "I'll beat the hell out of you, you coward!" At that point, both Conrad and my lawyer, Sam Holland, who was just as outraged as I was, said that it was time to end the deposition.

By this time, the media were having a field day with the case. They sent people to the courthouse every day to check the case file for developments and to find out where and when depositions would take place. They also sent camera crews to the place where Jimmy Campbell was being deposed. And that was how the story about Revé and Jimmy got out.

During Revé's deposition, the lawyers had asked her, "Well, what were you wearing that day, Mrs. Walsh?" By then, everyone already knew. It was there in the record. "A pair of gym shorts and a leotard," she answered.

"A pair of gym shorts and a *leotard?*" She told them that she was wearing it because she had been on her way to the gym, but they didn't care about the context. She was my wife, and they made her out to be some kind of terrible sleaze.

By that point, Revé didn't care about what happened to her personally. She really didn't care anymore. But I was not willing to see her dragged through the mud. I could not stand by and allow that to happen. We also both knew what the publicity would do to the Center, and to all of the people who were fighting with us. We might never get another piece of legislation passed, and the Center might get destroyed. Our personal reputation was one thing, but we did not believe that we had a right to sacrifice anything beyond it.

So, in the end, they broke us. We folded. On November 21, 1983, one week after what would have been Adam's ninth birthday, we decided to drop the suit. Of course the press had another field day: more suspicion, more innuendo. The hint that Revé had somehow been responsible for her son's death.

Whenever things got really bad, Revé remembered the day that she found out that Adam was dead. No matter what anybody did to her now, she would never be that low again. After the day that Adam was abducted, she never went into another Sears store again. Not once. Not ever. Revé already knew about the softer side of Sears.

By August of 1983, the second anniversary of Adam's death, I had testified a half dozen times to various congressional committees, had been to the White House and on *Donahue* and *Merv Griffin* and *Good Morning America*. We had accomplished some things, but we were a long way from finished. There was so much more that still had to be done.

"I came into this unaware of what was going on in this country—the random killings, the missing children, the helpless and powerless feelings of parents when their child is missing," I told a reporter at the time. "I have heard so many stories and talked with so many parents who are looking for their children. The Missing Children Act is only the tip of an iceberg. It doesn't protect children. It only makes it easier to identify bodies. It's only the beginning."

I had been going full speed, nonstop for two years since Adam's death, traveling constantly, going to different states, speaking in legislatures, lobbying in Washington. I knew that it was time to slow down. The doctors told me that I was pushing myself beyond what my body could handle. After the movie came out, I realized that I would have to try to take it easy for a while, start living a more normal life again, and spend more time at home with Revé and Meghan.

But it was hard to pretend that life could ever be normal again. There were too many reminders. Too much that could not be forgotten. And if there did happen to be a stretch of time—a few days, maybe—when I was not completely consumed with the memory of Adam, then there would always be something that yanked me back to the horror of what had happened to him. Something like the phone calls every now and then from Jack Hoffman of the Hollywood police, telling me about some possible lead or tip in Adam's case, some piece of information that would always, eventually, turn into another dead end.

For one newspaper story in 1983, pegged to the second anniversary of Adam's murder, a reporter asked me if I thought that Adam's killer would ever be found. I said that I believed it was possible, but that if it did ever happen, it would only be "by a fluke."

That was right about the time that police up in Duval County, a five-hour drive north of Hollywood, started questioning an itinerant drifter about a fatal rooming-house arson in Jacksonville. The drifter was being pretty forthright about his involvement in the case. And pretty forthcoming about something else, too.

He wanted to talk to the cops, he said, about some "trouble" that he had gotten into a couple of years back, down in Broward County.

Some trouble, he said, that had involved a little boy.

11

Law Enforcement

IN THE INVESTIGATION OF ADAM'S CASE, IN THE YEAR OR so after his death the police had questioned a lot of potential suspects, including at least two well-known pedophiles. One of these guys had raped and bludgeoned a six-year-old boy and left him to die near some railroad tracks in a remote area of Florida. When police checked the guy's house, they found a diary that had details on the rape and possible murders of twenty-five victims in two states, mostly young boys.

The second was a twice-convicted child molester out on parole. When police searched his room, they found a collection of newspaper articles about Adam and written descriptions of forty-five children that this guy had molested in four states. In a storage space, the cops found six sets of boys' clothing, sadomasochistic pornography and paraphernalia, and detailed letters to other child molesters. They also found a collection of audiocassette tapes.

The cops asked me to come down to the station. They said that I had to listen to the tapes to see if Adam's voice was on any of them. So I went over and, for what seemed like forever, had to sit there and listen to the screams, cries, and pleadings of little boys while they were being raped and tortured.

Adam's voice was not on any of the tapes. When it was finally over, I looked up, and six tough, hardened homicide detectives in the room all had tears in their eyes. I excused myself, and went into the men's room to throw up.

By now, I was pretty much ruined financially. I was still trying to hold up my end of the Paradise Grand partnership, still going to work at my office at the Harbour House. But I was overwhelmed with grief. At work, I would go into the bathroom and throw up and come back to my desk and pretend that nothing had happened. I sat there with the door closed for hours, telling my secretary to hold all my phone calls, pretending that I was going over projections and numbers. Instead, I would cry. I was having terrible fits of sadness and sorrow about Adam, constant thoughts about him and what had happened to him. The little desk we had set up for him was still there in my office with all of his things—pictures, drawings, little shells he had given me, the lucky sea beans that we had found together during our walks on the beach.

All of those things. Everywhere.

I was so torn. I had been obsessed with getting the Missing Children Act passed, and with doing something about how the FBI had refused to help search for Adam. All during that time, I had been traveling back and forth between Florida and Washington, at my own expense. Whenever things really went down to the wire on the Hill, whenever my presence was absolutely necessary, Jay or Robbie would call to say, "We've taken things as far as we can, but now you've got to come up and close the sale."

Besides Ray Mellette, there were two other partners in the Paradise Grand marketing company, one in Texas and the other over on the island itself. They were being very accommodating about my situation. I was using the Xerox machine and the phones incessantly, and the other partners were being very generous about it.

But after a while, they went to Ray and said, "The hotel is behind schedule, we're overbudget. Everything got thrown off track with Adam's murder and the search. We're paying John's salary, and every time we call over there to the sales office, he's gone somewhere or on the phone with someone else, another parent of a missing child. People are coming to see him, cops are talking to him. He's in the newspaper, he's flying here to go on this talk show, flying there to talk to that legislature. The hotel is overbudget. It's not going to open on time, and he's not focused. We love him, we care for him. But he's not focused on the work."

How could I be? I was frail and haggard and had lost thirty pounds. I couldn't even handle the normal, everyday tasks of life, let alone a staff that was sitting there waiting for me to tell them what to do. Ray was my defender. He'd say, "Come on, he's doing his job. He's doing his best. Give him some time. Have some decency. His son was murdered." But my partners wanted, quite rightly, to know if I was going to be a child advocate or a partner in our hotel management company. The trouble was, at the time I didn't know myself.

In Washington, I was learning a lot about the backroom workings of politics. How things really operate, behind closed doors and out of sight. But the things we were trying to do weren't limited only to politics. It began to seem as if a whole lot of things having to do with missing children were interrelated. So from other people, I was learning about a lot of other things, too.

From Ronald Wright, the Broward medical examiner, I learned that there were ten thousand unidentified bodies a year throughout the country, and that if anyone wanted to try to identify one of them, he had to send the corpse's fingerprints to the FBI lab, which had a three-month backup. And if the dead person had no criminal history and had never been fingerprinted in an arrest, then chances of identifying him or her were next to nothing anyway.

From police agencies around the country, I learned that the FBI's famous NCIC computer was so overloaded with burglaries and car thefts that it was virtually impossible for local police to try to use it to find missing persons. Even if the technology existed to keep a list of missing children or unidentified dead, small-town cops weren't necessarily looking for that kind of data—or entering it themselves.

I had also learned a lot about pedophiles. About how they had even formed a group that called itself NAMBLA, for the North American Man-Boy Love Association. These guys advocated the sexual molestation of young boys by adult males and were proud of it. I knew how sick these guys were. Someone had shown me a letter written to a convicted child pornographer in Pennsylvania from another collector. "One never can predict if or when the kid will squeal to the teacher or fuzz," it read. "That's one reason you see so many kids who had to be blown away after being molested. They couldn't be trusted to keep quiet."

At the Louisville conference on missing children back in 1981, a guy had come up to me one afternoon—short, kind of scruffy looking. What I remember most about him was how bad he smelled. He kept asking me all about the Missing Children Act. Not about what it would do to help missing and abducted children, but more about what kind of penalties it would carry—that sort of thing. I remember having a really weird feeling about this guy. He was wearing a name tag and everything. But something about him wasn't right.

The next day at the conference, Jay came up to me and said, "Jeez, John, have you heard? The cops are all over the place. Some guy who was registered here is a known pedophile with a warrant or something against him, and the cops came in and took him away." It was the same guy who had approached me. He had infiltrated the conference.

So I knew what these guys were all about. Later on, just to show how upstanding they were, someone ran an obscene love poem to Adam in a pedophile's newsletter. Something about how much they liked the sweet little gap in his teeth.

It was all well and good that the Missing Children Act was now the law of the land. But that wasn't the end of things. Our next goal was to set up a national center where parents of missing and abducted children could go for help, so that no one would have to go through what we had gone through without help from a centralized government agency. It was like what Revé had said: we still needed that skyscraper in Washington. That was how we arrived at step two in the overall game plan: a second proposed federal law, which came to be known as the Missing Children Assistance Act.

After those first hearings on the missing children's bill, Jay Howell and Paula Hawkins's subcommittee had kept on investigating all kinds of things related to child abuse and missing kids. As Revé had said that first time that we met Julie Patz and Kristin Cole Brown: the story of what had happened to Adam had opened up a Pandora's box.

For starters, Paula Hawkins's subcommittee had found dozens of cases of little kids who had been stranger-abducted, kidnapped under circumstances that looked like foul play. Yet when they started calling FBI field offices around the country to see how the cases were being handled, they found out that the Bureau wasn't doing anything. It wasn't involved. That was news because, according to the Federal Kidnapping Act, if a missing person had not turned up in twenty-four hours, then it was assumed they had been taken across state lines—which was when the

FBI would get involved. Yet in case after case, the FBI was obviously just plain foot-dragging. And now, for the first time, there was documented evidence of it.

The subcommittee had also learned about the case of a little kid who had been killed in the Midwest, under circumstances similar to Adam's murder. What was outrageous was that no one in Florida law enforcement had even heard about the case—and that no one in the Midwest case knew anything about Adam's murder. The Senate investigators realized that local homicide departments did not share their information, even in murder cases that involved children. Local police agencies had no idea what was going on in other jurisdictions. The cops were not using the NCIC computer bank as the potential crime-fighting tool that it was. As a result of these various investigations, on February 2, 1983, Paula's subcommittee held a joint House-Senate hearing on the FBI's law enforcement practices—and how they weren't doing a good enough job to protect little kids.

On the day of the hearing, it fell to a guy by the name of Oliver "Buck" Revell, the FBI's assistant director of criminal investigations, to take the heat for the agency. Their official position was that any bill that would tell them how to do their job differently was a bad thing. It would put a drain on manpower and be a bureaucratic nightmare and take away the Bureau's autonomy. As the number three man at the Bureau, it was Buck's job to sit in the hearing room and read a prepared statement that the FBI's lawyers had drafted.

Buck Revell and I later got to be good friends. We even testified together against NAMBLA before a congressional committee investigating underground child-pornography rings. But it was that day way back in 1983 when I first met him that I remember best. He was a big guy who wore a fur coat, and after he finished his testimony, he came up and shook my hand. "You know, I understand what the FBI lawyers say our policy is," he told me. "But I've got kids myself, and I was listening to you talk about how you couldn't get the FBI to look for your son. And I for one don't think our policy is the right one. It's just not right."

That same day, Buck Revell went back to the Bureau and drafted a several-page Teletype that he got approved by the director, William Webster, and transmitted to every FBI field office in the country. It said that, effective immediately, the FBI was to take a proactive role in the investigations of missing children, and that if any local police agency gave parents a hard time about entering their missing child's name into the NCIC computer, the parents could ask the FBI to do it directly instead. No need to wait twenty-four hours to file the report. No requirement for evidence of transport across state lines. No more need for a ransom note.

From now on, the Bureau would provide help in looking for a missing child as soon as it was asked.

A few months later I received a letter from a Dr. Ratray in Vero Beach. He said that as he was writing this letter, his little boy was asleep in the next room, and that were it not for me, the situation might be otherwise. A few weeks earlier, the man's son had been out playing on the front lawn when a stranger came by and abducted him. The doctor had called the FBI immediately, and this time agents jumped right into the case. Within hours they found the little boy and brought him home to his parents.

Later on, I talked to an FBI agent about how they captured the guy. The agent said that they had tracked him down on a golf course, and in some gunfire, the guy had been wounded. By the time the agents reached him, he was begging for a doctor. An FBI agent leaned over and said that if he didn't tell them where the little boy was, they'd let him bleed to death right there on the green. The guy did reveal the location, and that's where the agents found the little boy—not far away, locked inside the trunk of a car.

As far as anyone knew, this was the first case affected by the FBI's change in policy, and the dentist from Vero Beach was writing to thank me for my part in saving his son's life. We had raised hell to make the FBI aware that it needed to get more involved in cases of child abduction. Now that it had, my war with the Bureau was officially over. From here on in, the FBI and I would be allies.

In April 1983, I received a letter from Jay Howell asking if I would appear at a hearing before a Senate Judiciary subcommitte on juvenile justice, chaired by Arlen Specter (R-Pennsylvania). Specter's subcommittee was holding hearings on something called VI-CAP— the Violent Criminal Apprehension Program.

VI-CAP was the brainchild of a guy named Pierce Brooks, a retired LAPD captain. Years before, Pierce had worked on a case that became known as the Onion Field murder—the 1963 execution killing of an L.A. police officer that later became the subject of a best-seller by Joseph Wambaugh. Later on, Pierce got so burned-out by the violence in L.A. that he went off to be a police chief in Oregon, where he spent a lot of time studying murder cases—1,400 of them nationwide. Pierce realized that there were lots of patterns in the data that police might not have noticed before—odd habits and quirks that certain killers had, different pieces of seemingly random information that could fit together like the pieces of a puzzle. That gave him the idea that if a computerized network could be set up that contained specific information about these apparently unrelated murders, then maybe the cops could prevent a lot of horrible, violent crimes before they ever took place.

Pierce and other people who had been working on the idea wanted to start a nationwide computer system that would keep track of all kinds of information about violent crimes, detail it and catalog it, so that the FBI's behavioral psychologists could use it to put together profiles of the worst of the bad guys, then relay them to local police departments. It made a lot of sense to people on the Hill that this type of criminal was in the same sick bag as serial child killers and molesters. The subcommittee wanted me to talk about the fact that many victims of pattern murderers were children, and about how law enforcement could help prevent some of these crimes with the use of a centralized system.

"John, it would be real helpful if you would be able to make a plea for the VI-CAP tracking system," Jay wrote me in a letter dated April 27. "I believe that most people in America believe that we already have such a system. Most of the people believe that these kinds of horrible crimes are being tracked and analyzed. Most people believe that the individual police departments contact other areas to determine whether or not there are similar murders being committed in other parts of the country. Most people believe that nationwide Teletype alerts are actually read by other police departments.

"As you know, all of the above are not true."

On July 12, 1983, I went up to Washington to testify before a Senate subcommittee in support of a few million dollars in funding from the government to set up VI-CAP. By that time, everybody in the country had heard about Ted Bundy, a guy who had murdered thirty-six women in four states back in the 1970s. But what most people didn't know, as Paula Hawkins said in her opening testimony, was that "for every Ted Bundy who has gained national notoriety, there are dozens of unknown killers who have been responsible for untold deaths."

Up until that time there hadn't really even been a name for guys like Bundy or Gerald Eugene Stano, who had confessed to the murder of thirty-nine women in Florida, or John Wayne Gacy, who had murdered thirty-two boys in Chicago. Sometimes they were referred to as pattern killers or multiple murderers. But during this hearing, a new term to describe them was used, and it got picked up in the press. From now on, these vicious criminals would be known as serial killers.

A woman named Ann Rule, a former reporter and police officer from Seattle who had written a book called *The Stranger Beside Me* about Ted Bundy, also testified about what she had learned from studying more than a thousand murders nationwide. "The serial murderer is a relatively new breed of killer in this country," she said, "usually a male, who roves from state to state, killing one victim after another. Most serial murderers select a particular category of victim, usually women. In some instances, the victims are children. These killers are ruthless, conscienceless, and invariably cunning."

Another person who testified at the hearing was Roger Depue, who since 1974 had headed up a project at the FBI's training academy up in Quantico, Virginia. Depue was an FBI behavioral scientist and told the committee about how his group analyzed the characteristics and behavior patterns of these serial killllers. Depue was one of the real pioneers in the field; at the time, few people outside of law enforcement even knew that the FBI's Behavioral Sciences Unit existed.

When it was my turn to testify, I began by saying, "I'm going to talk about John Wayne Gacy, the man who murdered thirty-two boys in Chicago. And about the twenty in Atlanta and the seventeen in Houston. And about how the general public thinks there is a system like VI-CAP, but there isn't."

I said that I believed that my own son had probably been killed by one of these monsters who had been roaming around Florida, and that if VI-CAP could be established, we might be able to identify and track some of these serial killers before they went on to take so many lives. "It's a mobile society," I told a reporter afterward. "These guys go from state to state murdering people. It would be great if they could catch some of the murderers of children before the fact."

The more I learned about serial killers, the more convinced I became that this was the kind of person who had killed Adam. The nature of the violence that had been done to him made that much clear. People were also beginning to realize that these killers were smart, that they knew how to infiltrate places like schools and day-care centers, and that we had to do something to prevent predators like these from having easy, open-door access to children.

John Wayne Gacy used to dress up as a clown and perform at children's birthday parties. Half of his victims were from the same neighborhood, and many of those had all worked for a construction company that Gacy owned. All I could think of was that if something like VI-CAP had been in place, the cops might have been able to discover patterns, find things in common, that could have tipped them off to Gacy before he killed so many people.

As for Adam, there was no way of knowing if VI-CAP might have saved his life. But after the hearing, even Jack Hoffman, HPD's lead investigator in Adam's case, admitted to the *Hollywood Sun-Tattler* that local police departments didn't always use existing Teletypes to share information on most-wanted criminals. "Anytime you store information in a central bank," Hoffman said, "it gives the investigator that much more tools to work with."

Through Pierce Brooks I met Robert Ressler, who had started something called the FBI's Psychological Profiling Division—the group that put together profiles of some of the country's most dangerous and violent criminals. Part of Ressler's job was to go around the country making presentations about serial killers and pedophiles to groups of homicide detec-

My dad (center, light coat) was a B-24 lieutenant when he was only twenty-three years old. (Author's collection)

Me and my dad in the yard at the big house on North Street in Auburn, New York. I'm around two years old. (Author's collection)

One of six-month-old Adam's first swimming lessons, under Revé's watchful eye. (Author's collection)

Adam, two years old. (Author's collection)

Dive master Garfield
McCartney and me in
Eleuthera after one of our
underwater safaris.
(Author's collection)

Adam, with his
Gram, is wearing
his favorite hat—
the captain's
hat he had on the
day he was
abducted.
(Author's
collection)

Me and four-year-old Adam sailing in the Bahamas.
(Courtesy Adam Walsh Children's Fund)

We love this photo of
Adam relishing his
cotton candy.
(Author's collection)

Revé says that this is still the cutest picture in the world of Adam, who is five here. (Author's collection)

One of the things that Adam, here in the spring of 1981, loved most in life was baseball. (Author's collection)

The photograph that Revé took out of her wallet in Sears on the day Adam went missing—his official first-grade picture. In it, he's wearing the same shirt he had on that terrible day. (Author's collection)

Me with my great friends John Monahan and Jeff O'Regan at the press conference for the 1983 premiere of the first made for TV movie about Adam. (Author's collection)

Me, Revé and a tired Meghan fielding questions after the first airing of the movie *Adam*. (Dunn Photographic Associates)

Dan Travanti, best known as Captain Furillo in NBC's *Hill Street Blues*, played me in the TV movie *Adam* and proved himself a good friend. (Author's collection)

The whole clan at a benefit for the Adam Walsh Center, Palm Beach, c. 1989. From left: Jimmy Walsh, me, Callahan, Cousin Thommi Walsh, Jane Walsh, Meghan, Gram, Revé, Joe Walsh. (Author's collection)

Meeting Florida governor Lawton Chiles, ten-year-old Meghan shows the winning Walsh form. *(© The Orlando Sentinel)*

Right from the start, the FBI was one of the biggest fans of *America's Most Wanted*. Here, FBI director William Sessions visits the set. (Courtesy *America's Most Wanted*)

Nancy McBride, Nancy Jazvac (mother of eleven-year-old Staci) and me at the moment that a death sentence was handed down for Staci's killer. (Reprinted with the permission of *The Miami Herald*)

To Meghan Jane
With best wishes. *Ronald Reagan*

I've never played partisan politics. Three successive administrations have been friends to missing children and crime victims. President Reagan, who was always especially gracious to us, shown here with our friend Florida senator Paula Hawkins, is giving jelly beans to Meghan. (Official White House photos)

To John Walsh
Best Wishes,

Bill Clinton

Of all the awards that I've received, the one that I got in 1985, National Father of the Year, the Everyman category, is the one I'm most proud of. Other recipients were Ben Vereen, Mario Cuomo, Bruce Jenner and Gary Carter. (Author's collection)

On the streets with *America's Most Wanted*. (Courtesy *America's Most Wanted*)

David James Roberts. This scumbag's murder spree was what made me decide to host *America's Most Wanted*. (Courtesy *America's Most Wanted*)

Catching James Charles Stark, who tortured and murdered a little fourteen-year-old girl, became, for me, an obsession. (Courtesy *America's Most Wanted*)

John List murdered his entire family. The FBI tried to catch him for almost twenty years. We did it in eleven days. (Courtesy *America's Most Wanted*)

This is Ottis Toole, the man I believe is responsible for my son's murder. (Courtesy *America's Most Wanted*)

Me and Revé at our summer cottage with our 1946 wooden Chris-Craft. (Author's collection)

Here we are (from left: Cal, Hayden, me, Meghan and Revé) at the Emmy Awards in Pasadena in 1995. I had been nominated for an Emmy for my prime-time children's safety special. (Miranda Shen/Celebrity Photo)

tives and local law enforcement agencies—and to let agencies know what they could do to apprehend these guys.

In one of the first national conferences on serial killers, held in Baton Rouge, Louisiana, cops from different jurisdictions around the country began talking to each other and sharing information—and wound up solving seventeen outstanding homicides. Later on, the FBI and I began to push for joint task forces—meetings that would bring together city, county, and state law enforcement—to be held in different cities all around the country. One of the first, in Miami in the mid-1980s, led to the capture of three hundred criminals within six months—all because cops from different agencies around Miami got together for the first time and pooled their information on unsolved crimes.

As a part of that effort, I went up to the FBI's training academy in Quantico and started making appearances with Ressler around the country, talking about child pornography, serial killers, and pedophiles. When Ted Bundy's or John Gacy's or the Green River murders were happening, cops in other jurisdictions weren't necessarily even aware of the crimes. So I began by talking a lot about the lack of shared information. Why didn't homicide cops from different areas talk to one another? Why didn't they put information into the NCIC computer? Why did they resist working with the Bureau? All we were trying to do was let homicide cops know that if a woman had been trussed up and barbecued in their town, it might not be an isolated case. We wanted them to understand that the same guy responsible for a crime like that might well have done it fifteen other times.

The presentations were never open to the press; I was the only civilian ever invited to go out on the FBI tour. The reason was that we included a lot of slides and photographs that were incredibly gruesome.

Women who had been murdered and found with their breasts cut off, skinned, with logs shoved up their vaginas. Children engaging in sex acts with adults. Torture stuff. Nightmare stuff. Worse things than any human being could ever imagine. Things that would make anyone sick. Things that nevertheless existed. Our job was to make sure that the cops knew about the kind of guys who committed these crimes. That they were out there, hurting women and children in terrible, unimaginable ways.

Why was I doing all of this? Because I knew that Adam's murder was not an isolated case. That it was not a rarity, and that it hadn't happened in a vacuum. People knew about Adam's murder because of all the publicity that had surrounded it. But Adam wasn't the first kid abducted and killed by a pedophile. All anyone had to see were a few samples from some of the confiscated films and videos that Ressler and I included in our presentations—of fifty-year-old men sodomizing little boys and raping little girls who were screaming and crying—to know that these unspeakable crimes were a lot more common than people liked to think they were.

It wasn't easy for me to make those slide-show presentations with Ressler, but I did it anyway. And the cops we talked to seemed to understand and appreciate that. They would come up to me afterward and say, "Thank you, Mr. Walsh. God bless you." Before long, I knew as much about these things as any cop in the country.

At the same time, I was receiving tens, if not hundreds, of calls a week from all over the country—from people who had an agenda, didn't have an agenda, had heard about Adam's case, had a missing child, had a nonprofit organization, wanted to help the Adam Walsh Center, wanted me to speak, wanted to meet with me, wanted to thank me. A lot of calls also came from state legislators to tell me about spin-off programs and legislation happening in their state:

proposals for tougher penalties for child abduction, missing-children clearinghouses, bills dealing with every aspect of child exploitation.

I was also traveling more and more to Washington. In March of 1983, I met again with President Reagan, who reaffirmed his commitment to the Center. Then, that fall, not long after the movie *Adam* had aired, someone from Al Regnery's office at the Justice Department called up and said, "Give us a wish list of what you want your national center for missing children to be." Jay Howell did just that, covering all the issues in his proposal that we thought were important. The next week, OJJDP called back and said, "You've got the center. It's yours."

By that point, it was pretty obvious to me that my life was never going to be what it had been before we lost Adam. Things had gone in an entirely different direction, and there wasn't going to be any turning back. With all that was going on, it was crazy to think that I could continue to maintain my end of the Paradise Grand partnership. On top of that, one of the requirements for getting funding for the national center, to be located in Washington, D.C., was that I had to be part of the deal. "We want you either to run it or to be involved as a consultant," they had said. "But we want you directly involved."

The work would pay a small per diem—far less than what I had earned in the hotel partnership. But it would be enough to keep the family afloat. So we decided. It wasn't acrimonious. It was a sad parting. I sold out my interest in the Paradise Grand to the other partners, and in the spring of 1984, Revé and Meghan and I moved to Washington. Jay had left the Senate staff and was working as a Justice Department consultant for the Center. I was going to be the vice chairman of its five-person board of directors. A consultant. Which, technically, meant that I didn't have a job.

When they heard the news, the local press was

gracious about supporting the hometown boy. "Nation's youth will benefit with Walsh in Washington," one headline read. "In his new national post, he's the man who can make a difference for the nation's most vulnerable citizens."

We found a town house in a development in a Virginia suburb called Oakton, and I became a consultant to the new national center. It was pretty clear that Robbie Callaway and his friends on the Hill were interested in getting me to think about running for office, but I wasn't interested. If I had done that, I wouldn't have been able to get anything done. As a private citizen, at least I could take aim and criticize elected officials when I thought I should. I knew that I could get a lot more things accomplished as an outsider.

We were getting a lot of state bills passed, but I was having to do a lot of traveling to different states, cutting the deals one by one. Bills for state clearinghouses, background checks for people who worked in day-care centers, upgrades for local law enforcement. All related to children's issues—anything and everything that we could think of. It meant that I was away from home a lot of the time, and it was hard on Revé. But then we got some good news: she was pregnant again.

On June 13, 1984, Revé and Meghan and I returned to the White House, this time for the opening of the National Center for Missing and Exploited Children, a private organization funded temporarily by a $3.3-million grant from the Justice Department. It was the third time in a month that we had appeared with the president, and this time was the most emotional of all. Reagan held the ceremony in the East Room of the White House, quite an honor considering that that room is usually reserved only for state dinners and top-level diplomatic receptions. The president and George Bush were there, as was a group of parents of missing chidren—all wearing buttons with their children's pictures on them. During his remarks, the president mentioned the names of four children who had disappeared: twelve-year-old Ann Gotlib, of Louisville; John Gosh, thirteen, of Des Moines; Kevin Collins, ten, of San Francisco. And Adam Walsh.

Reagan gave a nice speech, and just as he got to a line about how our work was "a voice calling out to protect our children and keep them safe," a baby in the audience suddenly let out a cry. Then Reagan introduced me and invited me up to the podium. We presented him with signatures of support for the Center from 250,000 schoolchildren. And I talked about losing Adam.

"I beseech you not to assume it couldn't happen to you," I said, looking out at the audience. "It has happened to thousands of children and parents. We are all responsible for all the children."

This time, when Revé's due date rolled around that December, I had the whole Lamaze drill down: lots of ice chips. "You take deep breaths. I'll take your pulse while you scream and thrash."

And then, out popped a new little baby.

This time . . . a boy.

After Adam died, I had saved a lot of his things, the little things that seemed to be his alone—beautiful wooden model boats that I had given him, his shell collection, stones and sea beans that we had collected together. I never really knew what I was going to do with all of those things. Until now.

We named him Callahan—my mother's maiden name. In the hospital, after they cleaned him up and put a little hat on him and pronounced him perfect, I held him and rocked him the same way that I had with Meghan. Everything was going along just fine.

And then, without warning, everything suddenly got strange.

I remember a doctor coming up to us in the

hallway: "Mr. Walsh, I'd like to speak to you about Callahan. I'm afraid that we're not going to be able to put him in the regular nursery. Because it appears that he has a few problems."

It was like a body blow to the stomach. Revé was standing right next to me, and I zeroed right in on that doctor. "I do not want to hear any of your medical bullshit. You don't know who you're talking to. Don't give me any jargon. I don't want you to couch it. We had a little boy, and he was murdered, and I want to know right now, you tell me right now what is going to happen to my son. Tell me what the odds are. I want to know what his chances are. Fifty-fifty? Seventy-five/twenty-five? I have to know exactly what to be prepared for. No matter how bad the situation is, the one thing that I will not let you do is to torture us by not being straight with us."

I hate it when people screw around like that—trying to soften the blow by not telling you things. I needed to know whether Cal was going to make it. I could deal with that. But I was not about to sit around and wait twenty-four hours to finally hear that something was wrong—really wrong—with our new little boy.

"Okay, Mr. Walsh. This is the situation. Callahan has fluid on his lungs. It could be bad, and it could get worse. He's also got jaundice. We're going to monitor him for twenty-four hours. We're putting him on medication. And we don't want you to worry yet."

As if I could help it. Immediately, the thoughts started running through my head. I remember thinking to myself, "Well, wouldn't this be the ultimate test of Job. Waiting nine months for our new little boy. And now, this. If we should somehow lose this little baby, what more could possibly be done to us?"

I rarely resort to prayer. I believe that it is a testament of faith and commitment to religion. But I don't believe in praying just because you need a favor. I've never been one for the old "Dear God, if I don't get caught this time, I promise I'll never do it again" type of thing.

But this time, I prayed. I prayed hard. And I talked to Adam. "You've got to look out for your brother this time," I told him. "You have to watch over him. Because he has got to be okay."

It was a long, torturous twenty-four hours. Callahan was in intensive care. We could see him through the ICU window, but we could do nothing to help him. I felt so helpless. I was pacing, watching him, thinking to myself, "This would be just too unfair."

Revé was doing a lot better than I was. She seemed to believe that the doctors truly could make him well. She somehow had faith that he was going to be okay. Or maybe what she really thought was that no matter what, it just could not happen twice.

I stayed right there in the hospital until the doctors got the fluid out of Cal's lungs, and his fever broke and his color turned rosy. They came out and told us that he was going to be fine.

And he was.

Later on, after we got him home, he developed colic, and for the longest time, all he did was cry. We didn't care. He was a feisty little guy. Sweet.

Like Adam.

Revé said that living in Washington was the closest thing to being in prison that she had ever known. I was on the road for weeks at a time. She was home alone with a baby and a two-year-old, and all her friends were back down in Florida. She said that she had never had so much quiet in her life. So we talked about it, and not long after Callahan was born, we decided to move back home to Florida.

It was, after all, the place where we had won our first victories—where, in the mid-eighties, a local dairy first put the pictures of missing children onto milk cartons, and where a drug chain did the same thing on its shopping bags. By 1983 we had started a statewide clearinghouse run by the Florida Department of Law Enforcement, the FDLE, that would list the name of any missing child whose parents requested it. Almost as soon as we got that clearinghouse approved, funded, and operational, it had listings for 3,400 missing kids. We went on to a lot of other things, too: mandated background checks of teachers and child-care workers (after we learned that thirty-seven teachers in Florida were felons convicted of either child abuse, drug dealing, or murder), repeat-offender bills, laws that allowed the videotaping of testimony by children who were victims of sexual abuse so that they wouldn't have to take the witness stand in court.

But those weren't our only battles. As always, there were still other hurdles on Capitol Hill—this time about getting some sort of ongoing funding for the Center. Arlen Specter and Paul Simon wanted it to be administered by Al Regnery's office at Justice. Ike Andrews, a Democratic congressman from North Carolina who hated Al Regnery, wanted it administered instead by the Department of Health and Human Services.

The usual stuff.

Through it all, I kept learning about strategy and tactics. One of the things that I picked up was a habit of winging it whenever I had to give testimony at congressional hearings. Most politicians read from a prepared statement whenever they have to give a speech. But I learned to organize everything on two pieces of paper, then work from my notes. I tried a few times to submit testimony beforehand, but I just couldn't do it. I also found that if I didn't provide the staff with my remarks in advance the way most witnesses did, it didn't give them the chance to get a rebuttal together ahead of time.

Those were the kinds of things that I learned from dealing with politicians. A lot of passionate, dedicated, hardworking people hold public office in this country. But also, a lot of politicians are in love with the status and the game of power. I have no respect for those people—the ones who use the perks of office and forget that a lot of the constituents who put them there are poor, don't know how to work the system, and feel that no one cares about them.

Ever since my first run-in with Pat Schroeder and Harold Washington, I always made a point of addressing the committee members who leave the hearing room when victims are giving their testimony. That enrages the politicians. They think that I'm an egomaniac for daring to question their behavior.

I understand that everyone is busy—even elected representatives. But I also understand what it feels like to be the parent of a murdered child or a rape victim or a woman whose mother has been beaten to death, to have to pay his or her own way to Washington to attend a hearing, to wait for hours while all these politicians do their public posturing, and then to have to sit down at a witness table, finally, when three people are left in the room and everyone is shuffling papers and looking in the other direction. If a member of Congress has to get up and leave the room, I don't know why, out of common courtesy, they can't at least acknowledge the witnesses' presence before they leave.

I never was a psychotic, right-winged vigilante. I am not someone who goes off at the drop of a hat. But for someone who puts heart and soul on the line to try to get something worthwhile accomplished, working on Capitol Hill can be the ultimate frustration. At first, I didn't know the game. Now, I know it as well as anybody—I just refuse to play it. I've worked with people on both sides of the aisle. It never mattered to me whether someone was a Democrat or a Republican. The only thing I ever cared about was where he or she stood on children's issues.

To me, the situation is simple. Say there's a piece of legislation that has been endorsed by a number of people—a well-written, professionally drafted bill that has a measure of support. If it's a good piece of legislation, it proceeds through committees and hearings and eventually reaches the floor of the House or Senate for a vote. That's the American process. And if it gets voted down on the floor, I can understand and accept that. If it gets defeated, that is a reflection of the will of the people—their elected representatives saying no.

What enrages me is the way that so many small-minded, pompous, self-important little staff people and bureaucrats can muck up the process and prohibit people from even getting a hearing. Those times when the holy gatekeepers manage to keep their congressman from really seeing or considering an issue—that's where my frustration level goes right off the scale. And it's why, at the very beginning, I learned a valuable lesson. If you want to get something done, don't waste your time with four hundred staffers. Go to the top. Talk to the man or woman who makes the decisions.

Still, I had no idea that the battle would be so convoluted. That it would have to be won not only at the federal level, but also state by state. I began in the early days by spending most of my time in some outer office waiting to see a guy who could just as easily have been running a 7-Eleven, but had instead gotten himself elected to a state legislature. And then, pretty soon, I found myself addressing whole state legislatures.

That's how I did it: I worked my way up from staffers of state representatives to the state representatives themselves. Then to state senators, chairmen of the state houses, presidents of the state senates, U.S. congressmen, senators, and finally, to presidents themselves. Right on up through the whole food chain of politicians.

I've met some truly wonderful ones, both Democratic and Republican. Robbie Callaway always said that when I lined up legislative endorsements, party affiliation wasn't one of the criteria. The only thing that really mattered was whether the person I was lobbying happened to be at home.

I don't think that anyone in the history of this country has listened to more BS from politicians than I have. I have been patronized by the best of them. But it never stopped me. Long before it was fashionable to wear a ribbon on your lapel, I was knocking on congressional doors wearing a button with Adam's picture on it. I wish I could say that I remember all those years with crystal clarity, but I don't. They're a blur to me. They're generic. I don't remember the first time I addressed a state legislature. I can't say which politicians I met first. I do know that over the years I have addressed the legislatures in all fifty states.

What I remember most about those trips is what press people euphemistically refer to as "the photo opportunity." Day after day, year after year—the famous John Walsh Photo Op.

It would always start the same way: some politician shaking my hand, posing for a picture with me, saying, "Thanks so much, John. This is great. This picture's going to be in my constituent newsletter back home, and they're going to love it back in the district."

At which point I would say, "I'll be glad to stand next to you for this picture." And then I'd whisper, "Do you know one thing about this bill that's before you? Do you know anything about the bill at all? That's right. Of course you don't. You don't know one goddamn thing about this bill, and there's your staff over there and they don't know anything about it, either. So I'm asking you ... No, I'm telling you, learn about this bill. Learn about what it is that I have traveled all this way to talk about. This is an important bill. It's about children. We can get it passed if we work on it together. Today, I've helped you out. I've come here and made you look like a hero. But, please, please do learn about this bill."

Then I would turn to the camera and smile and say, "Okay, let's take the picture."

The amazing thing is that it usually worked. Nine times out of ten, the politician would look at me and say, "You know, you're right. I will take a good look at this bill, John. And the next time we hold hearings on it, I promise you, I'll know a lot more about it than I do now."

Over time, we learned never to crack open the champagne bottle until a bill was signed, sealed, and delivered. We wouldn't celebrate until it was. Because there were so many backstabbers in the world of politics. Things could be fine one minute, shot to hell the next. There was always so much changing of the minds.

Those were hard years. I was a man possessed, traveling nonstop on business for the National Center, adding paid speaking engagements as a way of keeping up with the bills. After every one of those trips, I would make a pit stop at the Center's office, turn my briefcase upside down, and dump out everything inside it in a big pile on the floor. Julie Cartwright, my assistant at the time, remembers hundreds of matchbook covers, napkin scraps, and random pieces of paper—all scribbled with the names and phone numbers of people who needed information or who had asked for help or who wanted to give it. That was our filing system after those trips: Julie jotting down whatever I could remember, sticking Post-it notes on everything to try to keep track of who needed what.

I remember speaking about missing children and victim's rights in the Midwest one time. After the speech, just as I was getting ready to leave, a guy came up to talk to me. Obviously drunk. Blitzed.

"You know better than anybody, don't you?" he

said. "How could they take my boy? They raped him and they tortured him. Well, I've got news for those two teenage punk bastards. I bought a gun and I'm going to that arraignment and I'm going to shoot them right there in that courtroom. I'm going to kill them, and I've got the gun right here under my coat."

The wheels in my head started turning, fast. There were still cops in the auditorium, but I wanted to get the gun away without a struggle. I didn't want to see the guy led away in handcuffs. So I was trying to think of what I could possibly say. I decided to ask the guy what his son's name was. He told me, then started saying how much he had loved his boy.

Then it came to me. "You know," I said, "you really ought to think about this. If your son could come back for even thirty seconds, do you know what he'd say to you? He'd say, 'Dad, don't do it. I'm in a better place now. Don't be bent on this vengeance. Don't do this thing. Don't hurt anybody else. Justice will be done. Don't do this to my mother. Don't do it to yourself.'"

I knew that that was the only thing that might save this guy: the idea that his son would not want to see him like this. That it wasn't the right thing to do. And that was all it took. "I'm going to get rid of this gun," he said. "I'm going to give it away to somebody." And then he completely broke down.

"Give me the gun," I said. "I'll take it for you."

I didn't feel that I had any right to give this guy all that crap about not taking the law into his own hands. How can you stand there and say that to the father of a murdered child? It's precisely what the father of a murdered child does want to do. I knew that much. I had thought about it myself at times. Quite seriously. About what I would do if I ever caught Adam's killer. What should happen to him. How he should die. People had actually said to me, "We could have him killed. We'll get him for you. It could all be done in a heartbeat."

But I also remembered everything that I was working for. And that it would be destroyed if I ever did anything like that. Friends said to me, "If you were involved in just one crime to get even for Adam, it would all end." What would that do to Meghan? To Callahan? I had thought about what it would be like if Adam came back, even for a minute or two. He had always been such a gentle person. I knew what he would tell me. He would say, "Don't do this, Dad. Don't do it to Mom, and to my brother and sister. Don't."

That's what it was like during those years. Unrelenting. Meet this guy. Take a look at that bill. Speak to this legislator. Let's draft this bill. Yes, I'll meet with this guy. Sure, I'll pose for that picture. Fine, I can make that speech.

Some people thought it was all very impressive. "Why, Mr. Walsh, you're going to address a joint session of the legislature of the great state of South Carolina," or wherever. That was when all the members of a state house and senate would sit together in the statehouse on a given night, and someone would tell me that it was a terribly big deal because the only other time it had happened was for the governor's State of the State message or something equally grand. I didn't care. I'd go to bill signings if they asked me to. I've been to more bill signings and had my picture taken more times with more politicians and gotten more commemorative pens than anyone else I know.

At home, I have fifteen big cardboard boxes filled with memorabilia. I always tell Revé that one of these days I'm going to go through it all and put everything on display. Hats, plaques, commendations, medals, awards. Somewhere in there is the one proclamation that means more to me than all the rest of the stuff put together. I got it in 1985, when the national Father's Day committee named me Father of the Year.

I knew that we had to work on more than just the political front. The courts were equally important. I wanted to educate myself about the criminal justice system, and the logical way to do it seemed to be to start attending trials. Especially the trials of men who had been charged with abducting and murdering children. I never made a big deal out of it. Most of the time I just listened, sitting in the back of the courtroom, not saying a word. Sometimes I did more than that.

One experience that will always stand out in my mind is the case of Staci Jazvac.

On January 30, 1986, Staci Jazvac, an eleven-year-old who lived in Fort Lauderdale, rode her bike to the drugstore to pick up some school supplies. When she still wasn't home an hour later, people started looking for her, and someone found her bike in a vacant field. Almost immediately, more than a thousand people began a full-scale search. The Adam Walsh Child Resource Center got a phone call right away and began helping to coordinate the search, printing and distributing fifty thousand flyers. Nancy McBride, who was then the program coordinator at the Lauderdale center, gave a lot of support to Staci's mother, Nancy Jazvac. It was the first major case in which the Adam Walsh Center took an active role.

We remembered what we had learned during the search for Adam—that rewards are useful in getting the media's attention, and keeping it. So the Center posted a reward. That way, if we had to go back to the press and ask for more coverage down the line, they wouldn't say, "Who needs you? We've already got Staci's mother puking and crying on camera. It's old news." Instead, they could report fresh news—that the reward had just been increased.

In most cases, no one actually collects the money. We didn't even have it. It was just a tactic to keep the case in front of the public. Except that two weeks later, on Valentine's Day, some guy having his lunch in a field a couple of miles from Staci's house discovered her remains. She had been raped and murdered.

We then had to come up with the reward, and after we did, we asked the guy if he would donate it to Staci's mother. We had been trying to help her out, paying her electric bill and things because she was lower income and having a really hard time. The guy's response was, basically, fuck you. I found the bones. I'm keeping the money. A useful insight into the general public.

As things go in the criminal justice system, Staci's case came to trial in a heartbeat—three months later, in April of 1986. The prosecutor assigned to it someone who would become very important in my life, a tough, lethal Broward County DA by the name of Kelly Hancock, then the chief homicide prosecutor in the state attorney's office.

Kelly had a plan. "John, life without parole is a sentence that juries can give relatively easily. But a death penalty is different. It's a much more difficult verdict for a jury to reach, and in order to get it, I have to prove heinous circumstances. Still, it's a verdict that will send a message. I can get the death-penalty conviction in this case—but only if you're in the courtroom, looking those jurors in the eye."

By that point, a lot of people in south Florida knew who I was. They remembered me as the father of that beautiful little murdered boy. And if that gave me influence, I thought, then so be it. During the trial, I sat in the courtroom, and it was torture. Nancy McBride attended every day and held the hand of Staci's mother. At one point the defense attorney stood up and said, "Your Honor, I want it entered into the record that if there is a conviction in this case, I'm going to base my appeal on the fact that John Walsh was in the courtroom influencing the jury." One of your basic "Fuck the victim" moves.

But the judge, God bless him (Judge John G. Ferris. I loved that judge. He had a lot of guts), said, "Let me tell you something. Friends of the defendant are here in this courtroom, and Mr. Walsh has every right to be in this courtroom as well. I want that in the record."

The guy charged with killing Staci was a pedophile, young, good-looking, a real scumbag. One day the judge took all the office secretaries on a tour to show them the new Broward County jail, and when this guy saw them coming through, he started masturbating in front of all of them. That's the kind of guy he was. At one point he turned around in the courtroom and looked me in the eye and gave me the finger: "Fuck you, Mr. Walsh. Fuck you."

Kelly did a great job, and at the close of the six-day trial, we got a conviction for the guy who had tortured and murdered Staci Jazvac. That, of course, wasn't the end of things. Then came the tough, tough time— the sentencing phase.

Kelly said, "John, I've got to convince this jury that there are heinous circumstances here in order to get their recommendation for the death penalty. Any suggestions?"

"Okay," I said. "Let me see the crime-scene photos."

"You don't want to see them, John. By the time they found her, she was only skeletal remains."

"Yes," I said. "I want to see them."

I looked at those photographs of Staci's remains, what was left of her, and what I saw, in close-up, were her hands. Two little skeleton hands that each had sticks and twigs and grass in them—whatever she could grasp while she was struggling as this guy was raping and torturing and killing her.

"Kelly, blow these pictures up. Get them in front of that jury and say, 'Want to know about heinous circumstances? I'll show you heinous circumstances. Look at these little hands. Want to know what this prick did to her in the last hour of her life? This is what he did to her. Just look at her little bony, skeleton hands.'"

Kelly enlarged those photographs and put them before the jury when he gave his final argument. On the day it was announced that the jury had reached its decision, I was supposed to be in Boston for some award ceremony with George Bush, but I turned it down because it wasn't as important as being in the courtroom that day with Staci Jazvac's mother.

We took our seats and waited. Then, the jurors filed into the courtroom.

In death-penalty cases, it's not hard to understand that there are often split decisions. But in the Staci Jazvac case, the jurors voted unanimously—twelve to nothing—to recommend that the judge impose a death sentence.

I will never forget what we did when that decision was finally handed down.

We bowed our heads and thanked God.

After losing their little girl in so horrible a way, Staci Jazvac's parents now at least had closure. It may have been small consolation, but they had the satisfaction of knowing who was responsible for hurting their daughter, and that this killer would never again be able to hurt another child.

Which was more than what Revé and I had. Five years after Adam's murder, there was still no arrest in his case. Sometimes police thought they had a good lead. Invariably, the tips would lead nowhere. By 1986 there had been no real movement in the investigation for nearly three years—ever since police up in Jacksonville had run across a drifter by the name of Ottis Elwood Toole.

On October 23, 1983, there was a sudden flurry of publicity when papers around the country announced that police had finally found the man who had killed Adam Walsh. The stories all said pretty much the same thing: that Toole, arrested as a suspect in a fatal arson case in Jacksonville, had told police that he was responsible for between thirty-five and fifty homicides around the country—and that one of them was Adam's.

Up in Jacksonville, Toole had given a confession admitting that he had picked Adam up outside the Hollywood mall, lured him into his car with toys and candy, and then killed him. But the cops weren't telling me much beyond that. Most of what I knew was from what I read in the papers. Toole had been traveling with Henry Lee Lucas, a known serial killer who was in prison in Texas and who was claiming responsibility for more than 150 murders. At a press conference, Sam Martin, the Hollywood police chief, said that the details Toole was confessing "make Charles Manson sound like Tom Sawyer or Huck Finn."

According to Hollywood's assistant police chief, LeRoy Hessler, Toole's stories were "grisly and heinous beyond belief," but for one crime out of all of them, he clearly showed remorse. "He breaks into tears," Hessler said, "when he talks about Adam."

At the end of their press conference, the Hollywood police announced that the following day Ottis Toole would be officially charged with Adam's abduction and murder.

Then, I made a statement of my own: "My heart will be broken for the rest of my life. But I hope that [Toole] receives due process. And I hope that Adam receives some justice."

Weeks went by. Then months. And years.

We kept thinking that the cops were working on the case, that there might be some reason for a delay that we didn't know about. But during that whole time, for whatever reason, Ottis Toole was never indicted.

I never received a full explanation for why that was the case. I learned that Toole had apparently recanted his confession a couple of times, and that he kept changing his story. And that when the Hollywood e went up to Jacksonville and brought Toole back wn to the spot along the Florida Turnpike where he said he had buried the rest of Adam's remains, there was no evidence. No trace of Adam. No sign of anything at all.

I believed that the cops were doing the best they could, and that if they did find out anything, they would let me know about it as soon as they could. But after a while, the bottom line seemed to be that they believed Ottis Toole had not really killed Adam. That he had just been lying to gain some notoriety. That he had just been bluffing. And I trusted them.

Throughout all of the legal battles and the court fights and the endless travel, Adam was never out of my mind. Never. Not even for a day. He was always the one I was fighting for, the one who kept me focused. And if the horror of what had happened to him ever began to fade, even for a minute, it always seemed that something would come along to reopen the wound.

Sometimes it would be a newspaper story. Or a phone call. Or some new piece of information from the Hollywood police.

And then, one day at an airport, it was something that Les Davies said he had to show me. Something that had arrived at the Adam Walsh Center, addressed to me. It was a letter, handwritten, carrying a postmark from Starke prison, near Jacksonville:

Dear Walsh,

I'm the person who snatched, raped & murdered and cut up the little prick teaser, Adam Walsh, and dumped his smelly ass into the canal. You know the story but you don't know where his bones are. I do.

Now you are a rich fucker, money you made from the dead body of that little kid. Oh, he was a sweet little piece of ass! I want to make a deal with you. Here's my deal. You pay me money and I'll tell where the bones are so you can get them buried all decent and Christian.

I know you'll find a way to make sure I get the electric chair but at least I'll have money to spend before I burn. If you want the bones of your little cockteaser you send a private lawyer with money for me. No cops. No State Attorneys. No FDLE. Just a private lawyer with a written contract. I get $5,000 as "good faith" money. Then when I show you some bones I get $45,000. You get a lawyer to make up a paper like that.

If you send the police after me before we make a deal then you don't get no bones and what's left of Adam's hot pussy can rot. I remember how the little bitch was crying for his mommy when I was ramming his asshole. I love to fuck a boy, and then I love to kill them. Now you want his bones or not? Tell the cops and you don't get shit.

Sincerely,
Ottis E. Toole

12

America's Most Wanted

NINETEEN EIGHTY-FOUR WAS A ROUGH TIME FOR US. It was the year that we moved to Washington when I didn't even have a real job—just a temporary National Center consultancy that was going to pay me about $32,000 a year. I was struggling—trying to get the Center off the ground, flying all over the country, lobbying, doing speaking engagements. Trying to keep all the balls in the air. At one point I finally collapsed and was put in the hospital in Virginia. I thought it was a heart attack, but it turned out to be exhaustion. They put me on IVs and everything, and the doctors told me that I had to slow down and start taking it easy. As soon as I got out of the hospital, I went right back to the Center and started up again.

After the two made-for-TV movies about Adam in 1983 and 1986, Linda Otto and Alan Landsburg had remained my guardian angels, supporting me emotionally and with career advice. They didn't just make the movie and then move on. They stayed in touch. Always wanted to know how we were doing, if we needed any help. And always telling me—just being nice, I thought—that I would be really great on television. "You know, you're killing yourself," they said. "And you've got the Center to think of. You can't keep staging bake sales, talking to two-hundred people at a time. Television is the most powerful medium. Think of how you could use it to get your message across."

Then, right out of the woodwork, up popped the opportunity to do a PBS special. The call had come from an independent producer for Westinghouse. "I want to do a documentary about parents of murdered children," he said. "About what it's like if your child is kidnapped and murdered. What does that do to a family? How do you get through it? It's obvious that you've found a way to channel your grief." Which was total BS, because anybody could see how angry and abrasive I was.

But this producer had a lot of faith in me. What he wanted was to film me, sitting down and talking to these parents. What happened to your child? How are you dealing with it? Straight documentary style. I talked to Linda Otto about it. "I don't know about stand-ups or anything," I said. She said, "John, you can do it. It's a documentary. Just go ahead and do it."

A Parent's Greatest Fear aired in May 1984, and I think we pulled it off. People watched the show and it was well received. I know that, for me, it was a heartrending experience. But it reminded me that other people out there were hurting as much as we were. It reminded me that Adam wasn't the only child who had been kidnapped and murdered.

A couple of years later, I got a call from a producer at HBO named Sheila Nevins. She was interested, she said, in putting together a documentary based on the book *How to Raise a Street-Smart Child,* written by Grace Hechinger. Sheila Nevins, who had known Dan Travanti for years—the actor who had played me in the two *Adam* TV movies—got him to host it. I suggested that she also line up Linda Otto, who signed on for nothing. Dan agreed to do it for expenses—a plane ticket to fly in and do the stand-ups.

The program *Street Smart* told parents how to educate their children about physical and sexual abuse. We reported that 70 percent or more of the crimes against children were committed by someone they knew—trusted authority figures—which reflected what we had learned over the years. That, unlike what we initially thought, kidnappings by strangers, while traumatic and horrible, were actually the rarest type of child abduction. That kids all over the country were being abused, physically and sexually, at home, and by friends of the family. And that, for the most part, the problem wasn't being discussed.

During the show, we talked about the criticism that we might be accused of unnecessarily scaring children. "I'd rather scare my kid than identify him in a morgue," I said. At first, none of the suits at HBO seemed overly enthused about promoting the show: "Who's John Walsh? Who's Dan Travanti? It's just a documentary. Who cares?" But Sheila Nevins kept fighting for that show. She got it produced, and after it first aired in 1987, it won a bunch of awards.

Although I certainly wasn't paying any attention to it at the time, two years earlier, the Australian media mogul Rupert Murdoch had bought Metromedia and Twentieth Century–Fox, as a foray into U.S. films and broadcasting. His idea was to try to turn a group of Fox affiliate stations into the nation's fourth television network, and he was willing to pour $110 million into the project over a two-year period to make it happen. Murdoch's people were trying to come up with a single night of programming for Fox's seven "O & O's," the local TV stations around the country that it owned and operated. Besides those, there were about eighty Fox-affiliated stations around the country—compared to NBC and CBS, who each had more than two hundred. The *Wall Street Journal* and the

New York Times were saying there would never be a fourth network. Murdoch was fighting an uphill battle—something that only someone with his ego and deep pockets could ever even dream of.

Fox's programmers knew that there were crime-fighting shows in Europe, such as the BBC's *Crime Watch U.K.*, that used viewer participation as a way to catch fugitives. And they wanted to start a show like that in the United States. This crime-fighting concept was already in development, and a guy named Tom Herwitz, who was the vice president of corporate and legal affairs for Fox televison stations in Washington, D.C., had already done a lot of homework. He had asked for a meeting with the FBI and wound up talking to none other than my old buddy Buck Revell, who was still there. Herwitz showed him a two-page treatment of the show, and Revell was impressed enough to see to it that the Bureau eventually gave its conditional blessing to the project. That left Herwitz with only one big problem remaining: finding a host for the show. Stephen Chao—Fox's vice president of program development—and an L.A. producer named Michael Linder sat down with Herwitz to discuss the possibilities. They considered the author Joseph Wambaugh, and a whole raft of actors—Treat Williams, Ed Marinaro, Brian Dennehy, Brian Keith, and Theresa Saldana, who had played herself in a TV movie about how she was nearly stabbed to death by some psychotic attacker. Then, during one of their marathon conference calls, Herwitz suggested me.

Everybody seemed to like the idea. What I had, they thought, was credibility. I had experienced a great personal tragedy, but had somehow managed to survive it and carry on with some pretty good legislative work. Herwitz, who was a lobbyist and knew me from the Hill, wanted to talk to me, but at first he had a hard time tracking me down. I was all over the place in those days, traveling something like a half million air miles a year. But finally, through Nancy McBride, my assistant at the Adam Walsh Center in West Palm Beach, he did get in touch with me. Nancy had already filled me in about the idea for the show. Herwitz wanted to know if I might be interested in doing a pilot.

"What's a pilot?" I said.

In the seven years since Adam's death, I had been asked to do all kinds of things—host TV shows, endorse home burglar systems, you name it. And I had turned them all down. So when this call came in, my immediate reaction was "No way. I'm not a celebrity. I'm the father of a murdered child." And then I talked for a while about Adam. Herwitz later said that that had only convinced him more. Besides my having the voice and the looks for TV, he thought, I was also a kind of card-carrying everyman—an ordinary person who had been hit hard by crime and who could reach audiences in a way that a standard TV actor couldn't.

At the time, Fox was still a start-up operation. The only hit it had was a show called *21 Jump Street*, starring a young unknown by the name of Johnny Depp. I knew that, in a grab for ratings, Fox might well try to make this new crime show something really exploitative. I told Herwitz and Linder that the show's content would be critical—as would be the way it treated victims. They told me that it could do some good; at the time, something like 280,000 fugitives were on the loose in the United States, wanted by the FBI, the U.S. Marshals Service, the DEA, Customs, the Bureau of Alcohol, Tobacco and Firearms, Interpol, and thousands of local agencies.

I told them that I wasn't going to move my family to California. No problem, they said. The show was going to be produced out of Washington. We went back and forth like that for nearly five hours. Afterward, Herwitz kept up the pressure. Persistent. Flattering. "We've screen-tested all kinds of people, but it keeps coming back to you," he said. "You're the guy we want."

I was being evasive. The idea certainly had potential, but this was still TV, after all. What would it do to my credibility on the Hill? And besides, what in the world made them think that I could handle the job? Sure, I had been on *Donahue* and in a couple of documentaries, but that was a far cry from appearing as the host of a weekly national television show. I didn't even know what the Nielsens were.

All I did know was that whenever I did a media appearance, there was always tremendous positive feedback. Every time I was on *Good Morning America* or some television interview, hundreds of calls would pour into The National Center, from state legislatures and ordinary citizens: "We were wondering if John could come to our state to help push our missing-child clearinghouse bill along." "I just saw Mr. Walsh on TV and I'd like to know what I can do to help."

I didn't know whom else to turn to, so I called Alan Landsburg and Linda Otto and laid it all out for them.

"Take it," they said. "You'll catch criminals."

"I don't know anything about it," I said. "I can't do it."

"Yes, you can. You can."

After thinking about it for a while, I finally told Tom Herwitz that I couldn't promise that I would do a weekly series, but that I was willing to host the show's first episode. He, Linder, and I arranged to meet the next week in Fort Lauderdale, where they were filming a segment about drug smugglers with the Broward County sheriff.

We wound up meeting at 1 A.M. on the morning of August 5, 1987, in the lobby of a Lauderdale hotel. I was nervous. We talked for an hour and agreed to meet again at 5 A.M. to shoot the show's opener at sunrise. They gave me a script, but I fell asleep back at the hotel before I even had the chance to look at it. My brother Joe, who was working for me at the time, was with me, and four hours later, we all met in the hotel lobby for the drive to the airport, where the segment was going to be filmed. They wired me up for sound, and at 5:30 A.M. I delivered my first lines. I was beat, and my voice sounded scratchy, but Linder later said that at that moment the producers knew they had their man.

After we finished the taping, Linder asked if I'd like to see a sample segment from the show—a tape of the first crime re-creation that they had produced. I said sure, so they popped a rough cut into a portable VCR monitor on the back of their rented station wagon. No studio. No screening room. Just the flipped-down back of a station wagon in an airport parking lot. The segment they showed me was about an Indiana man who had escaped from prison, where he was serving six life sentences for murder, rape, kidnapping, and a triple murder/arson. The convict's name was David James Roberts.

At the time the show's segment picked him up in 1974, Roberts had already been arrested for rape and convicted of robbing three women at gunpoint and locking them in the trunk of a car. He had served a prison term and was out on parole. Then, one day in 1973, he had ordered a new set of tires from a store. After they'd been put on his car, he just jumped in the car and drove off without paying for them. But he thought that the manager of the store might recognize him, so he followed the guy home. He broke into the guy's house, tied him and his wife up, raped the wife, then burned the house down. They found gas cans and the neckties that he used to tie them up. And when the firemen arrived, they found not only the bodies of the two adults but, in a crib in the back bedroom, their two-year-old baby daughter dead of smoke inhalation.

Although Roberts's fingerprints were on the gas can

at the scene of the crime and he was already a convicted felon, a judge set his bond at $10,000, which meant that he only had to come up with 10 percent of that and was out on $1,000. That November, he went on trial for three counts of murder, and it ended in a mistrial. That same week, at two-thirty in the morning, he spotted a nineteen-year-old single mother, divorced, who had just picked up her six-month-old baby son from the baby-sitter, because she worked at night. She was driving home down the deserted streets when she noticed a man walking down the road. Suddenly, he banged on the window, a gun in his hand, and jumped in the passenger side.

He made her go to an ATM machine and withdraw money, raped her repeatedly, and told her he was going to lock her in the trunk of her car. This was in Indiana in November. She was begging, "I'll do anything. Tell me what to do. Just, please don't hurt my baby." Roberts put the woman in the trunk, her baby in the backseat, and drove off with them. After a while, he pulled over and put the baby out of the car by the side of the road. The woman knew what was happening because, from inside the trunk, she couldn't hear the baby crying anymore. Later that morning, the cops found the baby, clutching blades of grass in his hands, frozen to death. He had crawled several hundred yards along the snowy roadside before he died.

In 1974, Roberts had been convicted for murdering the couple and their two-year-old, as well as for the kidnapping and rape of the Indianapolis woman and the murder and kidnapping of her baby.

The tape ran for five minutes, and I couldn't take my eyes off it. Watching that one segment changed my whole opinion of the show. I was so outraged and so heartbroken. I'll never forget it. Here was a suspect in a triple homicide, with a rap sheet as long as my arm. It brought tears to my eyes to see what he had done to two families. My brother Joe was standing next to me, and as I watched that tape, I felt like puking. All I could say was, "That son of a bitch."

"But here's the worst thing, John," Linder said. "In October of 1986, while being returned to prison from a medical facility, Roberts got a small handgun and escaped. He kidnapped two guards, who got away when he stopped to make a phone call." At the time of his escape, Roberts was serving six life sentences, three of which were commuted death sentences. Now, he had disappeared. The FBI had put him on its Ten Most Wanted list. "They've got their biggest man-hunters on this case," Linder said, "but they don't have a clue where Roberts is."

I couldn't believe it. "I'm the father of a murdered child, and here's a guy who killed two kids," I said. "Wouldn't it be great if we caught this guy? Wouldn't that be something? I'm going to go home and talk to my wife about this."

One of the biggest things on my mind was my family's security. At the time, Revé and I were living in a rented house in Boca Raton, and we had already received the occasional threatening call: "We're going to kill you. We're going to get you." Things like that. I wasn't sure who was doing it. I had certainly heard rumors that the pedophiles from NAMBLA weren't too happy with me. I had already testified against NAMBLA on the Hill and helped in something called Operation Glass Window—a Justice Department sting operation that had busted pedophiles and child pornographers all around the country. The judges saw to it that any money resulting from fines imposed at sentencing be donated to the National Center. So these pedophiles certainly knew that the National Center and I were their enemies.

In any event, not long before I was approached about doing the show, someone had called up our local utility company, Florida Power and Light, and said, "Hi, I'm John Walsh. You know, from the TV movie *Adam?* I'm at the airport, and I want to make sure that all my bills are paid before I go out of town."

The caller was told that FP&L's policy was not to give out any information without an account number. "Oh, come on. You know who I am. I really need to pay this bill. Blah blah blah. And, oh, by the way, I've changed my phone number to a new one."

The FP&L employee reconfirmed the old number with the caller.

"Great," said the guy. "I'll be sending you my check."

The first we knew about any of this was when an FP&L supervisor called us and said, "I think we've made a big mistake. We've given out your unlisted number to a stranger."

I was livid. The FBI had already starred our utility accounts, which meant that if anyone inquired about them, a notice was supposed to pop up on the computer screen warning that no information could be given out without a supervisor's approval. And we had absolutely no idea who had made the call—child pornographers, child killers, people just trying to harass us?

All we knew was that the horse was out of the barn. Both the Adam Walsh Center and the Broward sheriff advised us to get out of the house. So Revé took Meghan and Cal to the Bahamas for six weeks. And my brother Joe stayed with me in the house, going in and out so that it looked as if there was some activity. There were round-the-clock cops sitting in patrol cars out front. Once, a new guy came on shift without telling the other cop, who was inside. The new guy came around back, and the one inside freaked out and nearly shot.

In the end, nothing came of it. Except that now, in deciding whether or not to do this television show, I was extremely sensitive to the possible security issue. Fox was up-front about it. "You're going to be profiling psychopaths," they said. "And you're familiar enough with the world of law enforcement to know what that means."

I laid it all out for Revé: "If I'm profiling criminals as the host of a nationwide television show, it's going to change our life dramatically. Our visibility will be even higher than it is now, and we've got to consider the odds that some psycho may try to hurt us.

"I don't know where this is all going to go, Revé. I don't even know if this Fox network is going to fly. But you know, we may never learn who killed our own little boy. Wouldn't it be something if we could catch a guy who murdered two little babies?"

Revé was right there. "This is what we do," she said. "It's what we're all about. I think you should go ahead and do the show."

In my mind, some things still needed to be worked out. Because of the experience that we'd had with the two *Adam* movies, I wanted to make sure that this new show featured a toll-free number so that people could phone in their tips. And because of what I knew about interagency law enforcement task forces, I wanted to make sure that we included not just federal but also state and local crime-fighting agencies—and didn't set it up so that they were competing against each other. I knew that we would have to be careful about civil liability, adverse pretrial publicity, and the treatment of victims. But all of those considerations could be worked out, I knew. This was the kind of project that the big three networks would never tackle. Maybe this crazy, fledgling Fox could make it fly.

So after weighing all the considerations, I decided. Yes, I told them. I would host their TV show.

Before the show even went on the air, my existing relationship with the FBI was a big help. Two days before our Sunday debut, the FBI's director, William Sessions, a former judge, held a press conference along with me and Michael Linder at FBI headquarters. He said that the Bureau was willing to endorse the show, and the idea of citizen cooperation with it. Both, he said, were good for law enforcement. It was a pretty remarkable event, given that never before in the Bureau's history had it ever endorsed a movie or television show—even *The Untouchables*. But now, because of my history with the Bureau, the FBI's director was saying that the FBI and *America's Most Wanted* would have a kind of partnership.

By that point in my life, I can honestly say that I wasn't afraid of much. But on Sunday, February 7, 1988, the day that I walked into the Fox studios at WTTG in Washington to shoot the pilot, I was scared. It's still kind of painful for me to see those early clips today. It was rough. There I was in a suit, wearing makeup. The high-tech sets looked like cardboard (one TV critic said they looked like "the starship *Enterprise*"), and probably a hundred people, including a bunch of Fox executives, were all standing around, watching me. I had never done anything like this before. Nobody had told me anything—how to know which camera was on, how they count you down to let you know when to start talking. I was pretty green on that first episode. I was nervous— talking nonstop. Michael Linder was being really nice to me, telling me to stay calm and everything. I didn't know that if the light went off on the camera, you were supposed to turn away from it and toward one where the light had just gone on, or how you cut away to a commercial or cue the clips. I guess they figured they could just talk me through it as we went along.

So I just gave myself a little pep talk: "Now, John, just pay attention and do the best you can." People told me later how intense I was; that most TV personalities don't care if they don't get it right until take thirty-five, and I was trying to get it the first time. At 1 P.M., after a few hours of rehearsal, we began final taping of the show. The taping ran until 6:28. We had two minutes to get the final taped version on the satellite to six stations and to WTTG's master control. Then, at 6:30 P.M. on Sunday, February 7, 1988, viewers saw a pretty nervous guy on their TV sets at home saying, "I'm John Walsh. Welcome to the premiere of *America's Most Wanted,* a nationwide criminal manhunt, a partnership with law enforcement agencies across the country.

"Using actors, we will re-create crimes of dangerous fugitives, often at the location where they took place. We'll brief you on how the outlaws think and behave and where they may be hiding.

"Here in our studios, researchers are waiting for your calls on our toll-free hot lines. If you know something about these cases you're going to see, call us at 1-800-CRIME-88. You don't have to tell us your name.

"Some of the crimes you're about to see are tough. Parental discretion is advised, but we believe these stories demand telling."

Then the taped David James Roberts segment ran, followed by a segment where I talked about his description and background. Then we moved on to a profile of a guy named Ray Allen Minnick, who was wanted for multiple bank robberies and attempted murder. Then back to me, and I did some interviews with cops. After that, it was time to wrap things up. "I became a victim of crime when my young son, Adam, was kidnapped and murdered," I said. "I decided not to be victimized by fear or revenge. But each of us can help and must help stop crime. . . .

"I'm John Walsh. Remember—you can make a difference."

One of our biggest worries was that we would go the whole nine-week run of the show without a single capture. But after the very first image of David James Roberts appeared on the screen, the most amazing thing happened. Eight incoming phone lines lit up all at once. By the end of the first commercial, ten more calls were stacked up on hold. And two of those calls were from people in New York City who said they knew a man who looked just like the guy on-screen.

A few days later, I got a call from Tom Herwitz. "Guess what?" he said. "You're not going to believe this, John, but they've nailed David James Roberts." The cops had found him running a homeless shelter in Staten Island, where he had posed for a picture with Ed Koch, the mayor, in the *New York Daily News* a month or so before. Koch had gone over to Staten Island to give this homeless shelter an award, and David James Roberts, Top Ten FBI psychopath fugitive, was standing next to the New York City mayor right there in the *Daily News*. Roberts, our first capture, was sent to Indiana State Prison in Michigan City, Indiana, to serve six life sentences plus ten years (six in solitary) for escape.

Fox's initial game plan was to test *AMW* on its seven owned-and-operated stations. There weren't even any plans to move it out to the network. But the first show drew such sky-high ratings on the O & O's that they decided immediately to start running the show on the Fox network of 125 affiliated stations. No big discussion about it. No "Should we do a third show before we decide?" Nothing like that.

The show didn't look like anything else that was on TV. The editing style, inspired by a video that Linder had seen by the music group New Order, was full of energy and tension; it looked as if the footage had been shot with a handheld camera. Now they were calling us "reality TV"—and in some cases "tabloid TV." All of a sudden, we were everywhere: on the BBC, Japanese television, in *Paris Match* and the German paper *Der Stern*. We were also an instant controversy. Everyone was asking if this show had finally crossed the line. Had it gone too far? Were the crime reenactments too gruesome? Was this vigilantism run amok?

My position was that if the only thing we were ever going to show was still photos of criminals, then the only audience we'd get would be on PBS at one o'clock in the morning. And furthermore, that I was not some kind of vigilante. Vigilantes take the law into their own hands. *AMW* offered no rewards, and we kept the civil liberties of the accused in mind, no matter what we filmed. To this day, I still work within the system, hand in hand with law enforcement, trying to help them do their job. I was also trying to educate television people about how not to exploit victims. I was the one who kept saying, "We are not going to show that little molested girl's face on camera. And you are not going to broadcast her name. If she and her parents decide that she wants to talk, to let people know that it could happen to other little kids, then block out her face." The same for rape victims. If they wanted anonymity, but needed to tell their story to help regain some sense of control in their lives, then we would accommodate them in every way we could.

Reporters also wanted to know how, after doing the show, I could have the audacity to testify on children's issues on Capitol Hill. Hadn't the show completely destroyed my credibility? they asked. My response was always the same: "Do you ever watch the show? No? Well, how can you write about it, then. Go home and watch the show. And compare what we do with what's at your local movie theater this summer." We never showed graphic violence on *AMW,* and we didn't use exploding blood packs the way fictional cop shows do. None of that stuff.

We were being careful, and we still kept managing to do what we had set out to do—time and time again. In May of 1988, a guy who was wanted for a 1981 murder saw himself on the show, stopped a police car on a street in San Diego, and gave himself up. Which was probably wise on his part, since after his segment aired, three-hundred viewers called in with tips. That July, we caught another murder suspect, a guy named Robert Wayne Fisher, twenty-seven minutes after his profile aired. And it didn't stop. In March of 1990, *AMW* saw its one hundredth capture.

All that, and our ratings were great, too. During one working trip to California, I ran into Fox CEO Barry Diller on a boat where they were having a meeting of all the affiliates. He had hurt his leg, skiing, but he still managed to come over to me and say, "You know what? You're the star of the most popular show on our network. I know what your show's ratings are, I found out what we're paying you. And I'm going to double your salary."

In those early days of the show, a typical week started on Sunday, right after that week's episode had aired, when Michael Linder and I would sit down and work on the script together. He was a good writer and really captured my passion and my feelings. By that time, we weren't having any trouble finding cases to profile. They were streaming in from all kinds of sources—cops, victims, potential witnesses. A committee went through all the possible cases and would then refer the most promising to us, and then we'd talk about them. Is this case too far-fetched? Is this one too old? Do we stand a chance of catching this guy? Even in those days, I had lot of creative control in choosing which cases we featured. Which is how we came to air the story of a vicious killer named James Charles Stark.

Back in the spring of 1987, Nancy McBride, my assistant at the Adam Walsh Center, had handed me a photograph that had been sent to us by the National Center in Washington. This morgue shot of a little girl, about fourteen, sickened me. Her eyes were swollen shut. She had been battered. And the worst of it was that no one knew who she was.

The cops didn't know the little girl's identity, but they did know who had killed her. Because on May 1, 1987, this guy pulled his van into a gas station in Banning, California, and inside, an attendant saw the little girl screaming and trying to get out of the passenger side. At that point, the guy behind the wheel grabbed her by the hair, pulled her back down to the floorboard with his left hand, and with his right, shot her in the head. Then he drove off and, a couple of miles later, shot her in the head again and rolled her out of the van and down an embankment like so much garbage. This little girl, maybe thirteen or fourteen years old, had been kidnapped and kept in this van for two weeks. The guy had tortured her, raped her repeatedly, hit her with a ball-peen hammer in the elbows and knees, breaking her kneecaps. Later on, she was buried in an unmarked grave, and the only people at her funeral were a minister, a church social worker, and a funeral director.

The local coroner contacted the National Center to tell them about the case to see if they could help track down the little girl's identity. The Center put together a wanted poster, showing a close-up of the little girl's face as she lay on an autopsy table, along with a photograph of the man police suspected in the case: a three-time convicted rapist named James Charles Stark.

I carried that poster in my briefcase for nearly two years. No matter where I went, I could never get that little girl's picture out of my head. I was obsessed with it. If I was speaking to parents of runaways, or some local police agency, I would distribute photocopies of that poster. "Is this your daughter?" I would ask. "Do you have a missing little girl who looks like this? Have you got this guy in jail? Have you ever arrested this guy?"

And now that I had the forum of the show, I didn't even think twice about it. "We've got to do this Stark guy," I told Michael Linder. "I have to."

We shot a whole segment on the case—all about the little girl, what had happened to her, and as much as we knew about Stark. Two days before the show was going to air, Fox decided to promo it. So they ran a lead-in that featured the case. Based just on that promo, before the full segment even aired, we caught James Stark. He was working in a car wash in Ann Arbor, Michigan. People knew him as a strange guy; he used to brag about having killed people.

The real controversy came almost immediately. We were of course planning to go ahead and run the segment on Stark, even though he had already been caught. The story wasn't over yet. We still didn't know the identity of the little girl. I wanted to show that morgue shot of her on television. And some Fox executive said, "Why? Stark's already been caught, and we can't show it anyway. It's too graphic. Nobody shows morgue shots on prime-time television. We'll get all kinds of criticism for it."

I wasn't going to back down on this one. "Somewhere out there there's a grandma, a mother, a brother, or a sister who needs to know where this little girl is," I said. "That her remains are in an unmarked grave in California. That she was never given a proper burial. You don't know how terrible this is. You don't understand that, for a parent, there is nothing worse than not knowing. Nothing. I know what happened to my son. But the parents of this little girl don't even know that she's dead."

So Linder and I fought them on it. We hung tough. And we won. On the show that week, we showed the morgue photo of that little girl. And then a telephone call came in from a lady in Alabama who had been looking for her little girl, who had been mildly retarded and had either run or wandered away. The cops were finally able to put it all together, and this mother got her daughter's remains back. She buried them in a grave in Alabama and had a ceremony, and now she can visit her little girl's grave. She can put flowers on it and know that her daughter is in a better place. She doesn't have to worry anymore about whether her little girl is being tortured or if she is being prostituted or has drowned. I know all this because the mother in Alabama wrote me a letter and told me. The night that *America's Most Wanted* captured James Charles Stark was one of the best nights of my life.

After his capture, Stark fought being extradited back to California, because he was now facing the death penalty there. At the time, I knew that he had once escaped by faking trying to hang himself. He had been choking and gasping in his cell, and when the guards came in to cut him down and take him to the prison hospital, he escaped. He had planned the whole thing.

So when Stark lost his extradition battle, when the word got around that he was going back to California for this murder, he knew what he was facing. He'd been paroled three times already, and this was it. He knew the system. So in 1991 I said, "You know, we should do an update on James Charles Stark. He's lost his extradition fight, and he's back in California waiting for trial. Let's really tick him off and let those guards out in California know that he might try to feign illness or fake a hanging, in order to escape. It's a good story, and if he does try to fake his own hanging, wouldn't it be great if we could trip him up at it?" I wanted the prison to know that they had a child killer on their hands. They needed to be very aware of that.

So we went out to California, did a whole follow-up segment on Stark, and then, about a month later, he did try to hang himself. Only this time, no one came to cut him down. The official report says that no one heard him.

When I got that phone call telling me that James Charles Stark was dead, it was a great resolution to my obsession. Not only had the body of a little girl been returned to her mother, but the man who was responsible for her murder was now dead, too. And all because of the power of a television show.

Of all the stories that we've done, the one that really

shot us to national prominence was that of the notorious mass murderer John Emil List.

In 1971, List was an accountant living in Westfield, New Jersey. He looked like an upstanding guy. He went to work every day in a suit, had a big home, was a Lutheran Sunday-school teacher. He lived in a mansion with his wife and three kids, but when the money started running out, he robbed his mother's checking account and started selling off the furniture to keep afloat. List was a religious fanatic and apparently decided that because his wife drank wine and his kids were into rock-and-roll music, they were all in league with the Devil.

So one day, all very calculated, he sent notes to his three kids' teachers saying that the kids weren't coming back to school. He stopped the mail, the newspaper, and the milk delivery. Then he shot his wife in the head and dragged her into the ballroom. Next, he shot his mother and stuffed her into a closet. And then, as the kids came home, he shot each of them, two in the face: the sixteen-year-old, the thirteen-year-old, and the fifteen-year-old, who wound up being shot ten times because he fought back. Then List wrote a confession letter addressed to his minister. When the cops found the bodies a month later, funeral music was playing on the intercom sytem, the temperature in the house had been lowered to fifty degrees, and two bloody mops were in the sink. List's car was found parked at JFK airport.

John List had disappeared. For nearly twenty years there was an international manhunt for him, but no one found him. That still bothered a lot of people, including Westfield's retired police chief, James Moran, who wrote me a letter about how he had never been able to give up on the case. I was also getting some friendly sort of one-upsmanship from my buddies at the FBI: "Okay, Mr. Walsh. You think you're so hot. Let's see you solve the John List case."

We started by calling in an amazing guy named Frank Bender, an artist and forensic sculptor who worked with police to help try to identify the bodies of unknown dead kids. If some jurisdiction found the skull of a child in the woods, for example, Bender could do all kinds of research to re-create the child's face, so that the bust could be shown to the parents to see if it might be their child.

Bender really went to work, researching everything about List's background, his ethnic heritage, what his parents had looked like. How he lived, what he liked to do. Any small detail that might somehow fit into the puzzle. Bender did incredible work. He constructed a bust of what he thought John List would look like today, right down to the gray, thinning hair and the thick, horn-rimmed glasses. We featured that bust in a segment that we ran on List on May 21, 1989. And eleven days later, on June 1, we caught John List. One of those little old ladies who are the show's biggest fans called up and said that a guy who looked just like the man she saw on TV was living in a suburb of Richmond, Virginia, under the name Robert P. Clark. We later learned that, after murdering his family, List had moved to Denver, gotten remarried, and become an upstanding member of the community. Not once in twenty years did he slip up. But that didn't mean that he still didn't have to stand trial for cold-bloodedly executing five members of his own family. At the trial, which was held in April of 1990, List said he was sorry, and that he was now a frail old man throwing himself on the mercy of the court.

But the judge wasn't buying it. It was time, he said, to let the five dead members of the List family speak from the grave. The jury convicted List of first-degree murder and he received five life sentences. Not long after that, I got a letter from a guy who's now a lawyer in New Jersey. He said that he had been the best friend of one of John List's sons. Every year for twenty years this guy had gone to visit the son's grave, hoping and praying that, somehow, someday, there would be justice. "And that's what you did for my friend," the guy told me. "You got justice for my friend."

Frank Bender's re-creation was uncanny. His bust of List was on the front page of the *New York Times*, and it matched recent photos of List, right down to the receding hairline and horn-rimmed glasses. That bust now sits on a shelf in my office. It's one of my coolest mementos.

Our help in solving the List case turned into a big deal. It was all over the place. And when they interviewed the retired Westfield police chief, James Moran, about the capture, he gave us a pretty nice compliment. He said that it cracked him up that people were calling to congratulate him. "I'm not the one who got him," he said, pointing at his TV set. "They did."

All of a sudden, our little fourth-network TV show that everyone had called tabloidy and rough around the edges was finally getting some respect. Now, they were calling it a great vehicle. Now we had credibility. Now we were launched.

It was a big kick to get that kind of recognition. But it wasn't the biggest thrill that I've ever had from doing *American's Most Wanted*. The cases that have always mattered to me most are the stories of missing children. And of those, the one that I still think is closest to my heart is the story of Genny Krohn.

Genny was a beautiful little twelve-year-old who lived with her loving family in a subdivision in a remote area of the Florida Panhandle. One Wednesday afternoon, after asking her dad's permission, she rode her bike to get some candy at a convenience store less than a mile from her home. Genny never came back. A little while later, her father found her bicycle lying in the middle of the road. Almost immediately, Holly Adams, a friend of our friend Ginger Richardson, called Nancy McBride at the

Adam Walsh Center in West Palm Beach. Nancy called *AMW* right away and even arranged for a CBS satellite truck to transmit a home video of Genny to us so that we could include it in a segment on her that we were going to rush into production for that Friday night's show.

It was a bad time. Back in Genny's hometown, people were searching, sending out flyers, doing everything they could to find her, with no luck. Then, an agonizing three days later, Genny called her brother from a pay phone, saying that she had been kidnapped by some guy, but had been released, unhurt.

Genny was interviewed by the police and turned out to be a street-smart little girl. She told the cops that a guy on his moped had seen her, followed her down a dirt road, pulled a gun, and forced her to come with him. He had kept her in a motel across the state line in Mobile. And it was there, that Friday night, that the guy was watching TV and saw Genny's story on *American's Most Wanted*. "Jesus, am I in trouble now," he thought, and that was when he decided to take Genny back to Florida and let her go.

Genny gave the cops a great description of the guy, drew them a picture of his tattoo, and had got the license plate number of the truck he was driving. After the segment aired, another one of those die-hard older lady fans of the show called up and said, "You know that guy who kidnapped that girl on the Friday-night show? Well, he's staying in a trailer here." He had been wearing a blond wig to disguise himself, but the FBI found him and arrested him. After the guy was taken into custody, he said that the reason he had released Genny was because all the news on TV had freaked him out. Now he's doing life without the possibility of parole.

The best part of that story was yet to come. It happened when Genny's parents, Tom and Peggy

Krohn, invited me to fly down to the Panhandle to meet them. It was pretty emotional when I got there. I said hello to everyone, but I kind of hung back about approaching Genny herself. You should never try to touch a child who's been through an ordeal like that unless he or she approaches you first. And that's exactly what Genny did. She came up and threw her arms around me. It was just unbelievable. That single gesture made everything worth it. All the torture. All the hardships. All the horrible, horrible things.

Genny's dad took me aside and told me about the terror he had gone through. How all through those three days, his wife had kept saying to him, "We're going to get her back, aren't we? She's such a beautiful little girl." And of how he had tried to keep up the front. "I was so terrified," he told me. "It was better during the daytime because there was activity. There were cops at the house. But at night, when it got dark, that was when the terror set in."

I was remembering exactly what he was talking about. That was when Tom Krohn said to me, "Our little girl's going to be sleeping in her bed tonight because of you."

In 1992 Lance Heflin, the new executive producer of *America's Most Wanted*, came up with the idea of our Missing Child Alerts. What they are is pictures of missing children that we arrange to put up on the satellite, without the Fox logo on them, so that anybody can take the picture off the bird. That way, for example, if the local CBS affiliate in the child's hometown wants to run it on the local news, they can. As for the show itself, we've now run profiles of 287 stranger-abducted children. One hundred and thirty of those kids have been recovered—twenty-one alive as a direct result of tips to *AMW*. The remainder of those children are still unaccounted for, and we have a full-time person at both *AMW* and the National

Center working on those cases. Because it's one thing to catch a serial killer, but there is nothing to compare with the feeling of getting a missing child back alive.

We've learned a lot of surprising things over the course of *AMW*'s first decade. One was that one big demographic of fans aren't exactly where you'd expect to find them: in prison. But it's true: those guys are some of our faithful followers. We also track down a lot of fugitives who turn out to be already incarcerated for other offenses. At one point, for example, we hunted down Teddy Unterreiner, a notorious pedophile who, we believed, had escaped from the United States to Canada. He would sexually abuse little Vietnamese kids because he could speak Vietnamese, and he was wanted on more than twenty counts of molestation. At the time we ran our segment on him, we had no idea where he was. Until a prison guard in Canada called us up and said, "Hey, you guys, Teddy Unterreiner's here. Right here in our facility."

Another great part of the show was how much law enforcement loved it—all different kinds of agencies and jurisdictions. When cops first heard about the show, they, like me, were highly skeptical: "It's the media. They'll double-cross us. And they'll get into our case files." But right off the bat, we made it clear that they weren't going to have to worry about that kind of thing. Nor were we going to set things up so that different jurisdictions and agencies would be competing against one another. On one of our first cases, we made a point of inviting in three different police agencies—federal, state, and local—who, up until that time, hadn't been exchanging any information with each other.

"Look, you guys," I said, "why don't you all go into the corner over there and start comparing notes." Not long after that, the *New York Times* ran a big story about *AMW* in its Sunday magazine. Robert Morgenthau, the Manhattan district attorney, came out sounding like a big fan. "A couple of detectives or FBI agents can spend months or years searching for someone," he said. "It seems to me that this [show] is a wonderful way to save the taxpayers hundreds of thousands of dollars." It's always nice to hear stuff like that. I got a special kick in 1990 when, in recognition for my work on the show, I was named the FBI's Man of the Year. Me, the guy who seven years before had been bodily ejected from the Justice Department.

Being the host of *AMW* does have its drawbacks, though. Like the death threats. I had gotten my lecture from the FBI guys a long time ago. "If some nutcase tries to kill a guy like the pope," they told me, "imagine what some of these guys would like to do to you. Welcome to the world of reality." If people could see the death-threat file that I have, they'd puke from the things that people say they're going to do to me or my family.

Ever since the show started, I've had a rotating staff of three bodyguards who travel with me at all times. They're all New Yorkers, all detectives, and all the best—Ron Antoci, who for years worked serious organized-crime undercover, Paul Rossi, a homicide detective and veteran of the Manhattan district attorney's organized-crime unit, and through it all, John Riede, a highly decorated and now retired twenty-three-year New York homicide detective. Every day, I literally trust these guys with my life.

I remember the guy from Denver who sent me encrypted death threats every week for months, writing me and signing his sick, jangled letters in blood, like the Zodiac Killer. He claimed to have committed rapes, abductions, serial murders, but that the epitome of his life would be killing John Walsh. He was going to "kill the Manhunter," he said, because that was going to make him famous. The guy was a real nutcase. He tried to make me think that he was signing his letters with the blood of his victims. I sent some samples down to Quantico for analysis, and they said that the blood was most likely his own. So these are the kinds of lunatics I have to deal with.

There was another guy who broke out of prison and was wanted for murder. He used to call me up from pay phones and say he was going to kill me, and he wrote letters to that effect. He said that if he was ever cornered, he was going to take down an FBI agent with him. Two FBI agents—one an older veteran, the other a young guy who had just gotten out of the Academy—responded to a sighting of this guy. I never got to meet the older field agent, but the younger one came to Washington to be a guest on the show.

Later on, he told me that he had been playing tennis when he got the call, so he showed up for the shoot-out in his tennis whites and had to go get his gun out of the trunk of his car. By the time this young agent arrived on the scene, the psycho guy was out on the front porch in the middle of a big firefight. "I didn't even have a vest on," the young guy told me, "and this guy had automatic weapons and was firing through the screen door at us. My partner was down behind a fence and he was screaming at me to get down. John, the bullets were whizzing right by me. I'd only gotten out of Quantico six months before—and they never told us these guys were going to shoot back."

In the old days, agents had .38s that only held six bullets. Now they've got Smith and Wesson 9 mm that have twelve-bullet clips—good guns. So the old pro agent was down on the ground, firing away, shooting and shooting, telling his young partner, "Keep shooting. Keep firing. Distract him."

Finally, the psycho guy came out onto the porch, still firing, because, you know, sometimes these guys have a death wish. The two agents were winging him, and he kept firing back, and all the time the agents were moving in on him. They changed clips and kept firing and kept moving in, and finally the guy stopped moving. The older FBI agent shot him again anyway, and when they finally got right on top of the guy, the old pro shot him again, one last time.

All in all, the psycho guy had taken something like seventeen bullets.

"Jeez," the younger guy said to his partner. "What did you have to shoot him so many times for?"

"Damn it," the older guy said, "I just wanted to make sure he was dead."

No doubt about it, this show has changed my life. In obvious ways. And in at least one way that I could never have imagined.

In November 1990, a call came into the *AMW* hot line from someone who gave his name to the operator as Joe Matthews. The message finally worked its way through to me, and I knew immediately who he was. Joe Matthews, the Miami Beach homicide detective who had been imported by the HPD to polygraph me that terrible night nine years before, had once shown me some kindness in one of the darkest periods of my life. I never forgot it. And now, Joe said, he needed a favor himself. With a reputation as one of the best homicide investigators in the country, Joe had been working a case down in Miami that had become known as the Baby Lollipops case. The baby in question, a little boy, had been found dead in the bushes of an affluent Miami Beach neighborhood.

But that wasn't the worst of it. At three years old, this little boy weighed just eighteen pounds. He was what cops call a "closet baby." His body was covered with burn marks, and evidence of old abuse—fresh and poorly healed broken bones, skull fractures and lesions. The chief medical examiner called it the worst case of child abuse, neglect, and torture in Dade County history. Joe Matthews had worked the case as hard as he could, but there were no leads. He was at a bitter dead end, and in his mind, that just wasn't good enough. So, after much mulling, he decided to call *AMW* for help.

Three days after I got Joe's call, I was down in Miami with a film crew, ready to roll. I came out of my trailer and started walking down Ocean Drive. I hadn't seen Joe in nine years, but up ahead, a block away and walking toward me, was a guy I recognized immediately. When we met, neither one of us said anything. We just gave each other a hug, and we both had tears in our eyes. Joe, probably as well as anyone, knew what it had been like for me to lose my son.

The following week, the segment on Baby Lollipops aired on *AMW*. The odds were probably nine zillion to one against finding a suspect. But through tips, the baby was positively identified, which in turn led to the arrest of the person who had beaten and tortured him for the three years of his life and then finally killed him: his own mother. Joe got a confession from her. And later—after a trial that revealed that the woman used to put cocaine up the baby's nose and then spray him with insecticide because she liked to watch him go into convulsions—she received a death sentence.

Only afterward did I learn that, as horrible as the Baby Lollipops case was, it wasn't the only reason that Joe had contacted me. He had lost a lot of sleep trying to decide whether he should tell me about it, but something had been eating away at him for about nine years now, and it was time to get it off his chest. Joe had supervised and conducted over ten thousand criminal investigations—a thousand of them death investigations. And now, what he was telling me was the same thing that my buddies at the FBI had been hinting at for years: that the Hollywood Police Department's investigation of Adam's murder was one of the most screwed-up cases he had ever seen.

I never really knew. I had had my suspicions. Privately, I had begun to wonder if the cops actually knew what they were doing. It seemed to me that they were disinterested in Adam's case, that they were slow to follow up leads, that they hadn't really gone down every avenue or exhausted all the possibilities. I always remembered how, a few months after Adam died, a little boy had been abducted up in Vero Beach. Jay Howell had called the HPD, the detective division. He told them that a five-year-old boy had been kidnapped from his home in Vero the day before, and their response was, "Why are you calling us?" Jay laid it all out for them. That, several months before, Adam Walsh, a six-year-old boy, had also been abducted, and that when his remains were found, they were found near Vero Beach.

The woman on the other end of the line said, "Well, I'm sure that if the Vero Beach police think it's important, they'll contact us." Then she hung up.

All along, in the decade since Adam's death, the tips never stopped coming in. Boxes of them. Some of them were obviously crazy. Some of them weren't. Any letters that came to us, either at the Adam Walsh Center or to *AMW*, were immediately sent to the Hollywood police, ordinarily to Jack Hoffman, who was still the lead investigator in the case. HPD's attitude was always, "We're the investigating agency. We'll look into it." I don't know how many times I called Jack Hoffman myself after something had turned up. "Have you looked into this?" I'd say. "Have you checked that out?" Hoffman's response was always the same: "We'll get back to you." Sometimes it would be a month before he got back to me. Sometimes he wouldn't get back to me at all. Maybe I should have been more aggressive. But I didn't have access to all the confidential information that the police did, and I didn't want to compromise the investigation by asking too much about it. After all, I wasn't a cop. I was only a civilian. What did I know?

In 1983, we had ridden an emotional roller coaster when the HPD announced that they were going to indict this drifter named Ottis Toole. I didn't have much in the way of specifics—only that the case against Toole had apparently started falling apart when he couldn't produce Adam's body, even though the cops had spent a lot of time digging around the Indian River site where his remains had been found. That was when the *Miami Herald* started looking at whether the HPD cops were doing a good job. People were starting to question their methods and investigative techniques. This was also right at the time of our suit against Sears, and I was still hurting from all the vicious press that we had gotten. As a result, I lashed out at the *Miami Herald* for being so mean-spirited toward the cops. And on every anniversary of Adam's death—the fifth year, the tenth year—we always told reporters that we believed in the justice system and trusted that the Hollywood police were doing everything humanly possible to solve Adam's murder. Above all, I was always the solid citizen—the great defender of the efforts of the Hollywood police.

But over time, after all the experience I had gotten with law enforcement, all the investigations I had seen, all the bad guys we had caught, and all the joint task forces that I had been involved in, I began to think differently. My FBI buddies were clearly trying to tell me something: "You know, you really should get us involved in Adam's case," they were saying, "because those HPD guys haven't done anything on it in years."

From personal experience, I started thinking that maybe they had a point. In July of 1991, police in Milwaukee arrested a thirty-one-year-old sexual deviant named Jeffrey Dahmer. At the time of his arrest, Dahmer was on probation for a 1989 conviction for sexual assault of a thirteen-year-old boy. And when police opened up his refrigerator, they found three preserved human heads.

Apparently, although most of Dahmer's eleven victims were young homosexual men, he had also dabbled with children. In 1988, for instance, he had been arrested for molesting a thirteen-year-old Laotian boy, and to get even with the family, he then kidnapped the boy's fourteen-year-old brother. Dahmer took the boy back to his apartment in Milwaukee and sodomized and tortured him. The boy was found wandering in the street, naked, incoherent, drugged, and bleeding from the anus. Two Milwaukee police-men—who were later suspended for what they did—picked the boy up and took him back to Dahmer's apartment, writing the whole incident off as a lovers' quarrel. At the time, they noticed a horrible stench in the place, but they didn't bother searching it. Nor did they do a records check on Dahmer, who was on probation for having sexually assaulted this boy's younger brother.

Were these the two worst cops in North America? They returned the kid, they laughed about it, and then Dahmer finished him off. In the meantime, Dahmer had the stinkiest apartment in the building, filled with rotting body parts. But his parole officer said he never went down to see him because he lived in a rough part of town.

Not too long after Dahmer was arrested, his father, Lionel, called the *AMW* hot line. He told us that even though Dahmer had never been convicted for it, his father believed he was a pedophile. Lionel also told us that Dahmer had mustered out of the army in Holly-wood, Florida, in 1981 and lived in a motel on the beach near there.

I immediately called up Jack Hoffman and gave him the same information that had been in the papers. "Here's the tip," I said. "Dahmer's a pedo-phile, and his own father is saying that he was in south Florida at the time Adam was abducted." Hoffman called me back and said that Dahmer's lawyer wouldn't let his client talk to any police agency from a state that permitted the death penalty, which Florida does.

So I called the Broward County office of Florida's state attorney, Michael Satz, and asked him to write a letter. It basically said that I wasn't interested in pushing for the death penalty. I just wanted closure.

To know if Jeffrey Dahmer was the man who killed my son. I said I didn't care if he didn't die for it. I knew he'd never get out of prison. But he certainly fit the MO, and I just needed to know if he had really been in Hollywood and was the one who had kidnapped Adam.

Michael Satz responded that the state attorney's office hated to throw in the towel on a capital case. "Look," I said, "couldn't you just write a letter that would give the Hollywood police the entrée to talk to Dahmer? To see if he might confess to Adam's murder?"

So I went through channels. I had gotten the required letter. Then I called Jack Hoffman back and asked when he was going to talk to Dahmer. He told me that the HPD had already spent thousands of dollars on Adam's case, and there wasn't any money in the budget for that kind of trip.

"You know what?" I said. "I'm making a pretty good living on TV these days. *I'll* pay your way to go talk to Dahmer."

Hoffman said he'd think about it and see what he could do.

At that point, I received a call from two FBI agents in the Milwaukee field office who had been working the Dahmer case. "John, what the hell is going on with the Hollywood Police Department? Dahmer's lawyer has quit him. We've interviewed him on all kinds of unsolved cases around the country. We can get you in to talk to him. We can get the HPD right in. Where the hell is this detective? What if Dahmer was the guy who abducted Adam? Why the hell hasn't someone been up here to investigate it?"

The FBI guys were wondering about the abilities of an HPD investigator who seemed less than enthusiastic about pursuing the interrogation and suggested that an expert ought to be handling it. So I asked them how come they weren't involved. Because, they said, they couldn't just bigfoot the case. They had to be officially invited in by the local police agency whose case it was. And so far, they hadn't been asked.

I called up Hoffman again. "Why aren't you in Milwaukee talking to Jeffrey Dahmer?"

This time Hoffman said that he was going to go. But that he had to wait for a travel voucher.

Jeffrey Dahmer was a confessed serial killer, responsible for the deaths of at least eleven people, including a fourteen-year-old boy. He had a past history of child molestation, and he had three severed human heads in his refrigerator when he was arrested. In July of 1981, the month that Adam was abducted, Dahmer might have been living in Hollywood, Florida.

I had contacted the Hollywood police at least twice about questioning Dahmer. I had arranged for an official letter promising that I would not try to have him extradited. I had spoken to the state attorney's office, been in touch with the FBI in Milwaukee, offered to pay Hollywood police travel expenses out of my own pocket. I had passed along information that the lawyer who had put up all the roadblocks to an interrogation of Dahmer was no longer even involved in the case.

"Did you know that Dahmer's lawyer quit?" I asked Hoffman.

No, he said. He didn't.

On August 13, 1992, Jack Hoffman traveled to the Columbia Correctional Facility in Madison, Wisconsin, to interview Jeffrey Dahmer. It was a thorough interrogation, conducted for the most part by the investigator who accompanied Hoffman—FBI special agent Dan Craft of the Behavioral Sciences Unit. Dahmer was both cooperative and candid during the interview. Yes, he had killed all those victims. Yes, he had lobotomized one of them and kept him alive that way for days. Yes, he had dismembered and cannibalized his victims. But no, he had not killed Adam Walsh.

In their written report, both Craft and Hoffman concluded that Dahmer was telling the truth. There was no reason to believe that he had in any way been involved in Adam's murder. It had only taken thirteen months to find out.

By the end of 1994, the suspicions that I had had were now more than strong doubts. Joe Matthews, on his own, had been pushing the HPD to take another look at Adam's case. Matthews was convinced that Ottis Toole was still the prime suspect and couldn't understand why Toole had never been indicted. What Joe wanted more than anything was for the HPD brass to let him have a crack at interviewing Toole in prison up in Jacksonville. As it turned out, at the same time that Matthews was trying to get the case reopened, a new pair of supervisors over at the HPD were also coming to the conclusion that Adam's case deserved some renewed attention. They had tapped a young cold-case detective named Mark Smith to start focusing on it again. Over just the past few months, it seemed that the cops were taking more of an interest in Adam's case than anyone had in years.

I didn't know much about the specifics. I did know that thirteen years after Adam's death, no one had been charged in his murder, and that it was about time someone took a closer look at his case. I also knew that there is no statute of limitations on homicide.

If I hadn't been able to get any justice for Adam, I was at least getting it for other people. Week in and week out for eight years, *AMW* had featured hundreds of stories on bank robbers, rapists, murderers. But my favorite stories, the ones that I really loved, were the ones that led to the return of a missing child. There was nothing like it, absolutely nothing to compare to what it felt like when I suddenly got a phone call telling me that a missing child had been found, unhurt and alive. In 1996, we got the idea of holding an annual reunion of all the kids who had been returned safely as a result of the show. A big party was to be held in Washington on the Mall near the base of the Capitol on May 25, National Missing Children's Day.

Our plan was to tape the reunion to run as a special edition of the show that week, and for a lot of reasons, I was in a pretty good mood. Three days before, I had been told that *AMW* was definitely being renewed for the upcoming season. After I finished the reunion taping, I was going to fly up to New York for the big annual meeting with all the ad agencies and sponsors to introduce Fox's new fall lineup. I was thinking how phenomenal it was that this was going to be our ninth season. And here I was, heading to a reunion attended by all of these missing children who, thanks to the show, had been returned to their parents unharmed. I was thinking about how much I had to be grateful for.

We were driving down Constitution Avenue with my assistant Cheri Nolan and my bodyguard, John Riede. We were looking out the window of the car, and as we got closer to the Capitol, we caught sight of the brightly colored tent that had been set up for the reception. Just then the car phone rang. It was Chase Carey, one of the top guys at Fox.

"I don't know how to tell you this, John," Chase said. "You know that you're the most valuable guy at the network. But your show isn't going to be on the fall schedule. The show is canceled. Don't bother coming up to New York for the presentation."

It took a second for that to sink in. "Chase, what are you talking about? I was just out in Hollywood four days ago and they told me the show had been re-upped."

"John, it's the toughest decision we've ever had to make. And we want you to know that you're still a part of the network. You're the guy who made this network. We want you to do movies of the week, other projects for us. We want to keep you on contract. Just not for this show."

I was so stunned that I could hardly talk. I didn't know what to say. "Chase, I'm not an actor or a TV star. This show is what I'm all about. What I'm all about is this show."

"Well, when everything settles down, we'll talk about it. But for now, John, the decision's been made. Your show is canceled."

By that time, we had pulled up to where the reception was going to be held. Paul Sparrow, a senior producer for *AMW*, was tapping on the window, wondering what was taking me so long to get out of the car. He was worried about getting me into the reception on time because Dianne Feinstein, the California senator, was there and would be speaking, and all the kids, their parents, and the tipsters from those cases were lined up, waiting to meet me. And Sparrow still thought we were going to have to make the shuttle to New York.

If we were taken off the air, who was going to catch all the bad guys? Who was going to bring down the scumbags, if it wasn't us? Who would do that if it wasn't me? A million thoughts were going through my head. How was I going to tell the fifty loyal members of the *AMW* staff—people who had mortgages and families to support, who had worked day and night for this show—that they weren't going to have a job anymore?

And now, I had to get out there and put up the brave front at this wonderful reunion of missing children. It was unbearable. But no one knew. I made sure of that. I owed that much to those kids. I've seen the footage of myself, and there's no way you can tell. The *AMW* special on the missing children's reunion aired that Saturday night, and the only thing viewers saw were all those happy, beautiful little kids and their parents. And me, smiling and hugging people as if nothing had happened.

The very last episode of *America's Most Wanted* was scheduled to air on September 21, 1996. It seemed appropriate to me to have it finally feature the one case that we had never done. The most important story of all. The story of the investigation of Adam's murder. Nobody wanted to push me into doing it myself. So we hired a reporter named John Turchin out of Miami's Fox station WSVN, Channel 7, who put it together, using tips and information that Joe Matthews and Mark Smith had given him.

Turchin tracked down the former Sears security guard, Kathy Shaffer, who talked about how she had sent Adam out of the store that day. He reported that, thirteen years before, the cops had found a white Cadillac that Toole claimed was the car he had abducted Adam in. But that they had lost it. And that there had been bloodstained carpet samples taken from the car, but that those were now lost, too. Turchin also did an on-camera interview with a guy named William Mistler—a witness who had come forward to the Hollywood police five years before to say that he had seen a man in a white Cadillac put a little boy into a car in front of the Sears store on the day that Adam was abducted.

It was a powerful segment, and its conclusion was clear: all of the best evidence that had been uncovered to date still pointed to a man who was once the prime suspect, but who had never been indicted. A man named Ottis Toole.

We used something special to end that segment. Not long before, when we had moved offices, Cheri rediscovered an old cardboard box that she had packed up for me a couple of years before. In it were some film canisters that, I told her, maybe we ought to have developed. Maybe they were some old home movies, I said. Maybe there was even something of Adam on them.

Cheri did have the film developed. And that footage was what we decided to use for the final episode of

America's Most Wanted—our 427th—which aired on September 21, 1996. The segment showed Adam in his baseball uniform, running around the bases. Swinging his bat, making faces at the camera. The only remaining images of my son's last baseball game.

In those weeks before our final episode, the one thing that I could not understand was how a program that had gotten more than four hundred of this country's most dangerous fugitives—including eleven men on the FBI's Ten Most Wanted list—could summarily be taken off the air. We had helped recover twenty children. We had caught the guy who set a 1976 car bomb in Washington that killed a former Chilean ambassador to the United States. "We don't do UFOs," I told the press. "We save lives. When the parents of a missing child are desperate on Friday, we put them on on Saturday. We caught thirty-seven child molesters in one eight-month period."

I guess the executives at Fox thought that the outcry would die down in a month or two. That the public would say, "Well, I guess it was a business decision," and let it go. But the public didn't. By the time our last segment aired, something had already started happening. Letters—tens of thousands of them—began flooding into the Fox offices. By the time it was all over some months later, 185,000 people had written to Fox protesting the show's cancellation. Fifty-five members of Congress wrote in. So did thirty-seven state governors and all fifty state attorneys general. One postcard from New Mexico thanked Fox for taking the show off the air and was signed by "one of the criminals." A nurse from North Carolina stood outside the Fox network television lot in California for a week to protest the decision because a planned segment on her murdered brother had been canceled along with the show. A guy in New Jersey sponsored resolutions in twenty-nine townships calling on the network to reconsider. The FBI even issued a statement. Everyone was saying the same thing: asking, pleading, and demanding that *AMW* be put back on the air.

In the end, *America's Most Wanted* did go off the air—for a grand total of six weeks. On September 24, David Hill and Peter Roth, the newly appointed president of the Fox entertainment group, called to say that we were back in business, which then turned us into probably the shortest-canceled program in television history. During our hiatus, someone called us about a case that truly broke my heart. In Salina, Kansas, a guy had broken into a home one night and killed three members of one family—the great-grandmother, the grandmother, and a five-year-old grandson. In one horrible crime, this animal had devastated three generations. The police department in Salina was so small that it didn't have a chance of tracking down this murderer. But the letters and calls that we received from the people of Salina were begging us. "If you ever get back on the air," they said, "please, please profile this guy."

America's Most Wanted officially returned to the airwaves on November 9, 1996, and that night, I named the suspect in the Salina murders as *AMW*'s Public Enemy Number One. Twenty-five minutes after the show ended, we caught the guy hiding out in a homeless shelter in Boston.

It was a gratifying close to an unhappy chapter in the show's history. It made me feel good. But not good enough to erase the devastating news that I had learned just six weeks before.

During our segment on Adam's murder, we had included what, at the time, was the single best synopsis of his case that anyone had ever done. We said that the most likely suspect in the crime was still Ottis Elwood Toole, and that Toole, on death row in Raiford prison near Jacksonville, might still be coaxed into a confession. Toole was sick, suffering from cirrhosis and possibly AIDS, but he had hinted that he might be willing to talk to the right interviewer, and I was going to get him to talk. I knew that Mark Smith, the HPD cold-case detective, had spent two days trying to interview Toole, but that he hadn't really gotten anywhere. "If Ottis Toole gets sick, you've got to let me know," I told Mark. "Whatever you do, don't let him die without me knowing." I knew that I could get somebody into that prison who could wear a wire or bring a tape recorder or a video camera. Probably my friend Joe Matthews. I was willing to go straight to the Department of Corrections. The Hollywood police and the DA's office could go screw themselves. I had friends at the FDLE and the FBI. I was going to pull some strings and get Joe Matthews in to see Ottis Toole.

I knew that Toole was in prison, facing five life sentences, and I understood that he was never going to get out. But that wasn't what was important. A deathbed confession from Toole would be the only thing that could finally put everything to rest. A deathbed confession was my last best hope.

Two days after the September 21 segment on Adam aired, an anonymous tip came in to the *AMW* hot-line operator, who immediately transferred the call to my executive producer, Lance Heflin.

"How stupid are you guys?" said a voice on the other end of the line.

"What are you talking about?" Lance asked.

"Ottis Toole is dead," the voice said. "He died five days ago at Raiford."

Book
Four

13

The Case File

IN 1932, NOT LONG AFTER THE BODY OF ANNE AND
Charles Lindbergh's baby son was found in a shallow
grave in the New Jersey countryside, a reporter
bribed a funeral home director and a coroner into
letting him take a picture of the child's partially
decomposed corpse. The reporter's newspaper didn't
publish it, but bootleg copies of the photograph—
known to Lindbergh historians as "the coffin
shot"—later became an underground novelty item,
selling in bars and on street corners for a few dollars
apiece.

Over the years, I had learned a lot about the press,
both about its power and about how low it could
stoop. As early as six months after Adam's death, the
Miami Herald wanted to do a story on how Adam's
case was progressing. One of two reporters working
on the story went to interview Les Davies, one of my
closest friends, kicked off her shoes, and spent hours
interviewing him. She seemed to think that I had
some sort of gambling links because the plans for the
Paradise Grand called for it to be next to a casino.

"She was saying, 'Now, we've heard all the rumors, you know, about the drug retribution and all,'" Les remembers. "And I kept telling her, quite honestly, that I had no idea what she was talking about."

Still, when the story was published, it said that police "had heard the nebulous rumors of dealings with Bahamian casinos, of Mafia connections, of narcotics smuggling. One tale had Walsh refusing to be a drug courier, with Adam's abduction as retaliation." And they said that tips had "poured" into the HPD alleging that an "icy and stone-faced" Revé, had been involved in Adam's death—a suspicion, it said, "that had been shared, at one time or another, by more than a few Hollywood detectives."

On top of everything else that had happened to us, that kind of innuendo pained and infuriated me. Then, a year and a half later, when we dropped the suit against Sears, we had to go through it all again: the whole Jimmy Campbell episode and another slew of stories that dragged us through the mud. Stories that seemed to suggest that what had happened to Adam was somehow our fault, because Revé and I weren't really the all-American family after all. So from experience, I knew full well what the press was capable of. Or thought I did.

It was that experience that made me suspicious on the morning of January 12, 1995, when my executive assistant, Cheri Nolan, sent me a fax that had arrived at my Washington office. It came on the letterhead of the *Mobile Press Register* and was signed by a reporter named Jay Grelen. "Dear Mr. Walsh: I am writing to request an interview with you. I would like to discuss a range of topics, including your life and where you are emotionally and otherwise fourteen years after Adam's death."

Grelen went on to say that he wanted to discuss the status of Adam's case with me, that he wanted to meet me in person, and that he was willing to travel anywhere that would be most convenient for me. "I'm sure your schedule stays full and I will gratefully take whatever time you can spare," he wrote. "If I could watch you at work, with our interview squeezed in, that would be great."

Something about it just didn't feel right to me. I remember asking Cheri, "What do you think this guy *really* wants?"

Grelen kept trying to contact me, and I kept ignoring him. On February 21, he sent a certified letter: "My newspaper is committing much in time and resources to this project. . . . Won't you please help us in our effort to help you find Adam's killer?" Then on March 24, he showed up, unannounced, at the Fox studios in Washington, where my executive producer, Lance Heflin, told him in no uncertain terms that I was *not* going to be talking to him.

On the morning of Sunday, May 7, 1995, my instincts were proved correct. That's when the first of a three-part series of tabloid-style articles—sent to us by a congressman friend in Alabama—appeared in the *Mobile Press Register* under the screaming headline: "Adam Walsh: Myth and Mystery." Grelen, the sole reporter for the series, wrote that he had taken a special interest in the case ever since, as a copy editor fourteen years before in Baton Rouge, he had written some headlines for Adam's story. I guess that gave him some special expertise. Because now he had gone back into the library and looked at some of those old pictures of Adam, he wrote, and "as we stare into one another's eyes, a realization forms, an understanding. Adam's eyes seemed to ask for help. Adam Walsh became more than a story, and I had a whole new reason for telling it."

Grelen hinted that the "story" of Adam's murder was just that—a story. That there had been cover-ups in the case, and that he was going to be the guy to finally get to the bottom of them. "Something has stopped efforts to really get this [story] from the beginning," one unnamed source said.

He reported that I had refused to talk to him, as if I had something to hide. "Now you know what happened to the other reporters," said another source—who happened to be none other than Rex Conrad, the bottom-dwelling attorney from our Sears suit twelve years before. Conrad also said that he believed that Revé had left Adam in Sears not for ten or fifteen minutes on the day he was abducted, but perhaps for as long as an hour and a half.

Grelen reported that during a two-hour interview with Dick Witt, the Hollywood police chief, Witt had told him that, at the time of Adam's abduction, "there was no reason to suspect a stranger abduction." And that now, "the *probability* [emphasis added] is that there is no John or Revé Walsh connection to the death of their son."

All of that was hard enough to take. But in addition, the *Mobile Press Register* did something that I would not abide. They had also taken upon themselves to publish the location—and a photograph—of my family's house and yard, along with a description of my children's school.

My feeling was that if someone wants to hurt me for some reason, they can go right ahead and try. They could do it to me personally. But they had no right to do it to my wife and children. I had been getting death threats for years. I had bodyguards and security protection. I had lived with the sleazy innuendo that the press every now and then coughed up about Adam's murder. But I would not sit by, silently, when, to sell newspapers, they sent a photographer out, without my knowledge or permission, to photograph my home. The place where my wife and children live.

What in God's name did this newspaper hope to accomplish by doing such a thing? And you had to wonder what Jay Grelen thought was going to be in store for him once his opus had been seen by the world. Throughout the series, he kept mentioning the Pulitzer Prize.

I asked Cheri to fax the articles to Mike Christiansen, a trusted friend and attorney in Fort Lauderdale who had done a lot of pro bono work for the Adam Walsh Center, and who had handled some legal things for me in the past. At that time, I was still keeping in touch every so often with the HPD about Adam's case. And now, what I was hearing from them was that this Grelen guy was trying to write a book about Adam's murder that was probably going to talk about my "connections with the Mob" and God knows what else. I wanted to know from Christiansen if there was anything that I could do to stop this kind of crap.

But that would not be the worst of it. As it turned out, beginning in November of 1994, Grelen had been calling people up and trying to get them to talk about Adam's case. He went down to Hollywood, where, one morning at 9 A.M., he placed a call, requesting an interview, to the office of the Hollywood police chief, Dick Witt. Much to Grelen's surprise, Witt's secretary came back to the phone after checking with the chief and asked if Grelen could be there in an hour. Grelen talked to Witt—for two hours—and afterward called up Mark Smith, the HPD cold-case detective. Grelen told Smith that Chief Witt had said that it was okay for Grelen to see the case file—all of it. Smith was incredulous. No one in their right mind, let alone a chief of police, would hand over the confidential case file on a still-active homicide investigation. So, after he hung up with Grelen, Smith immediately put in a call to Dick Witt and asked if that was true. No, said Witt. He had never said any such thing.

Then, a week before Grelen's first article appeared, the most frightening thing of all had happened. That was when the *Mobile Press Register*, that great champion of the First Amendment, went to court in Broward County to try to get its hands on Adam's case file.

In the years since it happened, a lot of sickos had claimed to know something about Adam's murder. Some out of revenge; others in a twisted quest for glory. All I knew was what I had learned from my FBI contacts—that whoever had murdered Adam was a psychopath, and that it's usually hard to know whether these guys are telling the truth—or completely fabricating it. I had seen enough in my FBI presentations with Ressler to know that the normal Judeo-Christian ethics don't apply here. "Are you lying to me about how you killed that woman and stabbed her, sir? Was it really 147 times, or was it actually 192?" No, the only way to tell for sure if what these guys are telling you is true is to back it up with some hard, corroborating evidence.

If, for example, Adam's remains had been found next to the stump of a sawed-off maple tree and that was never publicized, and some lunatic came forward saying, "I killed Adam Walsh and I left his remains next to a sawed-off maple tree," that confession would certainly have some weight. If the same fact had been published in all the newspapers, it would be virtually useless. Hearsay. Public knowledge. Something that a smart defense lawyer could come up with in the blink of an eye. Even I, as Adam's father, had no idea what was in the case file.

I also knew that cases based on a suspect's confession are extremely tough to prosecute. The accused can suddenly claim in court that the cops beat him up to make him confess, or that he's just decided to recant. Anyone in law enforcement knows that the way cases are made is by keeping certain sensitive information confidential. And all the legal experts were telling me the same thing: "If the case files are opened up, John, you're screwed."

On Monday, May 15, 1995, a week after Grelen's

first article appeared, I walked through the glass front door of the Hollywood Police Department for the first time in fourteen years. I was there for a meeting that my lawyer, Mike Christiansen had set up between me, Joe Matthews, my bodyguard John Riede, the Hollywood police chief, Dick Witt, and an HPD officer named Paul Dungan. By that time, Joe Matthews and the HPD cold-case detective, Mark Smith, had begun looking into the case again. And we knew what we would have to prove to keep it confidential: that this was still an active homicide investigation. Because, as everyone knows, there is no statute of limitations on a homicide. The lawyers said that never in the history of this country had the media been allowed to look at the confidential case file in an unsolved capital murder case.

I had already decided that now, this time, I wasn't going to take it anymore. I was no longer going to be the humble, nonparticipatory victim. Right off the bat at that meeting I said, "You know, I've supported the Hollywood Police Department for years. I've done everything they asked me to. And now I want to know what's going on. What exactly is the status of my son's case?" By that time, I had addressed the International Association of Chiefs of Police. Been a consultant to the Justice Department. Been catching serious, dangerous criminals on my show for seven years.

And now, I wanted some justice for my son. I wasn't pounding the table, but I made myself completely clear. I said that we had heard that Grolen was planning a book, and I figured it would feature the famous John Walsh Mob Connection. "I want to know what you're going to do about this," I said. "I want you to tell the newspapers, clearly and for the record, that I have never had any associations with the Mafia, that I've never had my legs broken. That I'm not a drug lord and don't have any drug-related associations. And that—and who would know better than the Hollywood police—that John Walsh and his family have nothing to hide. Nothing."

At that meeting, Dick Witt, the Hollywood police chief, was asked point-blank if there was any official suspicion that I was somehow affiliated with the Mafia. We were all sitting there, expecting him to say how ridiculous even the idea of that was. Instead, what Witt said was, "Anyone who goes to [here he mentioned a well-known Fort Lauderdale restaurant] for lunch has something to do with the Mafia."

I knew that Adam's murder had happened a long time before Dick Witt came on board. But now, if Grelen really was going to try to get the files, then the ones who would have to fight him off would be the Hollywood police. Technically, I had no legal standing in the motion. I, after all, was just the father of the victim. Dick Witt and the HPD would be the defendants, the ones in whose official interest it was to keep their case file sealed. So now, whether I liked it or not, the HPD was part of our team. Above all, I could not do anything to alienate them. No matter what they had or hadn't done, I didn't want them to completely turn their backs on Adam's case. And I also believed that Mark Smith deserved a chance. He, after all, seemed to be making a lot more headway than anyone else had in fourteen years. After the meeting, Mike Christiansen sent a memo to the Hollywood city attorney, Joel Cantor, saying that I was "thrilled and delighted that HPD is taking a strong and affirmative stance on this case."

On May 18, the *Mobile Press Register* made it official: they asked the court to enter an order allowing them to have immediate access to the HPD file on Adam's case. When a reporter asked why he was pressing to open the file if Adam's family was opposed, Grelen stated, "The great irony in this is that I'm only doing what John Walsh has made a career out of doing."

At the first hearing, on June 12, there was more bad

news: the *Sun Sentinel* in Fort Lauderdale was joining the *Mobile Register* as a plaintiff. The papers were going to invoke the Florida Sunshine act. So now, they were turning it into a free speech issue. Of *course* this had nothing to do with them wanting to sell newspapers. At the hearing, Grelen admitted under oath that he had had an interview with Dick Witt. But that Witt hadn't really told him much. No specific information about the case. Just some generalities about how cold cases are worked. They never asked him if the interview went on for two hours.

For our side, Mark Smith testifed that Adam's was a cold case, and that no arrest warrants had yet been issued. But that Mark was working on two or three suspects. That was enough to make the court deny the papers' motion for immediate access to the records. Because of the assignment of Smith to the case, it should be considered "active," the judge, the Honorable Leroy H. Moe, concluded. But Moe wasn't going to let that ruling stand indefinitely. The *Mobile Register*'s lawyer, Thomas R. Julin, said he'd wait a month or so to see if HPD made any headway. And if they didn't, he said, he would resubmit the papers' request.

At a press conference the next day, June 13, the Hollywood city attorney, Joel Cantor, had to take a lot of heat. If this is an active case, the reporters asked, then what the hell have you people been doing for the last fourteen years? What are your leads? What evidence do you have? What have you found out lately? They were asking some pretty probing questions, and Joel was doing his best to tread water.

I wasn't at the first courtroom hearing, but I did a great job of sticking up for the HPD afterward. I made a point of telling the press what a great job the cops were doing. But what I really wanted to get across to everyone was one simple thing: that I wasn't trying to keep the case file closed to hide some horrible, dark secret. My wife and I, as I had always said, had nothing to hide. The reason—the only reason—that we were fighting so hard against the *Press Register* was because we were trying to keep Adam's case from being lost.

Then, on September 26, 1995, the other shoe dropped. The papers renewed their motion to open the file. This time, they were also joined by the *Palm Beach Post* and one of the really big guns—the *Miami Herald*. Three weeks later, on October 18, 1995, Judge Moe ordered the defendants—Chief Dick Witt and the Hollywood police—to make all of the records on Adam's case available by noon on February 16, 1996.

This was bad. Very bad. But not entirely unexpected. And we were still a long way from giving up the ship. For a couple of months, at first, things seemed to die down. Then, just before Christmas of 1995, while I was doing my first movie of the week out in California, I got a call from Mark Smith. He sounded a little nervous. "John, I just got asked this question, and I really don't have the answer, so I've got to check it with you. I'm assuming that they showed you these green shorts and the sandal back in 1984, didn't they?"

I was in the middle of a production meeting. I had no idea what he was talking about. "What is it, Mark? What are you asking me?"

I could hear him let out a long breath on the other end of the line. "I was afraid you were going to say that, John. Look, there's something I've got to tell you about. In 1984, they found a green pair of child's shorts and a yellow rubber flip-flop buried in Ottis Toole's mother's backyard in Jacksonville."

"You're lying."

"John, I was hoping that someone had shown them to you and Revé. Or that you at least knew something about them."

I started screaming. "Showed us! We didn't even know they existed! How could anyone not have told us? Green shorts and a yellow flip-flop? That's what Adam was wearing when he was taken. What if they're Adam's? You mean they've just been sitting there all this time and no one could take two minutes out of their busy day to pick up the phone and let us know? With all the torture that we've gone through? How could anyone on the planet possibly *be* so incompetent?"

On the other end of the phone, Mark was dead silent. It wasn't his fault. He was just the messenger. He had only been working the case for the last year or so. And he was doing a lot better job than anyone else ever had. He was the one, after all, who had gone back into the evidence room and found these things. What I could not believe was that neither Jack Hoffman nor anyone else had shown me or even told me about this. I kept thinking, "What if they're Adam's? What if they're Adam's?"

Mark said that after the holidays, we could come down and he would show us what he had found.

On January 16, 1996, we went back for another meeting at the Hollywood police station. We all got together beforehand at Mike Christiansen's law office in Lauderdale—me, Revé, my producer, Lance Heflin, my bodyguard John Riede, and George Terwilliger, a top-gun Washington lawyer and former deputy attorney general. George had special expertise in law enforcement; Cheri Nolan knew him from her days as a senior policy official in the Justice Department. Based on what he had seen already, George's take was that we'd better be prepared, because the HPD had not done anything right on this case so far—and there was no reason to believe that they were going to do the right thing now. We sat in Mike's office for a while, discussing how we were going to handle things at the meeting, and then we left for the HPD in a caravan of cars.

The whole way there, as we had for weeks, Revé and I were thinking about having to see those shorts. It was too much to consider. I had waited until the last possible minute to tell Revé about them. "I would always get information in bits and pieces," she remembers. "John never used to tell me much about the case. If there was something that I had to know, he'd usually wait to let me know. And even then, only if he absolutely had to. I guess it was all part of his protectiveness."

Representing the HPD were Dick Witt, the chief; Mark Smith, the cold-case detective; and the HPD officer, Paul Dungan. We all sat down around a big conference table, and it began. A few preliminaries. Witt looking all blown up, red-faced, and pompous. He was in charge here. This was his circus, and he was enjoying the limelight, talking on and on. Finally, he asked if Revé and I needed to collect ourselves before we were ready to view the contents of the envelope. By now, Revé, who had been waiting to see the evidence—any evidence—for fifteen years, was seething. *"Ready?"* she said. "We've been ready for years."

Witt gave the nod to Mark, who pulled an envelope out of a cardboard box on the floor and slowly opened it up. Inside was a mud-crusted pair of running shorts and a little yellow sandal. A tiny little flip-flop. No bigger than what a three-year-old would wear. Revé knew immediately that they weren't Adam's.

"They're not Adam's. Take them away," she said.

No one knows who those shorts once belonged to. There was no reason to think that finding them meant that a little kid was dead, the cops said. They didn't know whose shorts those were. It could have been that Hoffman, who described the flip-flop in his report as small enough for a two or three-year-old, assumed that both it and the shorts were not Adam's. Still, it was incomprehensible to me how those two items could have sat unopened in the HPD evidence room for nearly twelve years.

After that was over, Dick Witt said that from what he knew, Jay Grelen and Dan Christensen, a reporter from the *Broward Daily Business Review,* were "obsessed" with a conspiracy theory—that I was a "bad guy" and that someone had killed Adam to retaliate against me. And then Witt said the weirdest thing. He didn't say those charges were ludicrous. He said, "I think we're clean on the immediate family and all those in close proximity to the family." After fourteen years, that was his statement about me and my family? And this is the guy I was supposed to be relying on to fight the battle to keep my son's case file sealed?

Next, Mark Smith reported on the progress that he and Joe Matthews had made, beginning with a quick synopsis of some of the leads that had gone back over fourteen years, most now resolved. Smith had tracked down the security guard at Sears who ordered Adam out of the store—the garden shop door, along with three other kids. He had been standing next to the video game area, she remembered. At first, she hadn't recognized the little boy in the photograph that was shown to her. But by that night, when she was shown another picture, she realized that it had been Adam. Shaffer had been afraid to come forward with that information for fear of being blamed. Her parents made the decision that she would not speak any more about the incident, and over the following months, she was uncomfortable with the frequent telephone calls that her parents were getting from Sears and its attorneys.

Smith said that two witnesses from Hollywood had been found who were saying that they had seen Adam in a white Cadillac with a black vinyl roof. The same kind of car that Ottis Toole, the Jacksonville drifter, had told investigators he was driving back in the summer of 1981. Nothing suggested that they had read that in the newspaper. There might have been a photograph of the car, years before, up in Jacksonville when Toole first surfaced. But nothing else about it in the press.

Also back in 1983, some carpet samples with

blood—probably human blood—on them had been taken from the car's interior. DNA tests hadn't existed back then, but it would now be easy enough to determine if the blood was Adam's. There was only one problem: so far, no one had been able to find the samples. Mark had gone up to the Jacksonville Police Department and spent two days searching the evidence room. But no one seemed to know where the samples had gone since.

Also, in what was probably the single most compelling aspect of Ottis Toole's confession, Matthews and Smith had found that Toole had described a dirt access road off the Florida Turnpike, a road with a fork in it. Toole said that that was where he had decapitated Adam, and that he then drove about ten minutes north on the turnpike and threw the head into a canal. The information about the dirt road was in the case file, but so far no press reports had mentioned it. And, in fact, the road *was* four miles south of mile marker 130 in Indian River County—which, as we all knew, was where Adam's remains were found.

Mark reported that Toole had confessed and recanted several times. That he had apparently not been charged because the cops hadn't thought there was enough hard evidence to stand up in court. That, so far, the case still wasn't really prosecutable. Six months before, Mark had spent two days interviewing Toole, but hadn't gotten much. At the time, Toole was sick with a couple strains of hepatitis. But, Mark said, he was going to try again. On Toole's deathbed, if necessary.

What was clear from what we were hearing was that, based on Matthews's and Smith's work, this was still very much an active investigation. It may not have advanced much over the past decade, but now these two detectives were more than making up for lost ground. As for me, I was trying to think of whatever I could to help with the investigation of

Toole. I discussed the possibility of writing a letter to the state attorney, Michael Satz, to say that if the death penalty was what was keeping Toole from confessing, then I would agree not to press for it—the same as I had with the Jeffrey Dahmer interview. I talked about how we could approach Toole. Maybe send Joe Matthews in. Get someone who was willing to wear a wire.

Then, I asked Witt what his intentions about the case file were. And he announced them: that he wanted to release the case file to *bring pressure on Toole and force him to confess*. We all sat there just looking at him. No one could follow the logic. It made absolutely no sense. Why would you just hand over the only ace you had up your sleeve?

But it got worse. Witt said that the case file was ten thousand pages long, and that he anticipated quite a demand for it. Why, there had already been more than a hundred requests from the media for it—not to mention all those screenwriters and movie producers who had called. So what he was doing was putting all those stacks of pages *on microfilm*.

A police department putting its sealed, sensitive case file on microfilm—at taxpayers' expense—so that it would be easier for all the reporters to work from? I couldn't believe it. I just sat there with my mouth open. George Terwilliger finally said, "I'm a former deputy attorney general of the United States. Since when do police put files on microfilm for scumbag journalists?"

Now, I was really rabid: "Are you telling me that there are news organizations out there that already know you've capitulated and made a deal with the judge? I mean, are you telling the family of this murdered little boy, in the presence of their attorneys and friends, that you have already agreed to give up the files? This is a travesty. You're crossing a line that has never been broached. You're setting a new precedent in law enforcement here. You're giving it up on a capital murder case. And you are denying my family justice."

Dick Witt had been given every opportunity to redeem the Hollywood police in my eyes. He could have done the right thing. He could have hunkered down and taken the heat and fought for us. He could have brought honor and credibility to his department. And instead, every time he had the chance to be sensitive or responsible, he chose to be insensitive and irresponsible. After I got to see Dick Witt in action, all my hopes were dashed.

At the end of the meeting, Mike Christiansen tried to get a handle on things. "Now, wait a minute," he said. "Before we go, what should I be doing before we get to this next hearing? What do I need to write—an amicus brief, or what?" That was when the HPD's attorney, Joel Cantor, dropped the bombshell.

He said, "We've already agreed to it."

If Mike Christiansen hadn't asked the question, we would never have known. That was when I knew that it was all over. We were too stunned to do anything. During the whole meeting, Dick Witt had never taken a single note. Didn't even scribble on a notepad to pretend he had. And now I knew why. Dick Witt had no intention of keeping this file closed. The Hollywood police had simply decided to give it up. They caved.

I might have been naive when this whole thing started, but I wasn't anymore. By now I had a lot of experience with cops, the FBI, and law enforcement. The Hollywood police had just been hiding their decision from us. That they had been overwhelmed and intimidated by the press. And that Dick Witt showed no balls whatsoever. He was rolling over just to get the press off his ass.

Putting the case file onto microfilm meant that a lot of people would now be handling it. Joe Matthews already knew that some of his original polygraph charts—the ones for his interview with James Campbell—were not in the case file. Even though he had asked at the time that they be placed into evidence. Who knew what else might get lost or even removed? How would anyone ever know?

Just after that January 16 meeting, I saw two HPD homicide detectives out in the hallway. I didn't even know them. But at the risk of losing their jobs, they stopped me and under their breath said, "You've gotta derail this thing, John. Witt's going to give up those files. This is a train wreck waiting to happen."

I was completely irrational. The only possible recourse at this point was to get the state attorney's office to impanel a grand jury, which would prove, irrefutably, that the case was active. We didn't have much time. At the January 16 meeting, we learned that Witt had not even informed the state attorney's office—the people who had prosecutorial responsibility for the case—of his intention to open the case file. I told everyone that I was going to demand a meeting with the state attorney, Michael Satz, and his deputy, Ralph Ray.

At that point, we knew that we needed an intermediary, a sharp lawyer who knew where the land mines were and could help speak for us on the legal front. Mike suggested a former prosecutor he knew—first-rate—who was now doing civil work in Broward County. "Why don't I give Kelly Hancock a call?" he said. Fantastic. Kelly Hancock—the same wonderful prosecuting attorney who had won that death conviction back in 1986 for the guy who killed Staci Jazvac.

After leaving the prosecutor's office in 1989, Kelly hadn't done what most former prosecutors do—switch over to the big bucks world of the private criminal defense attorney. Kelly Hancock had too much class for that. He was now a private injury lawyer, trying to win damage awards in a lot of really rough cases. One, for example, of a little four-year-old boy who had been crushed to death by a sanitation truck.

On January 19, Mike met with Kelly, who, as it turns out, remembered quite a bit about Adam's case from the early days when Toole first surfaced back in 1983. That Toole had given a lengthy statement to the police that showed that he seemed to know a lot about the case. But that the case had had some problems, too. Enough to make prosecutors hold off on bringing the case to trial. But now, when Kelly was told what Mark Smith and Joe Matthews had uncovered, he immediately said that we should call the only person who had the power to initiate the first step in bringing Toole to trial—the order for a grand jury hearing. That man was the Broward County state attorney, Michael Satz.

Mike Christiansen filled Kelly Hancock in about a few more things. First, that horrible extortion letter that I had received from Toole back in 1988. Second, that a guy named William Carl Mistler had come forward to the Hollywood police, saying that he had witnessed Adam, on the day of his abduction, being put into a white Cadillac with a black vinyl top by a guy who looked like Toole. And that a polygraph hadn't ruled out what Mistler had said. On hearing all this, Kelly was astonished that the case had never been presented before to the state attorney's office. "With that information, the grand jury would indict," he told Christiansen. "In fact, there have been lots of cases that I've *tried* with less evidence than we have here."

On January 31, thanks to Kelly laying the groundwork, I went in for a meeting with Michael Satz and Ralph Ray, the chief assistant state attorney. Revé was there, as was George Terwilliger, Joe Matthews, Kelly Hancock, and Mike Christiansen. All in all, the meeting was my first chance to say, "Okay, you guys, the gloves are off."

It began with Satz telling me that no evidence on Adam's case had been brought to his office by the HPD since 1984. Not in eleven years. That it was only five days ago, on January 26, that the HPD first turned the case file over to Satz and Ray. Unbelievable.

Speaking as Adam's next of kin, I pleaded with them, begged them to review the case file before, for all intents and purposes, it was ripped wide open for all the world to see. We knew that there was other information now—leads and tips that Joe Matthews and Mark Smith had come up with recently—that also hadn't been forwarded to the state attorney. But at least they had seen that horrifying extortion letter that Toole had sent me back in 1988.

"What extortion letter?" they asked.

That awful one with all the terrible stuff in it, we said. The one that we had sent to the Hollywood city attorney, Joel Cantor, eight months before. And then, just to be on the safe side, sent again to Sgt. Bob Dunbar, the supervisor of the investigation. Satz and Ray had no idea what I was talking about. They'd never seen it. Those dumb sons of bitches at HPD not only didn't have it in the case file to begin with, but even after we sent them two more copies, it now seemed that they hadn't bothered to forward it to the state attorney. How could anyone possibly overlook a letter like that?

So, in the presence of Revé, George Terwilliger, Joe Matthews, Kelly Hancock, and Ralph, I showed a copy of the letter to Michael Satz. And on January 31, 1996, the state attorney of the Seventeenth Judicial Circuit, Broward County, Florida, read it, put it down on the table in front of him, and said:

"A jury would convict a man on the basis of this letter alone."

Ralph Ray then said that if the file was released, there could never be a successful prosecution or conviction. Which, of course, was what I had been saying all along. But now, for the first time, a responsible law enforcement official was agreeing with me.

We told them that we knew that the HPD had already agreed—way back in October, as a matter of fact—to make the file available in February. That there was no way that Dick Witt was going to stop release of the file. That he was already microfilming it.

Ralph Ray was flabbergasted. He sat right up in his chair and wondered aloud if, as he put it, the integrity of the file would be jeopardized by microfilming it. He seemed to suggest that that fact alone might be enough for the state attorney's office to act.

They couldn't believe what Witt was doing, that a police department they were supposed to be working with would have the audacity and stupidity to agree to give up a high-profile capital murder case this way without telling or conferring with them. They couldn't believe it. And I went through everything for them. I said, "Do you know what Joe Matthews and Mark Smith have found in the last six months? That they're a hair's breadth away from pinpointing Toole?" They didn't know. They hadn't heard any of it.

Which is when I finally lost it.

I had nothing to lose now. All bets were off. This is it, I said. Pleading. Desperate. You must join this suit. You must keep these files sealed for two reasons: for justice for my little boy. No one at the HPD gives a shit about him except Matthews and Smith. They don't give a shit if his murderer is ever even found. They're too busy covering their asses, playing a game. And the second reason you have to do it is because if they allow that case file to be opened up, it's going to set a dangerous precedent in these United States. Newspapers are going to start filing these suits all the time. What's to stop them? And then no one is going to get any justice in this country.

I was pounding the table with my fist, completely in tears. I said, "I cannot believe that for fifteen years I have defended the Hollywood police. Whenever the newspapers tried to drive a wedge—asking if I believed they were incompetent, if they had botched Adam's case, if they had compromised it and made mistakes—I always defended them. Every time. I have made more sacrifices than any crime victim I know. I have traveled to every state, testified all over the country on behalf of law enforcement. I have testified before Congress, spent my own money traveling all over this country to change laws and protect children. I am the number one supporter of the criminal justice system, and I have caught more criminals than any cop in this country. And now I am being screwed by the very police agency that is supposed to be looking out for my son's case.

"No one seems to remember that a six-year-old boy was kidnapped and beheaded. No one seems to care about that at all. It's all about lawyers, about freedom of the press and judges and covering your ass and bullshit. No one cares that Adam Walsh is going to be denied justice. No one except me.

"If it takes me the rest of my life to let the American public know what this police department has done to Adam's case, then I'm going to do it. Because I want justice. I *demand* justice for this little boy."

When I finally finished, there was total silence in the room.

Two days later, on February 2, Ralph Ray announced that the state attorney's office would intervene in the suit, requesting an emergency hearing to delay the judge's order. In response, Joel Cantor, the city of Hollywood's attorney, said that the HPD was going to do nothing to assist the prosecutor's office. Would not file anything to stop the release or even postpone it. Since HPD—the named defendants— had now completely turned their backs on us, Ralph asked if I was willing to file something under the Florida victim's rights statute—the same law that I had worked for passage of back in 1988—and join the suit, so that the state attorney's office wouldn't be in it all alone.

On February 13, three days before the file was scheduled to be released, Michael Satz filed an emergency motion to intervene. He outlined our whole argument. That opening the file "could adversely affect further investigation/prosecution." That it would have "irreparable consequences on the potential for apprehending the perpetrator."

I filed an affidavit, too: "I have asked only one thing of the prosecutor and ask only one thing of this court. To do whatever the law allows to permit the opportunity that there might be justice done for the murder of my son."

I kept telling reporters that I wasn't afraid of having the case file opened for any reason other than that it would jeopardize Adam's case. I kept saying, "We have nothing to hide in those files." Even so, the innuendo was always there in the press. I was a big TV star now; they were convinced that there must be some pretty ugly skeletons in my closet for me to be fighting so hard. On February 14, an editorial in the *Sun Sentinel* wondered why "'a complete review' of Adam's case doesn't take place until nearly 15 years after the crime?" The sunshine law, Florida's Public Records Act, "does not grant blanket secrecy for any and all unsolved crimes. Nor should it allow any further stonewalling on the Adam Walsh files."

"Do other decades-old crimes languish similarly . . . or is something fishy going on in the Adam Walsh case alone?"

The day before the hearing, we made our last public pitch to overturn the judge's order. "The judge's decision means that it will be next to impossible to identify the person who murdered Adam," the statement said. "Now, details previously known only to the police and the killer will be known to all—making it almost impossible to find out who the real murderer is. Witnesses who feared coming forward for various reasons now face an onslaught of media attention. How can this be justice? This decision is another example of how victims of crime are revictimized in the courts. . . . If we can't depend on a law enforcement agency to put the search for a killer above any other concern, what can we depend on?"

At this point, everyone—Kelly, Ralph, George Terwilliger, Mike—was saying that we'd prevail. This judge was never going to open the file. And they weren't saying that just to make me feel better. It was inconceivable that things could go otherwise.

Even if all our arguments failed, we still had a secret weapon. The judge had already said that the only way the files would remain sealed was if the state attorney announced he was going to bring a suspect before a grand jury. That would be enough to get us a postponement. Enough to get an investigator on the case and indict Ottis Toole.

The hearing was set for February 16, 1996, at ten o'clock. I wanted to be there, but everyone told me there was no reason for me to bother. In fact, my presence might cause a disruption. Revé would go instead, along with our lawyers.

At the time, I was down in New Orleans on location for *AMW*. Taping all night, out in the French Quarter during Mardi Gras. Thousands of people. Freaked-out cops. I'd been down there a bunch of times, and the cops were big supporters of mine. Let's not let John get shot. Let's keep a real close eye on him. Gotta keep all those drunken people back.

Before the hearing, I was talking on cell phones to find out what was happening. We were all so up. The best part was Kelly Hancock saying, "John, there is enough evidence to indict Ottis Toole. I've won three-hundred murder cases. I could do it myself."

We were all kind of laughing about the heat I would get from the media for fighting against the newspapers. I was saying, "Don't worry. They'll forget all about it when they hear Ralph Ray announce that he'll be indicting someone within three months. Won't *that* be a headline: 'Suspect in Adam Walsh Case to Face Grand Jury'? Can't you just see the guy from *USA Today* running to a pay phone with that one?"

We had been shooting until five o'clock in the morning and were supposed to start again at noon. So in the meantime I headed back to the hotel to get a few hours' sleep. I was tired, but I felt great. I told George Terwilliger to call me when it was all over.

Before the hearing, Revé went first to Mike Christiansen's office to go over what was going to happen. Everyone was so confident that it was going to go our way. We were so hopeful. It was the most hope that we'd had since Adam's murder.

When they got to the courthouse, it was the typical media frenzy. A billion TV cameras. Rubberneckers from all over the courthouse showing up at the hearing room. The courtroom was packed, and Revé was completely surrounded. Judge Moe offered her his private chambers so people wouldn't keep sticking cameras in her face. Later, after the judge went out in his robes and took his seat, Mike came back in. "Okay, they've started the case," he told Revé. "They have to listen to the arguments from both sides. So, you want to come out and sit in the courtroom? You might as well. You've come this far."

"Yes," she said. "I'd like to listen to the arguments."

Revé was seated in the courtroom and listened to George Terwilliger and the lawyers for the newspapers. Terwilliger said that there were a lot of new leads in the case, and that this was an active investigation, and that you couldn't open up the most sensitive details of the case right now. The opposing lawyers said, as Revé remembers it, "We've waited fifteen years and that's long enough and the public has a right to know. Blah, blah, blah."

The judge never wrote anything down. Never took a note. At the conclusion of all the arguments, George Terwilliger stood up and said, "Your Honor, may I address the court?"

He approached the bench and said, "Your Honor, Revé Walsh, the mother of the murdered child is here, and she would like to make a statement to the court. With the permission of the court, I would like her to be heard."

The judge looked at George Terwilliger and said no. He did not want emotion in his courtroom. If Mrs. Walsh wanted to say something, she could speak through her attorney. And that was when the judge made his decision. He didn't say, "I'm going to take this under advisement," or give the world at least the impression that he was going to weigh the grave First Amendment issues and statutory questions in light of the lawyers' statements. He didn't go back into his chambers to think about it or say that he needed some time to consider his decision. He knew what he was going to do before he had even heard the arguments.

And then he did it: he threw us to the wolves.

A photographer got a picture of Revé as she was leaving the courtroom. She looked as if she were walking away from the scene of an accident—the same way that she had looked that morning on *Good Morning America* when we heard that Adam might be dead. As if a bomb had just gone off in her head.

In New Orleans, I was asleep when the phone rang. It was George Terwilliger, and his first words to me were, "John, I'm so sorry."

George's argument had no effect on the judge. He had not even allowed Revé to speak. George said that Ralph Ray had told the judge that he would be willing to bring a suspect before the grand jury in three months. One of the newspapers' lawyers even agreed to a three-month stay. But the judge had made up his mind before he ever entered the courtroom. He came in with what appeared to be a prepared statement, and he read it from the bench. He released the case file. And there was nothing more we could do.

"What about Revé?" I said.

"She's devastated."

I kept asking George how this could have happened. I said, "George, isn't this against the law? How could that judge not let Revé speak? The mother of a murdered child?"

And George said, "John, that hearing today had nothing to do with justice. It had nothing to do with Adam. It had to do with selling newspapers, with lawyers, and with abuse of power by the press."

For fifteen years, I had been hurt, exploited, manipulated, and lied to. But I had persevered, because I believed that I could change things in this country, and that I would win justice for my son. I had tried so hard to get closure for my family. Now I knew that it was never going to happen. Because of people who didn't even know Adam—journalists and lawyers who were making money and going home at night to their kids. Didn't they have any conscience, any idea of justice or truth? I couldn't move. I was absolutely, absolutely devastated. I was thinking about Adam. Talking to him. Saying over and over, "I'm so sorry, Adam. I tried so hard for you. Daddy's so sorry . . ."

I was murdered twice that day. First, with the release of the file. And then, by the indignity that my wife suffered at the hands of that judge. I had nothing to lose now. Nothing. I had not felt this lost in fifteen years.

Using weird, convoluted logic that was impossible to understand, the newspapers kept trying to defend what they had done. "It is not a question of the media's claiming privileges that go beyond the rights of the public," Earl Maucker, the editor of the *Sun Sentinel,* wrote in an editorial, "but rather of the media's playing their role in the public's right to be informed." You figure that one out.

By this time, we didn't really care about any of that.

We were already looking at something else. Something that had reared up and become frighteningly clear during the court case.

On February 16, 1996, the day the file was opened, my attorney, George Terwilliger, a former deputy attorney general of the United States, gave a statement to the press. His hands were trembling from anger as he spoke: "The Hollywood Police Department gave up on a notorious homicide investigation because they were running scared from a bunch of newspapers.

"The only thing that releasing the files might reveal is that Hollywood police are the biggest bunch of bungling idiots since the Keystone Kops."

At the time, even he didn't know how right he was.

14

The Evidence

A LOT OF WHAT FOLLOWS IN THIS CHAPTER ISN'T EASY FOR me to talk about. Sometimes, in order to, I have to tell myself that it happened to someone else. I don't know how else to do it. To understand what happened—and why—you have to know the details. I didn't know most of this until the case file was opened in 1996. It was only then that I began to piece all of the details together. In the sixteen years since Adam's murder, no one had really done that. Not, that is, until now.

By the early autumn of 1983, cops all over the country were hearing through the grapevine about a serial killer named Henry Lee Lucas, imprisoned in Texas, who was confessing to an almost unbelievable string of sordid crimes—strangulations and shootings, disembowlings and stabbings—somewhere in the neighborhood of 150 in all. It was almost impossible to believe that one human being could have caused so much carnage, but Lucas was saying that he hadn't acted alone. His traveling companion, he said, was a guy named Ottis Elwood Toole. That came as big news to the cops in the Duval County sheriff's office in northern Florida, who at that time were holding Toole, a near-illiterate, thirty-six-year-old drifter, for his involvement in a fatal arson case the year before.

That was when the weird pilgrimage began. As the news spread, some dozen or so sheriff's deputies and homicide cops from places like Colorado, Texas, and Louisiana were beginning to descend on the Jacksonville jail with one thought in mind. They wanted to know if this Ottis Toole—who had been telling stories of some pretty grisly homicides himself—might be responsible for any of the unsolved murders in their jurisdictions—including some of the sickest rapes, mutilations, and knife murders they had ever seen.

In the middle of all this excitement, during the second week of October 1983, Toole began making vague references to a crime he might have done in the Lauderdale area, farther south, a couple of years before—the abduction and decapitation, as he told it, of a young boy. He was providing some interesting detail, enough for the local cops to put two and two together. It didn't take long for the cops to figure it out: What if Toole was referring to the murder of Adam Walsh?

HPD detectives Jack Hoffman and Ron Hickman had gone up to Jacksonville and spent quite a bit of time and energy looking into Toole's story. For a while, they thought they might have their man. They even called a press conference announcing his arrest. But then things started going downhill.

Toole was garbling details, coming up with implausible stories, even, several times, recanting his "confession." When they had taken him back to the Indian River County site where he claimed to have buried Adam's remains, he couldn't even come up with the body. In the HPD's eyes, Toole had provided some interesting details that might—or might not—be related to the Adam Walsh murder. Mostly, they saw him as a con artist who was trying to cash in on a crime he probably didn't commit—just for the sake of jerking them around.

Still, the HPD set up a task force to look into Toole's possible involvement. They ran an NCIC computer search, contacted other jurisdictions, traveled hundreds of miles checking bus tickets, employment receipts, and dozens of potential witnesses. It all led nowhere. In a report submitted to HPD assistant police chief LeRoy Hessler on January 10, 1984, Capt. R. S. Davis, then head of the Hollywood detective division, outlined the task force findings. In the three months since Toole had surfaced as a suspect, the six investigators assigned full-time to the case had traveled to Jacksonville, Georgia, Texas, Virginia, and North and South Carolina—at a cost of 3,500 man hours and $62,000. "All persons known to have had contact with Toole during the summer of 1981 have been located and interviewed," Davis wrote. And while Toole had not definitively been eliminated as a suspect, "detectives have been unable to uncover any evidence, other than his confession, linking him with the Walsh homicide."

"At this point in the investigation," he said in closing, "it has been determined that 'MAYBE HE DID AND MAYBE HE DIDN'T.'"

Over the years, nothing happened to change that belief. In the eyes of the Hollywood police, they had worked the investigation of Ottis Toole as far as any human could. In June of 1991, nearly a decade after Adam's murder, the local papers carried stories on the retirement of Hollywood police major James B. Smith, then head of the HPD detective division. In 1984, J. B. Smith had headed the task force on Ottis Toole and, on his retirement from the force, recalled all the work that his team had done. It was "probably the most complete investigation we've ever done to prove that somebody didn't do it," he said. In fact, "it took us almost a year to prove he didn't do it."

* * *

As I well remembered, my friend Joe Matthews's role in Adam's case first began back in 1981, twelve days after Adam's disappearance. A recognized expert in conducting interviews and polygraph exams, Joe, a Miami Beach homicide detective sergeant, was imported by HPD to handle my polygraph. But that was hardly the end of his involvement in the case. I wasn't the only one Matthews had polygraphed; the assistant chief, LeRoy Hessler, had also asked him to take a close look at a suspect named Jimmy Campbell. By that time, the cops knew about Campbell's relationship with Revé, and they were zeroing in on it in a big way. The theory was that Campbell might have killed Adam as a way of getting even with me.

As Joe has explained it to me, the first step in any successful polygraph is to get the subject to trust you. You have to spend a long time in the preliminary interview, watching the person's body language, seeing how they react to stress and structured questions. It's a delicate phase of the process, and Matthews had told Hessler that he needed to do the first interview with Campbell himself. Hessler had said that was fine, which was why, when Joe came in to start talking to Campbell, he was shocked to see that other detectives were in the interrogation room, raking him over the coals. "What the hell did you do that for?" Matthews said to Hessler. By the time Matthews got his chance at around nine o'clock that Friday night, there was no point in even trying to get a baseline reading from Campbell. The cops had been brutal—really leaning on him—and he was too exhausted and shaken up for an official interview.

Three days later, on Monday, August 10, Matthews went back to HPD and began his examination of Campbell. In the middle of it, there was a knock on the door. It was Hessler, asking Joe to step out into the hallway. He told him about the news that had just reached the station—that up near Vero Beach, a child's head had been found in a canal. They weren't positive yet, but it looked to be Adam. With that news, a difficult child-abduction case turned into a highest-priority murder investigation.

On hearing the news, Joe maintained his composure and went back into the interrogation room to continue with the exam. Over the next several hours, he talked to Campbell, cajoling him, drawing him out, getting him to open up. Campbell talked openly about his relationships with me, with Adam, and with Revé. He admitted to having smoked pot, and on a few occasions, snorting cocaine. It was sensitive information, but it only reinforced what Matthews's instincts were telling him: that Jimmy Campbell was coming clean—and that he would never in the world have done anything to hurt Adam.

At the end of the interview, Matthews came out into a conference room where cops and staffers were gathering to catch his official results. Things were tense. Everyone watched intently as Matthews took his time—methodically pinning his polygraph charts to a cork bulletin board so that he could make his interpretation. While he was still working, Hessler came in. "A positive ID has just been made: it's Adam Walsh," he told Matthews. "So let's get this son of a bitch."

Matthews, fighting to maintain his concentration, ignored Hessler.

"Jesus, Joe, what do they say?" Hessler asked.

Finally, Matthews gave the verdict. "Based on his response to structured questions, body language, and the polygraphs," he told the hushed room, "James Campbell shows no physiological reaction indicative of deception. It is my conclusion that he was not criminally involved, nor does he have guilty knowledge of whoever is responsible for the abduction of Adam Walsh."

Hessler exploded. "I don't want to hear that shit!" he shouted. "Joe, don't you give me that kind of crap!"

At first, Matthews was stunned. Then, when Hessler took him aside, he got the picture. This was now an extremely high-visibility case, and it was pretty clear who Hessler was convinced the prime suspect was. Hessler was the one who would have to face the music. And if the test was "not deceptive," as Matthews had called it, then why, Hessler asked angrily, couldn't it be called "inconclusive"?

That was when Matthews finally blew. "Listen, LeRoy," he said. "I'm not the one who asked to come over here and conduct this polygraph. You called me. You've got six of your own polygraph guys on staff, and if what you really wanted was for someone to call it the way you want it called, then get one of your own to do it. I'm nobody's whore. And what I'm telling you is that James Campbell did not murder Adam Walsh!"

Things cooled down, Hessler backed off, and James Campbell's polygraph was officially entered into the record as "not deceptive." But months later, when Matthews ran into Hessler at a local building-supply store, it was obvious to him that Hessler was still seething about it, and that he still believed Campbell was guilty.

"You really fucked it up, Matthews," he said. "You're the one who let the wrong guy go."

Years later, Joe would look back on that hot August night in the HPD as a turning point of sorts. It was, he says, "my first inkling that things were screwed up at home."

In really tough or high-profile cases, it's customary for neighboring police jurisdictions to offer to lend a hand. But when the Broward County Sheriff's Office offered to help the HPD with the Adam Walsh case, they were told to butt out. The general feeling at Broward was that whenever a break came in the case, HPD wanted to be the only ones to take credit for it. Whether the feelings were justified or not, it wasn't the only time that an offer of help would be rebuffed. Joe Matthews, who remembers the chaotic flood of reports and tips that were raining down on the department at the time, once made a friendly suggestion to the lead detective in Adam's case—Jack Hoffman. "You know, Jack, you really ought to put one guy in charge of all these tips," he said. "With all those reports all over your desk, it's too easy to lose a lead." A hostile Hoffman, recalls Matthews, "just blew me off."

Two years later, Joe, like everyone else, was relieved and elated to learn that a drifter named Ottis Toole was being indicted for the crime. He was a little dubious, though, when he heard that Hoffman and Hickman were the ones assigned to interview Toole ("Mr. Personality and his sidekick," he thought to himself) and baffled when no word of an arraignment followed. But what really disturbed him was what he heard every time he went back to the Hollywood station over the years to do a polygraph or give an interrogation-training seminar: the rampant scuttlebutt among HPD rank and file that my son's case was the most fouled-up investigation ever to come down the pike.

Joe and I didn't stay in touch after he polygraphed me in that horrible second week of Adam's disappearance. But after an experience as intense as that, you don't forget someone. As I would later learn, Joe never forgot about Adam, either. In every good cop's life, at least one case haunts him. For Joe Matthews, one of those cases was my little boy's.

In the spring of 1991, Matthews went up to Tallahassee to teach a three-day seminar at the University of North Florida's Institute for Police Technology and Management. He happened to get into a conversation with another of the instructors, an ex-FBI agent named Bill Haggerty. With all the shoptalk going on, somehow Adam's case came up. Matthews was surprised to hear that Haggerty had once interviewed Ottis Toole about it; he told Haggerty that he had been the one who had polygraphed me and James Campbell. Over drinks, the two were comparing notes when Haggerty, who had heard all about Ottis Toole's alleged confessions, casually mentioned that they were obviously phony.

"What makes you think that?" Matthews asked.

Because, Haggerty explained, the time frame was all wrong. Investigators knew that Toole, traveling alone, was on the road in the weeks before Adam's abduction and had been as far north as Delaware. A receipt from the Salvation Army showed that on July 24—three days before Adam's murder—Toole asked for help at a Salvation Army in Newport News, Virginia and was given $71.93 for a Greyhound bus ticket. Fourteen and a half hours later, on the morning of Saturday, July 25, he arrived back south in Jacksonville.

The next time that Ottis Toole turned up was in Jacksonville on July 31. There was no paper trail of any kind to say where he might have been during the five days in between—which included the day of Adam's abduction, on the twenty-seventh of July.

That proved that Toole couldn't possibly have killed Adam, Haggerty said. Because there was no way that, right after a fourteen-hour bus trip, he would immediately have taken off on a five-hour drive down to Fort Lauderdale. Even if, as he had told police, he had done it because he could make more money turning tricks in Miami than he could up north in Jacksonville. As Haggerty put it, "There's no way, after getting off that bus, that he would drive down to Miami to hustle fags, just to get a few bucks more for a blow job." Which meant, he said, that Toole could be ruled out as a suspect.

Matthews could not have disagreed more. "Bill, that's logical if you're talking about a normal person," he said. "But look at the way Toole had been living. He was a serial killer. He slept on the street, in parks, in his car. An overnight trip on a Greyhound bus that had air-conditioning and reclining, upholstered seats was probably the best night's sleep he'd had in months. When he got into Jacksonville that Saturday morning, I guarantee you, he was refreshed. It's entirely possible that he hopped into a car and headed south for a five-hour drive. You said yourself he didn't have a dime when he got into Jacksonville. And what he told the cops was true: he *could* make more money hustling in Miami than in Jacksonville."

The more he thought about it, the more astonished Matthews was. If this analysis was the reason that Ottis Toole had not been indicted, then the whole Adam Walsh case was standing on some shaky ground.

As soon as he was back in Hollywood, Matthews got on the phone to Jack Hoffman—still the case's lead investigator—and repeated his theory. Not surprisingly, Matthews thought to himself, Hoffman seemed totally disinterested. So Joe decided to go over his head; he called a longtime acquaintance, Gil Frazier, the head of the HPD detective bureau.

Matthews told Frazier the whole story. "I really think Toole's gotta be reinterviewed," he said.

"Fine," said Frazier, who picked up the phone and got Hoffman on the line. "Hey, Jack, I'd like you to go ahead and set up this Toole interview with Joe Matthews. I'm giving you my permission."

Matthews went downstairs to see Hoffman. "Okay, Jack. Let's get going on this," he said. "Why don't you give me a date and we can schedule it." Without even looking up from his desk, Hoffman said that he was too tied up at the moment to schedule an interview with Toole—who by this time was in Starke prison up near Jacksonville—but that Matthews should call him back. Which Matthews did, the next week. And the week after that. And every few weeks for the next several months. Each time he did, Jack Hoffman was either out, away, or busy.

Then, in October, Matthews ran into Bill Haggerty again at another Tallahassee training session. Haggerty seemed pissed off about something, and Matthews asked him why. Oh, said Haggerty, obviously irritated. He had gotten a call saying he had to meet Jack Hoffman and go down to the Florida state prison at Starke to interview Ottis Toole.

After all of his efforts to fan some interest in Toole, Matthews was angry as hell about being excluded. Even more so when Haggerty, who left the following morning for Starke, showed up again by late afternoon—with the news that he and Hoffman had gotten nowhere with Toole. Matthews believed that what Toole needed was the velvet glove; he had seen it pay off a million times before. You had to buddy up to guys like Toole. Work them slowly. Get them to trust you. "Of all the people they could have sent to interview Toole," Matthews thought disgustedly, "the Hollywood police pick the two guys who are absolutely convinced he didn't do it."

Not until three years later, in the middle of 1994, did Matthews see his chance: Jack Hoffman was being transferred out of the detective bureau. In what was officially termed a "career development" move, Hoffman, after a lengthy career as a homicide detective, was now being reassigned to the patrol division. Most cops saw "career development" for what it was—a demotion. But Matthews didn't care about any of that. The only thing he wanted to know was who would be taking over Hoffman's cases. The answer, he learned, was a young HPD homicide detective named Mark Smith.

Matthews called Smith up and, over coffee, reiterated his doubts about the case. That Toole was still the leading suspect, and that, with some legwork, the case might still be solved. Smith said that he'd have to talk to his superior about it. Two days later came the answer: thumbs-down.

This time, Matthews wasn't going to let it go. He called a plugged-in detective friend and asked him a question: "What's going on over there? Someone doesn't want the case reopened?" Well, said the friend, the guy who could make that call happens to be a good buddy of Hoffman's. And maybe he doesn't want to see his good buddy second-guessed. Who knows?

What Matthews didn't know was that over at HPD, two newly installed ranking officers—Maj. Brian Maher and Lt. Debbie Futch—were, for reasons of their own, concluding that someone ought to start taking another look at the Walsh investigation. It was an extremely high-profile case. It was still unsolved. And the same lead detective had been on it for some thirteen years. Maybe now was the time for a fresh eye.

A week later, Maher, Futch, and Sgt. Robert Dunbar attended a law enforcement seminar at Broward Community College taught by Harry O'Reilly, a retired NYPD homicide detective. As is customary at those conferences, they brought along an unsolved case—Adam's.

When Dunbar made the presentation, reporting that the two top suspects in the case were Jimmy Campbell and Ottis Toole, O'Reilly immediately noticed Campbell's polygraph.

"Who eliminated Campbell?" he asked.

Joe Matthews, they reported. "Then there's your answer," said O'Reilly, who knew Joe's reputation. "If Joe Matthews is the one who says it's not Campbell, then focus on Toole."

A few days later, Matthews was called in for a meeting with Smith, Futch, and Maher at HPD. In as diplomatic a way as possible, he said that he felt the case needed another look. That Toole was still the true lead suspect, and that investigators had made a big mistake in ruling him out. That was all it took. Within days, HPD took an unusual step: officially requesting that the Miami Beach Police Department loan them Joe Matthews to come in as a consultant and direct their review of the Adam Walsh case.

By August of 1994, thirteen years after Adam's death, the newspapers were still calling it "south Florida's most notorious unsolved murder." As a veteran homicide detective, Joe Matthews certainly knew his way around so-called cold cases; he had solved many of them. And Smith, who in 1990 cracked a contract slaying that had been open for thirteen years, was starting to feel the same way Matthews did about the investigation into Adam's murder.

As it happened, Smith wasn't really a stranger to the case, either. Thirteen years before, then a twenty-three-year-old patrol cop, he had been sitting in his squad car at 7 A.M. one hot July morning, parked across the street from the HPD in the Hollywood mall. A gray Checker cab pulled up to the driver's side, and a young couple who "had obviously not slept that night," as he recalls, told Smith they were looking for their son.

He knew immediately who we were. At roll call the night before, he had been given a photograph of the little boy, which he now pulled down from his visor. "I've got his picture right here," he said. "Don't worry. We'll find him."

By the time Matthews and Smith were assigned to review it, the official HPD case file on Adam's murder stood at nearly ten-thousand pages. There were photographs, transcripts, summary reports, interviews with prison witnesses, letters from crackpots, newspaper articles, car registrations, polygraph reports, Adam's birth certificate, his first-grade drawings, copies of our charge-account records from Sears. If anything was apparent right off the bat, it was how overwhelming this kind of case must have been for a small, relatively inexperienced little Florida PD. There were enough obvious goofs right in the paperwork to make that pretty clear. As Hoffman himself told a reporter in 1995: "Hollywood [had] never had a case like this. From the beginning, it was like a Chinese fire drill. The tips were on five-by-three cards. They were on matchbook covers. It was out of control."

So it wasn't hard to understand how some of the errors had happened. Others were not so easy to dismiss. Throughout the entire 120 pages of Hoffman's first official supplement report, for example, every time he referred to the video game that Adam had been playing at Sears, he had called it a "Hitari" game. In hindsight, that mistake makes perfect sense; back in the summer of 1981, video games were still such a novelty that Hoffman had probably never heard the trade name before. Later, he had gone back through the typed report, crossing out each *Hitari* and penciling in *Atari*, along with the initials *JH*.

Then how come he never bothered to correct another, far more obvious error? The one on the very first page of his official report, which describes—despite information on hundreds of thousands of missing posters to the contrary—the shorts Adam was wearing as "blue" and not green? And why was Joe Matthews's very first meeting with Jimmy Campbell—one that had taken place when Campbell was too shaken up to be interviewed—referred to as a "polygraph examination" in Hoffman's report, and characterized as "inconclusive"?

Other oversights were more troubling still. On page two of the report, for example, it states that initially the cops did not conduct "in-depth interviews" with potential eyewitnesses. Why in God's name not?

Because, as Hoffman wrote, "When the above mentioned witnesses were first interviewed it appeared
that this investigation was that of a missing child
incident." And one of those "possible witnesses" was
a seventeen-year-old Sears Roebuck security guard
named "Kathy Schaefer" [sic].

Accounts of the discovery of Adam's remains in
Indian River—included in a summary report Hoffman wrote three months later—were also frustrat-
ingly sketchy. It was clear enough that dozens of law
enforcement personnel had swarmed over the area.
Thirty-five miles of turnpike were searched for the
rest of Adam's body.

But it also looked from the report that this had not
been the careful, methodical examination of a roped-
off crime scene. In fact, nothing indicates that it was
preserved as a crime scene at all. There was no
mention of whether the canal had been dredged. No
hint of any tests performed to detect the presence of
blood at the site. Nothing whatsoever to indicate if
anyone had gone out looking for tire tracks, or maybe
a tossed cigarette butt. The kind of evidence that, as
Matthews knew, might now, all these years later, still
yield some DNA. Considering what the stakes had
been, it was a little puzzling.

What Hoffman himself wrote about it was this:
"This search did not reveal any additional evidence in
this case. Due to the above mentioned circumstances,
it appeared that this location was *just* [emphasis
added] an area to dispose of the severed head, and
that the homicide occurred elsewhere." The cops on
the scene evidently couldn't be bothered with minuti-
ae. What they were searching for was a body.

At the time, Hoffman apparently wasn't considering the possible outcome that Matthews and Smith
now knew to be fact. The eventuality that, sixteen
years after Adam's remains were discovered in Indian
River, the site would still stand as the only place on

earth where the cops could, with certainty, place Adam in the company of his killer.

In the following months, Matthews and Smith would sift through thousands of pages of case files, taking turns in a windowless third floor office of the HPD detective bureau. They agreed that Smith would write up any official reports; in the meantime Matthews would keep his own working notes. During his initial review of the file, Matthews drew up a list of all the facts that tended either to implicate or eliminate Toole; when he was finished, it stood at sixty-four pros to fourteen cons. Smith's first memo to his superiors, dated May 21, 1995, agreed with that finding. "Ottis Toole," wrote Smith, "has not been successfully eliminated as a suspect in this case."

Every investigation of a cold case starts the same way: by recovering old ground. A lot had changed in the past fourteen years. People had moved away or died. Even the Hollywood mall was different—now completely reconfigured. All of the entrances were changed around. A Target store was now where the old Sears had been. But lots of people who could talk were still around. Matthews knew that if Toole was the killer, then all other potential suspects had to be eliminated first—beginning, as had the initial investigation, with family and friends.

Smith tracked down the Sears security guard, Kathy Shaffer, who told him about that July day in the store. How a group of four kids—two white and two black—had gotten into a scuffle at the video game. When the two black kids told her that their parents weren't in the store, she sent them out the north exit. When she asked the two white kids if they were by themselves, the older boy had said yes. He seemed to be speaking for the one she assumed was his little brother, so she ordered them both out of the west, garden-shop exit. About a half hour later, she said, she was paged to the catalog department for the report of a missing child. She also remembered seeing Revé in the lamp department and being shown a photograph of the missing child.

Smith also talked to other witnesses. One, an employee in the catalog department, remembered seeing Revé walk in with a little boy, and that he had coaxed his mother into letting him stay at the video games. Another, who worked in Lamps, remembered that Revé had waited ten or fifteen minutes in her department before leaving. And that she had returned, very upset, about five minutes later, asking if anyone had seen her little boy.

Both detectives had, of course, heard all the rumors—that Revé had lied about the time she dropped Adam off; that she had left him alone in the store for hours; that she had been out that morning doing a drug deal. They knew that, a month after Adam's death, Revé had passed a lie detector test. But even so, Matthews still directed Smith to double-check the time frame against the statement from the secretary at St. Mark's and every living witness he could find. After a lot of legwork, Smith concluded—officially—that there was *no reason to doubt Revé's version of events.*

Next, Smith moved on to Michael Monahan, who had, at the time of Adam's abduction, been questioned by police after he waved a sugarcane cutter at some older kids who had stolen his skateboard. Over the years, some stories in the paper had made it sound as if Michael was a suspect. And now Jay Grelen—the reporter from the *Mobile Press Register* who by this time was trying to open the case file—was insisting to Smith that Michael "might have committed the murder of Adam Walsh as a favor for James Campbell." It was clear that Michael Monahan had never been considered a serious suspect by police, but Smith went ahead and reinterviewed him anyway. He also talked to Campbell, who once *had* been a prime suspect. Both Monahan and Campell were conclusively eliminated—as were, over the following months, the half dozen or so other peripheral characters whose names were mentioned in the file.

After several months of legwork, Matthews knew that only one true suspect was left: a gap-toothed sociopath named Ottis Elwood Toole.

At the time of his arrest in Jacksonville in July of 1983—for the arson death of a sixty-four-year-old man in a rooming-house fire—Ottis Elwood Toole, then thirty-six, had been a small-time fixture on the local crime scene for more than a dozen years. A sometime day laborer who had left school after the seventh grade, he had grown up in Jacksonville as one of nine children, living there with his mother until her death in May of 1981. According to a psychiatric evaluation conducted by the University Hospital of Jacksonville at the time of his arrest, Toole suffered from grand mal seizures that began when he was hit in the head with a rock as a child.

Toole always referred to his mother's death as her "going to sleep." He liked to lie down on her grave because the earth was warm there, he said, and he could sometimes feel it move. On and off he worked for the Reaves roofing company in Jacksonville, patching roofs, doing manual labor and picking up trash. He had access to guns, knives, and automobiles, and described his goal at the time of the examination as "to get straightened out."

The report continues: "The patient is a tall, huskily built man who is somewhat balding. He has very bad teeth. Effeminate mannerisms are noted. He is not hallucinated nor delusional. He is oriented to time, place and situation. He has poor current fund of information and only a fair general fund of information. He, for instance, misidentifies the president [at the time Ronald Reagan] as 'Johnson.' He can make simple change. He tends to reason concretely. His cognitive functions are intact with the exception of some minor memory problems." Toole said that his habits included drinking about a half pint of whiskey and several six-packs a night, plus a staggering array of street drugs. He described himself as homosexual and said that he did not have sex with children.

Toole had previously been picked up by the cops at least a dozen times for auto theft, larceny, lewd behavior, in Florida, Georgia, Kentucky, and Alabama. He was once arrested for propositioning an undercover officer in a pornographic movie theater. He had also been picked up for indecent exposure, cross-dressing, and window-peeping. The Jacksonville arson marked his first arrest for homicide. Which didn't mean that investigators didn't regard him as extremely dangerous. By this time, based on what Henry Lee Lucas was saying down in a Denton, Texas, prison, they knew better than to think that.

According to a 1983 Oklahoma police report, Lucas, then forty-six, was living on a former chicken ranch in Texas when he was questioned about the disappearance of a young woman named Kate Rich. Lucas, who had stayed with Rich for a few days that spring, admitted to police that he had "killed her, chopped her up, and burned her in a wood-burning stove." In fact, said Lucas, since 1975 he had killed 140 women in 25 states, usually by "stabbing them to death," although "he has admitted to strangling some and shooting others."

According to a psychiatric profile, Lucas, who had a glass left eye that "continually secretes fluid, causing matter around the eye," stated that "he did not feel comfortable having sex with women who were alive and practiced necrophilia. At times he would have sex with domestic animals, preferring dogs. He would kill the animal and cut away the sex organs."

Lucas's victims had been "anywhere from nine

years of age up to eighty years of age. He stated that he has no preference as to race, and some of his victims have been white, some black, some Indian, some Hispanic, and some Asian. He stated that the reason he killed all of these women was for sex. He admitted that he derives more satisfaction from having sex with a dead person. He stated that he has never killed a male and would have no reason to do so. He was known to bite nipples off the breasts and mutilate the body." Most of his victims were undressed before their bodies were dumped. Several were found nude except for their socks. "Lucas apparently has a phobia about socks," said the psychiatric report, "since he does not wear them at any time and will not wash his feet."

Lucas, who had done time in prisons in Virginia, Ohio, and in Michigan, committed his first murder at the age of fifteen. His first hard time—a ten-year term—began in 1960 in the Jackson, Michigan, State Penitentiary after he was convicted, at the age of twenty-three, of murdering his mother.

Henry Lee Lucas and Ottis Toole met in Michigan in 1976, and the two had traveled together sporadically in the years since, more frequently after the May 1981 death of Toole's mother. The picture that the cops were piecing together—based on police reports as well as information that the two were volunteering—was not pretty. They had stabbed some victims repeatedly. Cut others deeply along the arms, thighs, and legs. In some cases, disemboweled them. At least one victim, according to a police report, was decapitated, while the head of another "was carried in [their] car for several days." There were occasional attempts to incinerate the victims' bodies. Also, "efforts to cannibalize them." A second police psychiatric report said that if Lucas had sex with a woman either before or after killing her, Toole would then "mutilate the victim due to jealousy and anger."

While the dim-witted Toole was sometimes vague about the details of killing ("I got to thinking of it like smoking a cigarette," he would later say), Lucas, the brains of the operation, tended to recall specifics. "I can't get the people out of my mind," he told one interviewer. "It's . . . like watching a movie over and over." Also, unlike Toole, Lucas was almost exclusively heterosexual. "He likes girls," Toole once told the cops. In fact, "the only reason he would let me have sex with him was to keep me from raising hell with him."

For a time in the early months of 1983, Toole and Lucas had traveled with Toole's young niece and nephew. Later, after he and Toole split up, Lucas, who had been having a sexual relationship with the thirteen-year-old girl, got into an argument with her one day. Then he stabbed and dismembered her. "We had been all over Texas and she ended up getting killed," he later said. "There really wasn't no sense in it. That's the only girl that I can honestly say that I really loved."

In spite of all that, Ottis Toole cared to have only one thing on the wall of his jail cell in Jacksonville: a photograph of Henry Lee Lucas. The one, he confided to a prison psychiatrist, that he was "in love with." A man, Toole said, whom he "would do anything for."

Rootless and usually unemployed, Lucas and Toole would find a car and head out for days or weeks, covering thousands of miles at a time. From the spring of 1981 until the time of Adam's murder at the end of July, for example, police records showed that they had been in Louisiana on April 4; in Jacksonville on May 13; in Houston on June 15; back to Jacksonville, June 19; in Wilmington, Delaware, on July 11; and then in Pikesville, Maryland, on July 22, where Lucas was taken into custody and held until October 7.

Matthews knew that HPD investigators had been

unable to account for Toole's whereabouts for the five days surrounding Adam's abduction. The next order of business, then, was to see if their work still held up.

Early on the morning of Saturday, July 25, 1981, Toole had stepped off a bus in Jacksonville. He was then unaccounted for until the following Friday, July 31, when, receipts showed, he had rented a room in Jacksonville. Now, as then, it seemed that no one could remember seeing him in the interim. In fact, no hard evidence placed him anywhere during those crucial five days. "I didn't find that he had gotten, say, a traffic ticket in Daytona," says Smith. "So is it possible that Ottis Toole was in Hollywood for a couple of days on July twenty-seventh, 1981? Absolutely. It's only a five-and-a-half-hour drive south of Jacksonville."

When Ottis Toole was taken into custody in the Duval County sheriff's office back in 1983, his handler was James "Buddy" Terry, a local detective who had known Toole, through his various scrapes with the law, for the past eighteen years. The familiarity made for a relationship of sorts. Terry knew what a weird character Toole was; Toole, for his part, seemed to trust Terry. It only made sense, therefore, that Terry should be the one to help coordinate appointments for all the law enforcement types who were descending on Duval.

One of them was Paul Ruiz, an investigator with the Travis County, Texas, district attorney's office, who had flown over to question Toole about four unsolved homicides in Austin. With so many cops and detectives trying to get in to see Toole, Ruiz learned that he was going to have to wait awhile. In the meantime, Buddy Terry asked if he might sit in on some of the other interviews, helping brief the visiting cops on how best to handle Toole. Over that week, Ruiz got to know Ottis pretty well. Like almost everyone who came in contact with Toole, Ruiz would not soon forget the experience.

Ottis was weird to begin with. Ruiz saw that. "He rambled, and he liked to BS the guys who were coming in to interview him. That's just how he was. You really couldn't quite tell a lot of times whether or not he was telling the truth." But after a while, Ruiz could tell when Toole was going to lie and kind of pull their leg. So once he started, Ruiz would say, "Now c'mon, Ottis, don't be doing that to these guys." Then Toole would laugh and kind of come back to being straight with them.

Ruiz remembers Toole as uneducated and virtually illiterate, but also as cagey, and very street-smart. He had to be, considering the kinds of things that he'd been getting away with. Toole also liked to play games. He would say the most grotesque things just to see how people would react—going on and on about how he and Lucas cut women's breasts, for example.

Still, the cops were learning that patience with Toole had its rewards. If they were willing to wade through the BS, the payoff was sometimes the solution of a case. Toole was jerking one Colorado detective around one day when the cop finally decided just to put it to him straight: "Ottis, have you ever been to the Denver area?"

"Oh, yeah, I been through there," Toole said. "I remember driving . . . You know, in fact I ran out of gas in this real nice neighborhood and I didn't have that much money. I know what you want to know. You want to know how that woman died that was in bed. Well, I needed some money, so I walked up to the window and looked inside and I just shot her through the screen." When the woman didn't die right away, Toole said, he had tied her up and stabbed her.

The Colorado detective's mind was completely blown. He knew full well the case that Toole was talking about. And every one of the details was true.

During those interviews in Jacksonville, Toole was providing a lot of sick detail, some almost beyond comprehension, about his and Lucas's exploits.

About how they had left a knife blade sticking out of the top of one victim's head. How Toole had ejaculated twice on a car's dashboard while Lucas was raping a nineteen-year-old girl in the backseat. About how "the blood flew all over" when he shot a girl through the wrist as she was driving down a highway. How later, when he dragged her body out of it, he noticed that her car had a pinstripe down the side, and that she had been wearing a "college-type ring" on "the pointing finger" of her right hand. All details from right out of the blue. All details that actual police files in three different jurisdictions showed were entirely correct.

Buddy Terry knew that Toole was certainly capable of lying, and that he was also enjoying all the attention he was getting. But he had known Toole for nearly two decades now, and had never once seen him confess to a crime he didn't commit.

Just before noon on Monday, October 10, 1983, Steve Kindrick, a Florida detective who was in Jacksonville to interview Toole about a murder in the town of Rockledge, near Cocoa Beach, introduced himself by saying that he was "from Brevard County." Toole, he remembers, looked pretty bad—dirty and unshaven, with bad teeth and a terrible stench. The two made small talk for a while, and then Toole began rambling about the sixty-five murders that he said he had been party to. What most struck Kindrick about it was how casual Toole seemed. "Like two people talking about the weather," he wrote in his report.

Still, Kindrick wasn't getting anywhere about the Rockledge case. So, after about a half hour, he shut off his tape recorder and started packing up to leave. At that point, Toole looked at Kindrick and asked if he was from Fort Lauderdale. No, Kindrick said, he wasn't.

"Are you sure?" Toole asked.

Kindrick assumed that Toole was confusing Brevard County—in the central part of the state—with Broward, the county farther south that includes Fort Lauderdale.

"Ottis, for the last hour we've been talking about Cocoa Beach and Rockledge," Kindrick said. "I'm from *Brevard* County. What's the matter? You expecting someone from Lauderdale?"

"Yeah," Toole said. "Yeah, I am."

"What's the matter. Did you get into something down there?"

"Yeah, I did."

At that point, according to Kindrick, Toole's whole demeanor suddenly changed. Where he had been relaxed, jovial almost, he now, in the words of Kindrick's report, "held the sides of his chair, shifted from side to side, and started looking into the floor." Further: "Reporting Agent felt for a man to admit involvement in sixty-five murders, but get upset about Fort Lauderdale, it had to be something appalling."

The abrupt shift told Kindrick that he had stumbled onto something, and that, rather than taint somebody else's case, he'd better back out of it. He left the interrogation room and immediately told Buddy Terry what had happened.

Terry, who was getting ready to leave for a Louisiana task force conference on the Toole/Lucas crime spree, had a conversation with Toole, who asked him, too, if he had ever been to Lauderdale. "Why do you ask, Ottis?" Terry said. Because, Toole replied, something had happened down there two or three years back that he wanted to speak to someone about. The murder of a boy.

At the time, Terry had no idea what Toole was talking about. But when he mentioned the exchange to Kindrick, the Brevard detective did. The "something" that Ottis Toole was referring to might be the Adam Walsh case.

Kindrick told Buddy Terry about the exchange, and the next morning, Tuesday, October 11, at 9 A.M.,

Kindrick notified the HPD detective division. They didn't seem particularly interested in the information. "Like, 'Oh, yeah, we know all about that,'" he recalls. "We were all thinking, 'Hey, did you guys just wake up or something?' I was surprised that they weren't more receptive. To me, it seemed like it should have been a priority call."

A week later, on Tuesday, October 18, 1983, Lt. Joe Cummings, the Louisiana homicide investigator who had set up the Lucas/Toole task force conference, arrived in Jacksonville along with a colleague, Sgt. J. Via, who was on assignment for the Ouachita Parish sheriff's office. The two were interested in seeing if Toole had anything to do with the brutal murder of a sixteen-year-old girl in their jurisdiction.

Cummings and Via's first interview with Toole began at ten that morning. Toole was remarkably casual in talking about the murders he had committed, until the talk turned to the murder of blacks. When Via asked Toole why he was reluctant to talk about those killings, Toole said that he was worried that, if they knew about them, black inmates might try to kill him.

Via asked if he was reluctant to talk about killing children for the same reason. According to Via's written report, Toole suddenly "smiled and stated, 'You are talking about the kid that got his head cut off around West Palm Beach, Florida.'"

Like Buddy Terry before them, Via and Cummings had no idea what Toole was talking about. But they let him keep talking. He said that he had abducted a six- or seven-year-old boy from a shopping center near West Palm Beach and taken him to a remote area along the turnpike, where he decapitated him and threw his head into a canal. Toole emphasized that he had not performed the actual murder himself. He told them that Henry Lee Lucas had.

Cummings and Via immediately called Buddy

Terry into the room, and Toole kept right on going. After abducting the boy, he said, he and Lucas had driven about an hour to an isolated dirt road leading into a swampy, wooded area where, he said, he decapitated the boy with "a machete or bayonet." He then placed the child's head inside his car—a white, 1973 Cadillac four-door with a black vinyl top and black interior—and headed south to the Florida Keys. Toole told Cummings that at one point he hit the boy, hard, in the face. Not to hurt him, but because he wouldn't stop crying.

During the conversation, the three watched as Toole's body language did a major turnaround. He suddenly got subdued and quiet, staring at the floor and rocking in his chair. There was "a striking change in Toole's emotional attitude and behavior," Via wrote, "which had not been noticed in any of the prior interviews." Afterward, in the hallway, Cummings remembers, "I walked out and said, 'Who the hell is this kid in Florida he keeps talking about?'"

On Wednesday, October 19, it was Paul Ruiz's turn, and during his first official interview with Toole, the subject of child-killing came up again. "Oh, I would never hurt any kids, you know," Toole said. "I would never do anything like that." Ruiz noticed how quiet Toole suddenly became. His leg started jumping up and down, as if he were nervous. He stopped talking and clasped his hands together between his thighs. He looked at Ruiz and said, "I would never do anything to any kids." Then he trailed off. He didn't say anything for four or five seconds, which, as Ruiz knew, was unusual for Ottis. He was denying that he had ever done anything to a little kid, but Ruiz didn't believe him. He basically thought that Toole could have done anything to anybody at any time.

Ruiz's written report included one final exchange. Of how, at the end of the interview, Toole suddenly volunteered that he would never have killed a young child. Although, he said, "I could kill a fourteen-, fifteen-year-old . . . and it could have been in Florida."

And if he *had* done such a thing, Toole added, "I wouldn't necessarily know the exact location."

It wasn't until 3:10 P.M. on October 19—more than a week after Kindrick first notified the Hollywood police, that they finally heard back from Ron Hickman.

"We were all thinking, 'What the hell is wrong with these guys?'" Steve Kindrick remembers. How could it take a neighboring police jurisdiction eight days to track down a lead about the notorious unsolved homicide of a child? A case that, it seemed, they had an unsolicited confession for?

When the HPD reached Terry, he repeated the message Kindrick had left the preceding week: that he had a suspect who was saying that two years before, he had abducted a young boy from a Sears mall in Fort Lauderdale and had decapitated him. This time, six hours later, Hoffman and Hickman arrived in person at the Duval jail.

It was immediately apparent that the two didn't have any intention of sharing information or buddying up with other cops. That was all right. Proper police procedure dictated that they play it close to the vest. But what irritated some of the other cops, who, after all, were trying to help out on a case that didn't even belong to them, was the HPD cops' attitude. Hoffman's nickname at HPD was, like my father's, Gentleman Jack. But he and Hickman didn't seem very gentlemanly—at least not to the cops in Jacksonville. It wasn't just that the two of them didn't introduce themselves. It was that they barely even said hello. "You got the idea right away," says one cop who was there. "They were too big for that. They were wearing their nice dress suits, and their attitude was 'What are we even doing here? We've heard all this before.'"

At 10:00 P.M. that night, an hour after they arrived, Hoffman and Hickman took their first sworn statement from Toole. During the interview, with Buddy Terry sitting in, Toole claimed that he and Lucas, driving a 1973 black-over-white Cadillac, had traveled down to Fort Lauderdale a couple years before, slept in the car, and paid cash for gas. They had gotten into town around noon and gone to a single-level mall that had a Sears store in it. How did he know it was a Sears? they asked.

" 'Cause I know a Sears when I see a Sears," Toole replied.

Toole said that he might also have gone window-shopping in the mall itself. He remembered a wig shop, where he had stopped to look at the wigs. "Could we be talking about a beauty parlor?" he was asked.

"No," said Toole. "Regular wigs. Wigs that you put on your head."

And had he actually gone into the Sears store?

"No," said Toole. "I didn't go into the Sears store. But I could have went in it, came back out, and forgot I went in it. I do that sometimes." Part of the reason for his vague recollection on that point, he said, was that he had been drinking heavily that day, and popping pills.

According to Hoffman's summary report, Toole then described the boy he had abducted, whom he had first spotted outside the store in the parking lot, as being about seven to ten years old, with blond hair, curly, and wearing blue jeans, a blue shirt, and sneakers. (A transcript of the interview shows that when asked what kind of hair the little boy had, Toole said, "I'd say it could have been curly or wavy or in between. I'd say it wasn't no straight-bodied hair.")

"Was the child in the front seat with you and Henry or was he in the back?" Hoffman asked.

"If you snatch up somebody, you damn sure ain't gonna let 'em get in no backseat," said Toole.

After abducting the boy, Toole said, he and Lucas had driven northbound on the Florida Turnpike for about an hour and a half. When the boy became uncontrollable, Lucas told Toole to pull over. Toole said that he found a dirt road along the turnpike and removed the boy from the car. As the boy lay face-down on the ground, Lucas had decapitated him with three or four blows. Toole had been drunk when all of this occurred, and when they asked him why he was confessing to the crime, he said that he wanted to tell about it and then forget it.

During the interview, Toole was shown a photograph of the turnpike in the area of the canal where Adam's remains were found. He said it looked familiar. When he was shown Adam's picture, Toole said that he didn't think it was the same boy. Although "it could have been 'cause I was too, ah, fucked up in the head, you now. I ain't really sure. . . . Maybe that was because I was drunk and I ain't drinkin' now."

Toole was then shown a photograph of Adam's remains. For a long time, he didn't say anything. Then, finally, he said, "Since the kid's head is wet, it does kinda look like the kid some." Because "the kid was sweaty in the parking lot, and his hair was all sweaty."

That was Toole's story. Some of the information was right. Some was wrong. When, at 10:47 P.M., Hoffman and Hickman stepped out of the interview room that night, leaving Toole with Buddy Terry, they didn't seem impressed. "They were saying, 'Nah, this guy don't know anything. Same old stuff. He doesn't really have anything to say,'" Paul Ruiz remembers.

A few minutes later, Terry came out to tell Hoffman and Hickman the same thing he had just told Toole: that Ottis must be lying about at least one thing. Records in Maryland showed that during the time Toole was talking about—from July 22 until October 7 of 1981—Henry Lucas had been in police custody in Baltimore. Now, said Terry, Toole wanted to give another statement.

One thing was clear to almost every cop who ever interviewed Toole: it was going to be an uphill battle, and he was going to sensationalize all kinds of things. But anyone who had done interrogations saw people like that all the time. The best way to deal with Toole was to let him ramble on for a while, then tell him, "Now, come on, Ottis. Don't tell me something happened that way when I know it didn't." He would say, "Okay. Okay, yeah, it really didn't quite happen that way," come back down to earth, and start giving you the truth. The one thing you didn't want to do was act as if you thought he was an idiot.

Hoffman and Hickman reentered the interrogation room at 12:30 A.M.

This time, Toole said that he had abducted the little boy himself. That, when the child started crying, he had hit him in the eye, knocking him unconscious. That he had driven out of the mall to the turnpike and headed north. That he pulled off the turnpike onto a dirt road to kill the child because he was a smart kid and would probably be able to identify him. That he had decapitated the boy, put his head in the car, and scattered the rest of his body, without burying it. When asked what kind of weapon he had used, Toole said "a bayonet."

Hoffman and Hickman were of course familiar with Adam's autopsy report. Ronald Wright, the medical examiner, had made a number of findings two years before: that before death, there had been a broken nose and injury between the eyes. That Adam was already dead, and lying facedown, when he was decapitated. That there were five blows to the base of the skull. That the killer was right-handed and would have had to use both hands.

With those facts in mind, the two started asking Toole about what he had done: How many blows?

With one hand or both? Where—down low or up high? Toole said that he had had both hands on the weapon. That it had taken "four or five" strokes. Not down by the shoulders, but up "close to the head." That afterward, he had traveled north on the turnpike for "about ten minutes" before stopping to throw the head into a canal that had "a little wooden bridge."

"Are you right-handed or left-handed?" they asked.

"Right-handed," said Toole.

During the interview, which went on for ninety minutes, they also asked Toole why he had lied about Lucas being involved. He had done it, Toole said, to "get even with his ass."

It was at the end of that second interview, Ruiz remembers, that Hoffman and Hickman "came rushing out, got on the phone, and started really getting involved in the situation. That's when they decided they were going to have to take Ottis down to Hollywood."

The next day, Thursday, October 20, Ruiz spoke to Toole again. Had strict police procedure been followed, no one would have breathed another word to him about Adam Walsh, for fear of tainting HPD's case. But that isn't the way things were. A lot of different interviewers were around—quite a bit of excitement. And Toole was volunteering information to anyone who would listen. He talked to Ruiz about going to the shopping center that day. How he had gotten the little boy into the car, but had not planned to kill him at first. That what he actually wanted was to keep the little boy for himself and raise him. He really wanted a little baby to raise, Toole said, because he knew "how to change diapers."

Toole also told Ruiz the rest of it: that Adam was a baseball fan, and that he wanted to get out of the car, and that he kept saying that if Ottis would just take him back, he wouldn't tell anyone. And that when Adam kept yelling, it had gotten on his nerves. That he backhanded him several times, hitting him in the head. Toole said that he had decided to kill Adam when he realized Adam was "too smart" and might be able to identify him.

Toole recalled pretty clearly what he had done to the little boy at Indian River, but he didn't seem able to remember exactly what he had done with the rest of Adam's body. His exact words to Ruiz were "all the body parts seem to be all jumbled up." But he thought that the body should be in the "pond" where the head was found. Then Toole asked Ruiz if the pond had been dredged. "I know they must have found blood on the dock," he said.

By that time, Toole had heard that he was going to be flown down south to Hollywood the next day, then taken up to Indian River. His last words to Ruiz, in fact, were that "he would try his best to help these Hollywood guys find the body."

At 9:00 A.M. the following day, Friday, October 21, Toole, along with Hoffman and Terry, arrived at Perry Airport in Pembroke Pines, near Hollywood. First, Toole was taken to HPD. Then, at 3:30 P.M., he was put into a Chevy High Top van, and, to test him, the cops drove to a Sears store at the Broward mall. Toole said it wasn't the place. When they pulled into the Hollywood mall, he said he was pretty sure that this was it, although he had been pretty drunk at the time and was having a hard time remembering the sequence of events. At the mall, Toole pointed, correctly, to the west entrance, describing it as where he picked up the little boy. He had lured him into the car with candy and toys, he said, and had used the driver's-side control to lock the car's four power windows. Then he redirected the driver toward what he said had been his route: out Hollywood Boulevard, around Military Circle, and about ten minutes farther to the entrance to the Florida turnpike. After the van drove northbound for about an hour and a half, as Toole said he had done, he pointed out an area off the turnpike that he said looked familiar. The area where he had pulled off and decapitated the little boy, who was by then no longer moving.

Hoffman later told Dick Hynds, who had not come along, that on the turnpike, just as the van was passing the precise spot where Adam's remains had been found, Toole, out of the corner of his eyes, seemed to shoot a glance toward it.

"Did you see something?" they asked.

"Well, I think I might."

"But again," said Hynds, "Toole didn't say anything positive."

That exchange is not mentioned in the case file. Nor, for a time, was the input of HPD detective Larry Hoisington, who was the van's designated driver that day.

According to Hoisington, Toole said that when he first pulled off the turnpike, he hadn't paid a toll. Which meant something to Hoisington, who was particularly familiar with that stretch of road. He remembered that two years before, there had been a construction site near mile maker 126, with a temporary access road leading into it. At the time, a fence around it had been removed, which meant that there was nothing to block a car from pulling off the northbound lanes. In fact, Hoisington recalled, at the time it was the only place for miles that you could exit without having to pay a toll.

Hoisington never mentioned any of that to Toole. But later that afternoon, just as the van neared the construction site, near mile marker 126, Toole suddenly said that this looked like where he had first turned off the turnpike the first time, when he decapitated the little boy. Hoisington stopped the van and pulled off onto the road. Yes, said Toole, this sure looked like the place. Hoisington pulled into the access road and everyone climbed out. Days earlier, Toole had described the place as a "triangle road." And sure enough, there was a fork in the road, right there beyond them.

At that point, a Florida trooper stopped by to see what was going on, and Hoisington double-checked his recollection: Had this been a construction site back in July 1981? Yes, said the trooper. And also the only exit from the turnpike at the time that didn't have a tollbooth.

Talking with Hoisington, Toole said that he had placed the little boy's head on the rear floor of the car, behind the driver's seat, and pulled back out on the turnpike, northbound. After driving north for about ten minutes, he said, he had pulled off the turnpike again and walked toward a canal—out onto a small wooden dock—and thrown the head in. He wasn't sure if it was a bridge or a dock, exactly, but it was made out of wood and stuck out over the water.

The group headed north on the turnpike to see if Toole could point out the area. Ten minutes later, about four miles up the road, just as he said it would be, Toole seemed to think they were at the right spot. He told Hoisington to stop. A canal ran along the turnpike there, which was not far from mile marker 130. When they all got out of the van, Toole looked around and said it looked like the right location. He then walked over to what Hoisington, who was seeing it for the first time, would later describe as "a wooden walkway-type bridge" into the canal. Toole said that this was where he had gotten rid of the boy's head.

Hoisington had no idea if any of what Toole was saying jibed with the facts. Not, that is, until Hoffman came up and told him that, two years before, this was where Adam's remains had been found.

After a couple of hours at the canal, the group then drove back to the construction site to look for evidence. For an hour and a half, while others searched, Hoisington sat with Toole, who started talking to him. The only reason he had killed the little boy, Toole said, was that he wouldn't stop crying for his mother and father. That the only way he knew to quiet him was to kill him. Hoisington asked why he had kept the little boy's head. Toole said that he wasn't really sure. Maybe, at first, as some sort of keepsake. But then he got scared about having it in his car, which is why he pulled off the road again and threw it into the canal. Toole kept saying how drunk he had been at the time. Later, after telling Hoisington about some of the other murders he had committed, he said that the only one he was ever sorry for was Adam Walsh's.

Det. Larry Hoisington's information about the Indian River trip certainly seemed compelling to Mark Smith when he heard about it. But it was not in the case file. Not until October of 1995, during the reinvestigation of Adam's case, when Hoisington was finally interviewed about it. Up until that time, he had never filed a report on what he saw and heard that day. For one simple reason, he told Mark Smith. Because none of the detectives on the case had ever asked him to.

On Friday, October 21, at 9:30 P.M., Hoffman and Hickman interviewed Toole again for nearly two hours. Again, he talked about the crime. About parking his car at the Sears store that day, about how warm the weather had been. He might actually have gone into the Sears store itself that day, he said, instead of just cruising through the mall. Referring to his first interview with Toole, Hickman asked, "Can you tell me how you described the child, his looks?"

"I said his hair didn't look straight-looking."

"Like little waves in it maybe?"

Yes, said Toole. "It could have been 'cause it was hot outside, you know. He was kind of sweaty from the heat."

On that day, Toole had drunk a half case of beer and taken quaaludes. "I wasn't feeling no pain," he said. He had kidnapped the little boy to take him back to Jacksonville and raise him as his own.

Why this particular boy? Hoffman asked.

Because, said Toole, he was well-spoken, could

carry on a conversation, and "acted kinda like he was real smart."

Toole talked about how "I told him I was going to take him to Jacksonville with me. And he spoke up later and said he didn't want to go. He wanted me to take him back where I got him from and I told him no. Then, "he was yelling [that] he wanted to get out of the car." That, said Toole, was when he had "hit him real hard in the stomach one time. And I slapped him clean across the face."

"When you say across his face," Hoffman asked, "do you remember what part of his face you struck him in?"

"Across his eyes."

"Was that with an open hand or a closed fist?"

"Both."

After that, the little boy didn't wake up again. But Toole was still afraid that he would be able to identify him. Which is when he found a place to pull off the road. Recounting the details, Toole began to cry.

By now, the press had gotten wind of Ottis Toole's confession, and things were heating up. Assistant chief LeRoy Hessler thought that the best thing to do was to go public with the news. So, on October 21, he called a press conference, announcing that Adam Walsh's killer had been found, and that Ottis Toole would be arraigned the next day for the crime. In Hollywood, the news came as welcome relief.

The next day when the paper arrived at the Hollywood home of Arlene and Wayne Mayer, their fourteen-year-old daughter, Heidi, took one look at the front page and hollered out, "Mom, look! It's that guy!" As soon as Arlene Mayer saw the photograph of the scruffy, gap-toothed man in the paper, she knew exactly what her daughter was talking about.

Two years before, around 6 P.M. on a warm evening at the end of July, Arlene, her daughter, and her husband had made a quick stop at a K Mart not far from the Hollywood mall. Wayne, in his work clothes, said he'd wait in the car. As Arlene and Heidi, then twelve years old, walked across the parking lot, they noticed a weird-looking guy watching them. He got to the front entrance of the store before they did and was still watching them. He seemed to be talking on the outdoor pay phone. Except, they noticed, he hadn't dropped any coins in the slot.

Inside, Arlene went to the layaway desk while Heidi headed for the toy department. A few minutes later, Arlene saw Heidi running toward her, screaming, "Mom! Mom! It's that guy again!"

In the toy department, the man had come up to Heidi, pushing an empty shopping cart and asking if she wanted to go for a ride.

Arlene, by now really frightened, tracked down a security guard, but by that time the man had disappeared. For a long time, the two were afraid to leave the store. Finally, they spotted Wayne walking up to the entrance and ran out to tell him what had happened. "They were both shaking," he recalls. "Scared to death."

That night, Arlene reported the incident to the Hollywood police, who seemed interested only in what kind of car the man was driving. Arlene hadn't noticed the model, she said, and Heidi hadn't, either. And that was the end of it. Because just a couple of days later, what had happened to Arlene and Heidi Mayer got lost in the explosion of news about the abduction of little Adam Walsh.

Not until two years later, there in the newspaper, did Heidi see the man's face again, in the photograph over a story about his being charged with the murder of Adam Walsh. The papers had said the guy's name was Ottis Toole. Again, Arlene Mayer telephoned the HPD to tell them what had happened. This time, on October 24, two detectives, Jack Hoffman and Ron Hickman, came over to interview them. It was a rough experience, Arlene remembers; the detectives frightened Heidi. They kept hammering her about what kind of car the man had driven, and Heidi kept saying that she didn't know, except that it was "a good-sized car . . . not a small one." Still, in separate sworn statements, Arlene and her daughter told what they knew: that the man had thin hair, used the word *ain't*, was between thirty-five and forty, and was scruffy-looking. Also, according to Heidi, it had looked as if one of his front teeth was missing. Both she and her mother picked the man's picture out of an official photo lineup.

All of the pieces seemed to fit, with one possible exception: the time frame. The Mayers recalled that the incident had happened "about two days" before Adam's abduction—either on a Friday or Saturday. They were sure about that because those were the only days they ever went shopping. What the Mayers had no way of knowing, of course, was that Ottis Toole could not have been in Hollywood on Friday, July 24. His bus from Newport News had not gotten him into Jacksonville until early Saturday the twenty-fifth; if you factor in the five-hour car trip, he could not have been in Hollywood much before early afternoon.

Recently, Wayne Mayer, who was never interviewed by the police, said again that he was sure the incident had taken place on a Friday—because he was working construction at the time and was still in his work clothes. He had been too grimy even to go into the store—which meant that it had to have been after work. Yes, he was positive that it had been a Friday.

Positive, that is, until he was asked one final question: "Wayne, is it possible that you ever worked on a Saturday?"

"Why, sure," he said. "I worked Saturdays all the time."

Today, Heidi Mayer, now twenty-eight and the mother of two, knows that the man she saw that day was Ottis Toole. "Nothing," she says, "will ever change my mind."

She also understands the full implication of that fact. As she puts it, "I'm the one that got away."

Arlene Mayer is just as certain as her daughter. Still, she is frustrated that she doesn't have a clear picture in her mind of the man's car—sitting, as it was, out there at the edge of the parking lot. Only that it was "big." And "light-colored." And "kind of beat-up looking." A "hillbilly car" that looked as if someone had been living in it.

Her husband says that she always described the car as being white. Arlene says she doesn't remember that. Or much else about it. Even the model.

"Except what I told the police before," she says, still turning it over in her mind. "That it was something like an old T-bird or a Cadillac."

After Toole's initial confession back in 1983, Hoffman and Hickman spent a lot of time trying to find out how Toole, if he was making it all up, could have gotten hold of so many telling details of the crime. They knew he couldn't read, but maybe there had been some other way. One hunch was that he had gotten them from Adam's made-for-TV movie, which aired at 9 P.M. on the night of October 10, 1983—the night after Toole first spoke with Kindrick. Toole had already denied seeing the movie, which meant nothing. But, as the detectives learned from interviews with five of Toole's fellow inmates a few weeks later, the only thing anyone was watching on TV at the Duval jail that night was the Monday-night football game.

According to transcripts, a number of those inmates had some other interesting recollections about Toole. One, Julius Wilkes, who had known Toole in Jacksonville and shared a cell with him just before he was taken down to Lauderdale, once heard Toole talk about having killed a little boy. "He was saying, 'They found the head. I hope the body ain't where I put it,'" recalled Wilkes, who at the time had known nothing about the crime. "I do remember him saying that: 'I hope the body ain't there.' How did he know the body and the head were separated? This is what made me say, 'I got to watch this son of a bitch.'"

Toole, said Wilkes, "kept asking questions about the jail and how the dudes in there would take him if he was a child killer. He was really frightened about that part . . . like he was worrying about his life." Whenever Toole talked about adults he had killed, Wilkes said, "he was boastful, you know. But when it came to the kid, he was, like, hurting. All the guys in the cell felt that he had gotten guilt struck."

Another inmate, Bobby Leroy Jones, recalled that one day Toole "started talking about his niece. He said he knew she was going to get killed. But he didn't give a damn. He just sat down on his bed and started laughing about it. I just figured the guy was out of his head. Everybody in here thought he was going crazy—the way he would talk about killing people and laughing, and getting mad about it and starting all over again."

A third inmate, James Poole, said that Toole had once said that he was in the "child repossession business," and that he had talked about having had a "seven- or eight-year-old son" in Broward County, whom he once dropped off somewhere along the highway during a drive north to Jacksonville.

And a fourth, Gilbert Boyd, remembered that Toole once told him that he had murdered a little boy down in West Palm Beach, and that Toole thought the boy had been a policeman's son.

These last two stories could have been, as the cops seemed to think, just more evidence of Toole's BS. But they could also have contained some grain of truth—of the time, in Toole's hazy, booze-soaked recollection, that he did drive a young "son" up from Lauderdale.

And of that little boy's hat—white, with a brim, and way too big for him. Kind of like what a police captain might give to his son.

It never seemed to occur to the cops that the most maddening part about Toole's confessions—his inconsistencies and fuzzy recall—might actually have a reasonable explanation. Any normal person would certainly remember having committed a homicide. But to Toole, as he himself once said, murder was no more memorable than "smoking a cigarette." Factor in his heavy drinking and drugging, and it makes sense that—even when he was really trying—he might not be able to remember exactly what he had done with the body of one victim out of the hundred or so killings that he had been a party to. As one cop remembers, sometimes when Toole couldn't remember something, he would have a special way of prompting himself. "Goddamn it," he would say, punching himself, hard, in the temple with a balled-up fist. "Come on now, Ottis. Get it together."

Then, after coming up with all of those details, Toole had started recanting. Saying that he hadn't killed Adam after all, and that he had made the whole thing up. In addition, he seemed completely unable to lead searchers to Adam's body. On Wednesday, October 26, 1983, at 9:45 P.M., Jack Hoffman took another sworn statement from Toole, this time with Buddy Terry in attendance. Earlier in the day, Toole had said that he wasn't so sure that he had done the killing. "Ottis, were you lying today?" Terry asked. "Are you sure you didn't kill Adam Walsh? Now, come on now, let's don't do it this way. Look at me. Look at me, Ottis."

Toole began crying. "My mind ain't gonna take much more of this shit," he said.

"Just tell the truth. That's all I want to know," said Terry.

"No, I didn't kill Adam Walsh."

"Are you sure or are you not sure?"

"I'm sure I didn't."

"How are you sure? What makes you sure you didn't kill Adam Walsh?"

"Because, if I was really sure, I could come up with his body."

There was no doubt about it. Ottis Elwood Toole had been one tough nut to crack. As everyone knew, hardball didn't work with Toole; you had to coax him. But Hoffman and Hickman apparently used a different method.

According to Steve Kindrick, who talked to him again some months later, Toole finally decided to clam up entirely. Toole told Kindrick that when they took him back to where he had disposed of the body, they had called him "a son of a bitch and an asshole. And it finally made him mad. 'I wasn't going to tell them anything more,' he said. 'I told them to just take me back home. And you know, we weren't that far from where the body was at.'"

"Well, Ottis, if you were that close," said Kindrick, "then why'd you change your mind?"

It was, Toole replied, "because of the way they treated me."

In May 1995, when the *Mobile Press Register* started trying to get its hands on the case file, the state attorney's office appointed its own investigator to reexamine the case—Phil Mundy, a tough, retired Fort Lauderdale detective with some twenty years' experience. Mundy and Mark Smith both looked into another allegation—the rumor that had been swirling for years that Buddy Terry had fed information to Toole in hopes of lining up a book deal. It was a serious charge, one that, if true, could shed doubt on the whole investigation. Terry had certainly been smeared in the press about it. So Smith and Mundy checked with cops, investigators, and Terry himself—

who, they were surprised to learn, had never officially been interviewed about the charges.

What they found was that Buddy Terry was a good cop who, back in 1983, had basically been trying to help everyone out. Terry was the one who had led Hoffman and Hickman to Toole's white Cadillac. Terry was the one who had learned about Henry Lee Lucas's incarceration at the time of Adam's murder. It may have been fair to say that Buddy Terry had been a little overzealous. But it was clear that he had been wrongly accused, perhaps out of sheer jealousy on the part of other cops. There was not a shred of evidence to suggest that Buddy Terry had tainted the case.

Which still left the question: Why had Toole talked so freely? Was it bravado? Stupidity? Did he just do it for the attention? Steve Kindrick once put it to Toole directly: "Ottis, why are you talking about all of this?"

The response was ugly. But perfectly in character. And maybe as close to the truth as it was possible to get. Toole was talking, he told Kindrick, because he had been given a court-appointed public defender—a black man—who had told him in no uncertain terms to keep his mouth shut. Who told him that the last thing he should be doing was shooting his mouth off to the cops. That had done it, Toole said. As he so delicately put it to Kindrick: "No nigger lawyer's gonna tell me what to do."

After the initial flurry of publicity surrounding his arrest, interest in Toole receded. By May of 1984, he was sentenced to the electric chair for the Jacksonville arson murder, had given statements in connection with thirty other killings, and was charged in nine. One courtroom observer remembers Toole's appearance. "You know how you can tell a lot about a person by looking into their eyes?" she says. "Well, with

Toole, when you looked in his eyes, all you saw was a blank page." At the trial, she says, even while prosecutors were saying all kinds of terrible things about him, Toole sat there the whole time with a stupid grin on his face. Like, "Yup, I'm the one they're all talking about. They're talking about me."

Back in 1983, I was as excited as anyone when the cops announced that they were going to indict Toole and was disappointed when the case against him seemed to start falling apart. I never really understood why. I just figured that the cops knew what they were doing and were working the case as best they could. Sometimes Jack Hoffman would call with news of a tip, but I certainly knew that the cops weren't going to share sensitive, confidential details with me. That kind of thing might jeopardize the investigation. So I tried to keep on top of things as best I could, without butting in.

Sometimes, I couldn't help finding out about things—as when, in 1988, Toole suddenly seemed to rear up again, sending me that horrible extortion letter. As it turned out, Toole had dictated the letter to a cellmate who could write, a guy named Gerard Schaefer, a former state trooper who had been convicted for a series of rapes and murders. For a while there, the two had a little cottage industry going, writing letters all over the place, trying to extort money for alleged "information." They were all the same. Long on ghoulish detail. No hard proof.

But most of what had happened I didn't find out about until much later— 1996, as a matter of fact, when the case file was opened up. Such as the call that had come in from a guy named William Carl Mistler. On July 1, 1991, Jack Hoffman got a call from Mistler, who lived in Hollywood and had just seen an article in the *Miami Herald* about Maj. J. B. Smith's retirement from the HPD, in which Smith talked about how thoroughly HPD had worked to eliminate

Ottis Toole as a suspect. Mistler was under the impression, like everyone else, that Toole had been indicted long ago. On hearing that he hadn't been, Mistler was appalled. Because, he told Hoffman, he had seen Toole abduct Adam in the parking lot that day.

Mistler told Hoffman that on the afternoon of July 27, 1981, he had been in the west parking lot of the Hollywood mall and had seen a man matching Toole's description put a little boy into a white, four-door Cadillac with a black top and then drive off. At the time, Mistler didn't think much about it. The little boy hadn't seemed frightened. And the next day, he and his family had left on a camping trip. Not until they got back to Hollywood did they first hear about Adam's abduction. Even then it didn't occur to him that the two incidents might be related. Because, after all, the newspapers said, there had been eyewitnesses. And the police had narrowed the search to a blue van.

Two years later, in 1983, Mistler, like everyone else, saw the articles about Ottis Toole's arrest. He recognized the man as the guy in the Cadillac that day. Other witnesses must have seen it, too, because Toole had clearly been arrested and was being charged in the crime.

Hoffman told Mistler that he was going on vacation, and that he should call back in a couple of weeks. Hoffman didn't take down a phone number.

But two weeks later, Mistler did call back. He agreed to a polygraph, which an HPD examiner called "inconclusive." And consented to being hypnotized by someone from the Broward sheriff's office. Mistler described the man he had seen as having reddish brown hair, a two-week old beard, weird eyes, greenish teeth, and a yellow-stained shirt "the same color of a manila envelope. It was that filthy. Along with . . . what looked like a morning cup of coffee . . . right down the center." He described watching the man kneel down and talk to the child. Take him by the hand and put him into the car.

During an interview with Hoffman, Mistler got upset when he started talking about how, if he had done something, he might have prevented Adam's murder.

Because Mistler came forward, on October 17, 1991, Jack Hoffman and Bill Haggerty went up to reinterview Ottis Toole at Starke. During that interview, Toole said that the only reason he had ever confessed was for personal gain—that he had enjoyed being given food and cigarettes at the Indian River location.

"It is this detective's opinion," Hoffman wrote at the conclusion of his report, "that Ottis Toole was being truthful and sincere about his noninvolvement in the Adam Walsh homicide."

By this point in their review of the case file, Matthews and Smith knew some hard evidence was still needed. The most compelling kind, of course, would have been Adam's body. But it was never found. By the time the canal, the land along the turnpike, and even Toole's mother's backyard in Jacksonville were searched, two years had lapsed since the murder. It was now fourteen years later.

But some physical evidence was still left, as both detectives knew. One of Joe Matthews's first suggestions, in fact, was that every piece of existing evidence be reexamined—and compared to whatever appeared about it in the written case file. In doing just that, Smith knew where he had to start: in the HPD's fourth-floor evidence room, an interior office filled floor to ceiling with industrial metal shelving and boxes, bags, and envelopes of evidence from hundreds of burglaries, rapes, and murders. The Adam Walsh evidence took up an entire shelf of its own, and Smith started making his way through it. One of the first things that he found shocked him: there, in an envelope, was a yellow flip-flop and a pair of a child's green shorts.

Those were the items that would be shown to Revé and me at our meeting with the HPD in January of 1996. Then, as now, there was no explanation for why they had never been shown to us before. The two items had turned up during an excavation of Toole's mother's backyard back in 1983, after which Jack Hoffman had taken possession of them. "This evidence was then brought back to the City of Hollywood," he wrote in the final line of his 143-page report, "and placed into the evidence room."

Which is where it had sat, unopened, for nearly twelve years.

Matthews had read the reports about Toole's black-over-white Cadillac—and about how, when it was found, the car's interior and window locks were exactly as Toole had described them. Matthews also saw that carpet samples had been taken from the car and had tested positive for blood back in October of 1983. The bloodstains were right where they should have been, if Toole's story was to be believed: on the driver's-side floor, both front and back.

Finding those evidence reports was one of the most exciting moments of the entire search. Matthews knew what could be done now with DNA testing that hadn't been possible back in 1983. Now, the samples could be retested and compared with samples of Revé's and my DNA, which would be similar to Adam's. Any matchup with those blood samples would end all the speculation, once and for all.

Except that, although Smith spent months trying to track down the carpet samples, there was no longer any sign of them. Anywhere. Not at HPD, and not up in Jacksonville, where they had been sent back in 1983 for tests. The samples had last been signed out of the FDLE's lab by someone with the initial *J*. Maybe a local cop named James Geisenberg. Maybe

James "Buddy" Terry. Neither man recalled anything about it. And the bottom line, no matter what had happened, says Smith, is that "it was an HPD case, and it was our evidence. We were responsible for it, and why it sat there for six months without being picked up was not that person's fault."

Like the carpet samples, the car itself was now gone, too—last registered to a man in St. Augustine in 1985, who later had it towed to an unknown junkyard in Jacksonville. "Based on this information, it is believed that this vehicle is no longer accessible," Smith wrote in his report. "Any attempt to locate it for the previously mentioned test would be futile." As the press would later write it, a two-ton piece of evidence had simply disappeared.

After reexamining all of the available remaining evidence, Matthews and Smith agreed that it was time to reinterview Toole. Except that now Dick Witt, the HPD's police chief, suddenly declared the Toole interview strictly an HPD matter. It was not Matthews, but an officer from the juvenile division—one of Matthews's polygraph students, who was completely unfamiliar with the case—who was ordered to accompany Smith up to the Union Correctional Institute at Starke on June 27, 1995. Despite his interviewing expertise—and all of the work that he had done on the case—Joe Matthews was edged out yet again.

At 8:45 A.M. that morning, Toole was brought into an interview room next to the administration building from the medical facility where he was then being housed. Smith had been told that, because Toole had active hepatitis B and C, everyone would have to wear surgical masks. Toole's abdomen was distended and he was tired, but he didn't seem feeble. He was coherent and could walk unaided. At first, he was soft-spoken and cooperative—at least until Smith told him why they were there. Then he suddenly became agitated, saying that he was not in any way involved in

Adam's case, or in any other case—even the ones he was convicted of. After thirty minutes of general conversation, he agreed to be tape-recorded, but the interview went nowhere. Toward the close of the interview, Toole became tired and was returned to his ward in the medical unit.

After nearly a year of investigation, this was the first time that Mark Smith had ever come face-to-face with Ottis Toole. "I wasn't really comfortable being in the same room with him," says Smith. "And I don't mean because he had a contagious disease." Toole was interviewed again several times by Smith, but the response was always the same. Asked about Adam, he would shake his head and say, "No, no, I didn't do it." People had forced him to say things, he insisted.

By 1996, Toole, serving five life sentences in the Florida State Prison at Starke, was not in great shape. He was only forty-nine years old, but all the years of drinking, drugging, and God knows what else had taken a toll. Smith says that because he knew how desperate I was to get a "dying declaration" from Toole (which would stand up in court as a confession), he asked to be notified if Toole's condition worsened.

But that's not what happened. When Toole was later transferred to a medical facility off prison grounds, someone must have dropped the ball. No one notified Mark when it happened. No word came. On September 15, 1996, Ottis Toole died of hepatitis, cirrhosis, and—according to unconfirmed reports—AIDS, at the North Florida Reception Center in Lake Butler. His body went unclaimed, so it was put into a grave at the Union Correctional Institute in Raiford. He left a Bible and a few personal effects.

And I lost my chance for a deathbed confession.

After our *AMW* segment on Toole aired on September 21, the *AMW* hot line got a call from a woman who was angry because she assumed, mistakenly, that I had been officially notified of Ottis Toole's death.

No one had bothered to call her, she said. And after all, she was Toole's niece.

My assistant, Cheri Nolan, asked Joe Matthews to call the woman back. He did, and spoke to her for nearly three hours. She told him the whole sorry story of her childhood. How Toole had sold her as a prostitute when she was thirteen, and would watch while men came in to have sex with her.

Matthews listened to her for a long time and finally decided there was no harm in asking. Did she believe that Ottis was the killer of Adam Walsh?

"I have no doubt of it," she said evenly. "I know my uncle too well."

Matthews asked her how she could be so certain.

It was, she said, because of what happened the last time she ever saw him. It was Christmastime of 1995, and she had gone to visit him at Raiford. Toole was obviously sick. His health was failing. She knew that she might never see him again.

And so she asked him directly. "Uncle Ottis, are you the one that killed Adam Walsh?"

"Yeah," he said. "I killed the little boy. And I always felt kinda bad about it, too."

She began to ask how and why he could ever have done such a thing. But that was as far as she got. Because Ottis Toole said that he had already talked enough about the murder of Adam Walsh.

And that, now, he didn't want to talk about it anymore.

After Toole's death, just one small ray of hope was left to me. The murder weapon.

Over the years, police had taken into custody a total of five bladed instruments that they thought might have been used in the crime: Michael Monahan's sugarcane-cutting knife; a machete found at the roofing company where Toole sometimes worked, a different machete, taken from one of Toole's relatives; a third, found in the trunk of Toole's Cadillac; and a bayonet, taken from over a mantel at Toole's sister's house in Jacksonville.

Back in 1983, blood had been found on at least one of those blades, but there was no way to tell whose it might be. Now, fifteen years later, there was no material left to be tested, not even for DNA. That left a single, remote possibility. Back in 1986, Matthews had worked on a case—the first in the country—that had been solved using a new forensic technique. By comparing minute striations on a steak-knife blade with corresponding markings on a victim's chest cartilage, scientists were able to prove conclusively that the knife was the murder weapon. And now, even though it took a full year to set up, Matthews arranged for a lab at the University of Florida in Gainesville to run the same kind of test on the bayonet and four machetes.

The five weapons were sent up to Gainesville, along with Adam's remains. In May of 1997, the results came in. All four machetes were definitively ruled out, but the bayonet was a different story. The minute etchings on its blade were not inconsistent with markings on the bone. The lab could not call it a definite match. Nor could they rule it out.

At first, the findings didn't seem to mean much. Over all the years, and in all the police reports, the murder weapon was always described as "a machete." Always, that is, with just a few exceptions.

A review of the records shows that in that first conversation with the Louisiana detectives, Via and Cummings, way back in 1983, Toole said that he had used a "machete or bayonet."

A month later, as part of the investigation, Hoffman had interviewed one of Toole's acquaintances, a guy up in Jacksonville named Charles Lee Hardaman. At the time, Hardaman, who had sometimes worked with Toole, remembered that Toole sometimes carried a large knife. According to Hoffman's report of a sworn statement from Hardaman in November 1983,

"Mr. HARDAMAN indicated that the knife was approximately 18 inches long, and would fit on the end of a rifle. This detective asked Mr. HARDAMAN if this knife would be that of a bayonet and Mr. HARDAMAN indicated that it would be. Mr. HARDAMAN had knowledge of this bayonet due to the fact that he was one time the owner of this knife and that he gave it to OTTIS to sharpen for him and that OTTIS TOOLE never returned it to him. As to the time that Mr. HARDAMAN gave this bayonet to OTTIS TOOLE, he recalled that it was prior to . . . May of 1981."

And then there was the 1988 memo from Jack Hoffman to Dick Witt—a report outlining how two sergeants from the Broward sheriff's office had gone up to Raiford to interview a prisoner there, one Gerard J. Schaefer. Schaefer was the same guy who, back then, had sent out all of those horrible extortion letters with Toole. In the words of Hoffman's report, "Gerald Schaffer [*sic*] informed [the two Broward sergeants] that Ottis Toole told him that he used a bayonet to commit the Walsh Murder." He said that they would be able to find the bayonet hanging over the mantel at Toole's sister's house.

The two cops went to interview the sister, Vinetta Ciphers, who told them that she didn't know if her brother had killed Adam Walsh, but she was sure of one thing. That the bayonet had been hers since 1979, and in all those years it had never once left her house. If Ottis had taken it, she would have known about it. The sergeants asked if they could take it for testing anyway, and she agreed.

In 1996, Mark Smith decided to track down and reinterview Charles Hardaman. Smith showed him a photograph of the bayonet that had hung over Vinetta Ciphers's mantel, and Hardaman immediately recognized it as his own. He had always wondered what happened to it, as a matter of fact. Because he had loaned it to Toole to sharpen, he said, and Toole had never given it back. The knife wouldn't be the kind you'd forget, Smith thought. It was a full foot and a half long, fairly heavy. And not a typical bayonet. It wasn't a thin, narrow blade that slipped into the tip of a rifle barrel. This had a full, wooden handle attached to it. It was actually more like a sword.

Back in 1988, Hoffman hadn't seemed too excited about the recovery of that bayonet. In the very last line of his report, detailing how it was handed over by Vinetta Ciphers, he reiterated, in closing, that "there is no evidence at this time to link Ottis Toole to the Walsh Murder."

Nine years later, it suddenly looked as if that same bayonet *could* be the murder weapon. Now, of course, it could never be proven. But if this bayonet *had* been the murder weapon, what would account for the dozens of references in the case file to the searches for, and descriptions of, machetes—while there were so few about bayonets?

Maybe the answer is contained in the transcript of Hoffman's very first interview with Toole in the Duval jail back in 1983. The record shows that during that interview, when Toole first described the murder weapon, he did refer to it as a "bayonet."

"What kind of bayonet are we talking about?" Hoffman asked. "When you say 'bayonet,' are you talking about . . ."

"Bayonet is a big knife about like that," said Toole, indicating the length.

"You're saying almost eighteen inches long?"

"Yeah."

"Similar to, like a machete?"

"Yeah," said Toole. "Like a machete."

While Joe Matthews and Mark Smith were working their end of things, the state attorney's investigator, Phil Mundy, was doing his thing, too. For starters, he reinterviewed Steve Kindrick, the first person Toole ever mentioned Adam's murder to. One of the things that Mundy asked him was what Toole had said he used to lure Adam into the car. As Mundy knew, almost every reference to it in the case file vaguely mentions "candy and toys." But that's not the way Kindrick remembers it. According to him, the very first time Toole ever mentioned it, he said that what he had actually offered the little boy was a small, handheld video game. Something like a Game Boy.

Mundy also saw that no hard information in the case file indicated that Toole might actually have been inside the mall that day, let alone Sears. But Mundy noticed that in Hoffman's very first interview with him, Toole did mention going into the mall and spending some time looking at wigs in a wig store. Toole's fixation on some wigs seemed almost comical, given his own thinning hair—and the round bald spot that had been clearly visible on the back of his head. Mundy knew that there was no wig store at the Hollywood mall. At least not anymore. But he located an old crisscross phone directory from 1981. And found, under the street address for the mall, a listing for a wig shop, right along with the one for Sears Roebuck.

But even that was not the most compelling information Mundy would find. That wouldn't come until the fall of 1996, not long after our *AMW* segment on Adam's case aired. That was when a woman in central Florida called the Hollywood police and said that she had some information about the case of Adam Walsh.

I will only give her name as Mary H. She is seventy-six years old. She lives in a quiet retirement community. And I am not going to be the one responsible for having the press descend on her. It was not easy for her to come forward after all these years. I know what the press is capable of. And I am not going to be the one to throw her to the wolves.

On an afternoon in February 1997, Mary answered

the door of her spotless second-floor apartment, wearing a navy blue skirt and a white blouse with a Peter Pan collar. She was a little nervous at having visitors, but cordial and cooperative. Back in 1981 she was working as a waitress and living in Hollywood with her husband, Lou, on a street not far from ours. In fact, she says, she knew who Adam was. Another little boy she knew from the neighborhood, whose name she remembers as Scott, had pointed him out several times in the neighborhood. Around noon on the afternoon of Monday, July 27, Mary went over to Sears because, she said, "I had seen in the paper that they were having a lamp sale." On Saturday, she had bought the table lamp that still sits next to her chair. She had decided, on the following Monday, to go back and get another one. She remembered the New York bake shop that was in the mall. And the wigs that were "in the corner, on stands." But maybe that was in Kresge's or Woolworth's—she's not sure. She never really paid much attention to wigs because she always had a lot of hair.

Not many people were in Sears that day, Mary remembers. On her way into the store, she passed the garden section, where she had earlier bought some tulip bulbs, and was heading back to the lamps when, in the middle of the toy aisle, she saw what looked like a television monitor. "It was new, kind of, and I think it was only for games," she said. Three children were at the computer, along with one who was younger and standing off to the side, about three feet away. One kid was operating the game, and the others were watching. Two of the kids were kneeling on the floor. The younger boy was about the same age as Mary's little neighbor boy, who at the time was about six years old.

Mary couldn't quite get past the group, though, because as she tried to pass, they were standing in the middle of the aisle. That was when she noticed a man standing with them, talking to the little boy she recognized as Adam. She stopped until the man stepped back, allowing her to pass and, in the meantime, got a good look at him. "He didn't look like somebody that a little child would be talking to, or who would be working in the store," she said. "He was sunburned, and he looked kind of shady." The man's skin tone was "real brown, like somebody that lived outside." And she couldn't hear what he was saying, because he was mumbling.

Finally, he looked at her, grinned, and moved to the side. "And when he grinned, the one thing I noticed was that he had big round freckles across his face. And he had a big gap in his front upper teeth." His hair was "shiny" and "laid real close to his head." It looked thin to her, and a little fuzzy at first. Until after she passed him, when she turned around and noticed that he was bald in the back. "Not on top, like most people," she said. "It was on the back of his head, and it was kind of a round spot."

Mary says that she had no trouble remembering the man. She had passed by him close enough to touch and had watched him from only seven or eight feet away. Besides, she says, it was easy to remember how he looked because "I never saw anybody who looked like him."

Mary tends to pride herself on her recollection of detail. She seems unsure of exactly what he wore. A red shirt and blue pants with some kind of paint on them White, really heavy-looking spots all down the front of them, actually. "Like paint or caulking." Dirty sandals of some kind. She can't quite remember his hands, so he must have had them in his pockets or else was wearing long sleeves. "He wasn't holding them up, talking, not like my husband, Lou," she says, who's Italian and "you're liable to get hit when he's talking."

One thing she did remember clearly about the man.

The way he smelled—terrible. Like beer and onions. Overpowering. Something she could smell even from a few feet away.

The man was talking in a low tone to the little boy, the one who was standing off to the side. And the little boy was looking up at him. The guy wasn't tall, but he stood with his shoulders hunched up. The little boy never turned his head toward Mary. He never took his eyes off the guy. "Whatever he was doing to hold his attention," she said, "this guy really had the child's interest."

The little boy, slim, with a thinnish face, was wearing a cap. A little big on him, she remembers, because he had it pushed back on his head. It had a bill, a long bill. Or maybe it just looked that way because his face was so small. But anyway, the child definitely had his head back. He was looking straight up into the man's face. The little boy had on shorts, which Mary thinks could have been blue, but maybe, she said, she is wrong. What she most remembered is how the three older kids were all dressed alike, in everyday clothes. But this child was clean-looking, clean and neat. And he looked as if he didn't stay in the sun. He was pale-looking, at least compared to the man, whose skin was dark.

The little boy had on flip-flops, what Mary called "sand shoes." They're not shoes, exactly, she said. You wear them at the beach. Rubber, spongy-looking shoes that were just a little big on him, she noticed. "I remember that. They were kind of large," she says. Or maybe his narrow feet just made them look that way. His toe went through a strap in front. The way, she thinks, that all the kids were wearing them.

After Mary passed the toy section, she went into the lamp department, where she saw only one other woman—a customer who seemed to be waiting for something. The woman was slim, with light, straight hair, parted down the middle. Probably in her thirties. Mary looked around for a bit, didn't see anything she liked, and went back out. But by that time, when she got back to the video game, no one was in sight. "All the children and that man," she said. "Everyone was gone. There was nobody in the aisle. There was nobody at the computer." She had wanted to take a look at it herself, but someone had turned it off, and she wasn't sure how to turn it back on.

Mary said that she hardly ever watches TV. So later that day, it was her neighbors who told her that a little boy named Adam Walsh had gone missing over at the Sears. "I said, 'Well, I'm sure I saw him in the store. He was talking to somebody, but I didn't know him.'"

At the time, Lou, Mary's husband was away for a few weeks on vacation. She was at home by herself and got the impression that others must have seen the guy, too, because the police seemed to have some idea of who had taken Adam. Then, after Mary's husband got home, he took her on a car trip up to Washington, D.C., for a few days. On the way back, on the turnpike, they saw a blue van. They had heard all about a blue van on the news, and Lou even tried to chase it for a while. It was all pretty frightening. And then, when they got home, came the news that terrified her even more. That the police had found Adam's head up near Vero Beach. "I was afraid to go out," she remembered. "I didn't know if the guys who had done it were caught or anything. I knew the guy had seen me, and I didn't know that he didn't live around here somewhere."

Because she has a hard time speaking to people sometimes, for a time she wrote all of her recollections down on paper. She let Lou read what she had written "so he felt like he was there." She intended to give her notes to the police, but Lou said, "Why don't you leave it alone? The policemen will do their job." And so, when she moved out of Hollywood some years back, she just threw all those old papers away.

Over the years, she never forgot about what had

happened that day. And then she saw the man's picture again. He was older, but he still looked the same. And it got her pretty upset. "I said, 'My God, you mean he's still living? And they didn't get him?'"

Not long after that, she sat down and wrote a letter. It was hard for her to do. But she felt that she should have done it long ago. She tried to offer an apology.

When the policeman first came to interview her, she picked the guy's picture out of a lineup. Mary knew that she probably should have come forward sooner. But she didn't know any detectives and had never met any policemen. She is the kind of person who would never have had any reason to.

And there was the day, right after Adam was found, that she and Lou did go over to the Hollywood police station. "I was going to tell them about seeing this man," she said. "But there were so many people over there. So many telling things that were no help. And the police had other jobs to do."

One policeman was outside, at a bench, and all kinds of people were waiting in line to talk to him. The policeman looked a little annoyed, she said, and didn't act as if he believed anything. Or maybe he was tired. "I decided not to tell it," she said, looking down at the floor. "I guess I just chickened out."

We fought so hard to keep that case file closed. We thought that if it was unsealed, it would take away all our hope. And it did. But for a reason different from the one we thought. We believed that it would forever destroy whatever evidence could still be used to prove who killed our son. Instead, it showed what a disaster the investigation was right from the start. How filled with laziness, stupidity, and arrogance. It showed that there had never been a chance of convicting Adam's killer. Not from day one.

At the beginning, the Hollywood police wanted it to be Jimmy Campbell. If it had been, it would have made for one great headline: "Wife's Lover Killed Adam." There was just one problem with that theory, though. It wasn't true. And that marked the beginning of a bad situation for all of us.

Once Campbell and the rest of us passed those polygraphs, the cops should have bored down. They should have said, "There's the possibility of a stranger abduction here." Even if they were 100 percent sure that the family was involved, in those critical first days they should have been more willing to focus on other things, too. They should still have run a parallel search.

Two years later, when Toole confessed, instead of regarding him as the most logical suspect, the Hollywood police basically ruled him out. I've watched hundreds of interviews with guys like that. The weirdest things come into their minds. Through a drunken haze they remember some horrible detail of a crime, or how they slept with some guy or ate some particular kind of food. They couldn't care less about who, what, and where.

If you're a habitual serial killer who's planning to turn a trick or score some drugs, chances are you won't be able to look that date up in your Filofax later on and say, "Oh, yes, Tuesday the twenty-first. Let's see—yes, I was home watching *Friends* at nine o'clock." That is not the world that the Ottis Tooles and the Henry Lee Lucases live in. These guys are nomadic, opportunistic predators who live from one moment to the next. That's what the average citizen—and maybe these investigators— could not grasp. Supposing they asked Toole what he was doing during a three-month period two years ago, and his answer was, "Well, I was in Tampa for about a week."

Do you know what "about a week" is to a guy like Toole? Ten days to a month.

So what do *I* believe happened? This:

That on July 23, 1981, Ottis Toole goes to Riverside

Hospital in Newport News, Virginia, complaining of depression. His longest stretch of employment has been for four or five years, on and off, at a roofing company. His mother, with whom, we can assume, he has had one swell relationship, has just died eight weeks ago. Before that, he had been in the company of a psycho named Henry Lee Lucas, whom he just adores. Then Lucas gets his ass thrown in jail, leaving Toole to fend for himself. On his own, he has been in New York City, Texas, and Arkansas. Hitchhiking all the way, sleeping outside and in vacant buildings.

The hospital report describes him as "disheveled and dirty." He's drinking a half-pint of whiskey and several six-packs per night, along with God knows which bizarre, street-traffic drugs. He goes to the Salvation Army, where he gets a handout—$71.93 for a bus trip back down to Jacksonville.

He is aimless, weird, and angry. Unable to form normal human attachments. And he has no money—but he knows how to get some. He can turn a few tricks down in Miami, where they pay pretty good. In the meantime, he can live in the car. Park it at the edge of one of those malls. Who's gonna know?

And while he is down there around Lauderdale, somewhere in his sick brain he decides to get himself a new traveling companion. A pet. A little kid. He knows how to do that, too. You go to the K Mart and get yourself a shopping cart. It doesn't work with that little girl, though. She had too much of a mouth on her. But two days later . . . well, how about Sears?

Same deal. You wander around. Head over to the toy department. Some of the kids are causing a ruckus. Yelling. Shoving. But not the little boy, younger than the others, standing over to the side, by himself.

A few minutes later, outside the store, you see him again. Without his mother, and a little scared. But now, you're not a stranger anymore. He remembers you from inside the store. And you tell him you have a new video game over at your house around the corner. Why, not even three blocks away.

Four power windows with the control on the driver's side.

He was so quiet and respectful. Delicate, almost. Why did he have to start hollering like that . . . ?

It was all over relatively quickly. Within the day. Within hours. Within 120 miles. It was not drawn out, and my little boy did not have to live for days or weeks that way.

But however it was, it was not so fast that he didn't know what was happening to him. However it went, it was not easy.

Not for Adam.

Why was Ottis Toole never indicted for my son's murder?

The simple answer is that it was because the Hollywood police never presented the case to the state attorney's office for prosecution. The more complex answer is tougher to figure out. It involves conjecture and speculation, and—ultimately—a judgment.

It's not that the HPD cops were simply lazy or stupid. Maybe they honestly believed that he didn't do it. Maybe they were sick of the case. Maybe, once they heard about James Campbell, they didn't think we were worth the effort. Maybe they thought, "Toole's in prison anyway. What's the difference?"

If someone doesn't see what is hiding in plain sight right in front of them, there must be a reason for that. Maybe a combination of ego and arrogance. Pride—the worst of the seven deadly sins.

What astounds me is how the truth was always out there, just waiting to be seen. And of how many people refused to see it: the cops, the courts, and especially the media. Aren't journalists supposed to be the big guardians of truth? They certainly worked hard enough to have the case file opened up. And then, after that whole battle, what did they do with it—except flip through it, looking for dirt?

The week after the case file was turned over to the press, a columnist for the *Miami Herald,* Fred Grimm, wrote what journalists call a "thumb sucker" or "think piece." Grimm was patting his paper on the back for upholding the First Amendment. It was a good thing that the case file had been opened, he wrote, because "Ottis Toole's ghastly lies do nothing to shed light on the enduring mystery of little Adam Walsh."

He went on to say, "The only mystery left unsolved was how any cop, without supporting evidence, could have believed Ottis Toole."

Kelly Hancock says that if he had prosecuted Ottis Toole, the jury would have come back within hours with a guilty verdict, and Toole would have died on death row for my son's murder. Buddy Terry, too, always believed that Toole was telling the truth. So, too, to this day, do Joe Cummings, Paul Ruiz, and Steve Kindrick—all those cops from the early days. Not to mention Joe Matthews and Mark Smith.

There was also an exchange that came during a fateful meeting on November 12, 1996, in the office of Ralph Ray, the chief assistant state attorney for Broward County. At that meeting—attended by Ray, Kelly Hancock, Phil Mundy, Joe Matthews, and from the HPD, Mark Smith and his superior, Lt. William D'Heron—I demanded to know why the HPD had not given me the simple dignity of letting me know through official channels that Toole was nearing death. I knew that Toole would never have confessed to any cop. But it was clear that he had been crying out to make a deathbed confession to someone. And that in not being notified, I had lost my very last chance.

At that point, D'Heron seemed to offer an apology for what he termed a "miscommunication" between

HPD and the prison—as well as for all of the mistakes in the case that had been made over the years. It was an acknowledgment, yes. But after everything that I and my family had been through, I couldn't believe the way in which it was finally being offered. "And that's it?" I said. "This is how it's all supposed to end?"

At that point, Ralph Ray and Phil Mundy began to give me a synopsis of their investigation—the places they had been, the people they had talked to, the solid evidence they had gathered—that all pointed to Toole. As I listened, I was heartbroken at what had *not* been done. But I also realized that these were two men who, more than any other law enforcement officials, had proved that they cared about a little six-year-old boy's brutal abduction and murder. They had demonstrated to me that they, too, wanted justice for Adam. I told them that in three months they had advanced the investigation more than had been done by the HPD in fifteen years. And I made it clear how grateful I was.

And then, at the end of that meeting, I turned to Phil Mundy, the state attorney's veteran lead investigator, and told him that I still needed an answer. Something—anything—that might give me peace. So I asked him, man to man, who he thought had killed my son. And Phil Mundy's words to me were: "Toole's your man. I'm absolutely convinced of it."

To my mind, the evidence is overwhelming. I know that certain people, some even at the FBI, are convinced that Toole was not the killer.

They can think what they like.

I am Adam's father, and I know what I believe.

And finally, there is what Toole himself said in an interview with Det. Jack Hoffman and Det. Ron Hickman in Jacksonville, Florida, on October 21, 1983, recorded as an official transcript on page sixteen of a Supplement Report, Hollywood Police Department, page 5570 of case file no. 81-56073. What

Ottis Toole, an itinerant drifter with an I.Q. of 70, told these lead investigators in the case:

Q. Let me ask you a question. Did you kill that little boy? Did you abduct him from the Sears store in Hollywood?

A. Well, if I didn't kill him, I wouldn't know where the Sears store was, and I wouldn't know where the forks in the road was . . . would I?

15

The Upshot

I BELIEVE THAT THE TWO ADAMS ARE ALWAYS UP THERE, looking out for me. Every day. They're my inspiration—my father and my son. And no matter how heartbroken I get, or how much I get into the depths of despair, no matter what happens, I truly believe that they're proud of me.

People who haven't been hit by crime can still enjoy what Revé and I call "the luxury of being naive." They go around thinking that it could never happen to them. I envy those people; I truly do. They don't know any better. They don't understand that, once it happens to you, everything changes. Every tiny aspect of your life. And even though you may look the same on the outside and may be acting the same way, on the inside you're coming from a totally different place.

To us, even back in the early days, our most basic understanding was always unspoken: Adam cannot have died in vain. If we had not gone on to do what we eventually did, we would have remained as we were: two grief-stricken, hand-wringing parents whom other people looked at and felt sorry for. But what we both came to believe was that if you are given an opportunity to change things, then how can you not at least try?

There will always be murdered children. There will always be abductions. But at least we tried to pull something out of the ashes. Even today, you can, at the very least, try to get some of these kids back and maybe cut down the odds that it will happen again. And somewhere along the way, somehow through it all, we learned that, yes, there are other things in life besides your murdered child. There are other things to talk about, other things to live for. Other things to feel proud of.

It seems sad to me that people gravitate only to the Adam Walsh case or the JonBenét Ramsey case or the Ennis Cosby case and pay so little attention to all of the lesser-known others.

I learned, and I've said it for years, that there have been thousands who have died since Adam died, and many more thousands of people who have learned firsthand that anybody can be a crime victim in this country. That there are people out there who do terrible harm to others without ever considering the consequences. And no matter how much you think you're prepared for it, no matter what you've done with your life in the past and what you hope to accomplish in the future, you are still vulnerable. You are at the mercy of these people.

Revé says that we never did get our skyscraper in Washington, at least not literally. What we do have is a red-brick building in Arlington, Virginia, that houses the National Center for Missing and Exploited Children. In 1990, the Center, now thirteen years old, merged with the four Adam Walsh Child Resource Centers, located in California, Florida, New York, and South Carolina. Together with these branches, the National Center has worked with law enforcement on over 53,000 missing-child cases and helped reunite over 35,000 of those kids. On any given day, the

Center's hot line receives more than seven-hundred calls, and its new Web site more than two-hundred-thousand daily hits. In 1986, NCMEC began some pioneering work in the use of computer-generated age enhancements, which help show authorities what a missing child might look like with the passage of time. People like the mayor of Tuzla have visited the Center, in this case to get ideas about how to locate and identify missing children displaced during the fighting in Bosnia. Not long ago, the prime minister of Belgium also paid a visit after a string of brutal kidnappings and murders of children in his country. He wanted to talk about what might be done to create an international center for missing children.

We've had a series of directors, all of them good. Ernie Allen, whom we first met back at that Louisville conference in 1981, is an especially strong voice. He's now the Center's director. Robbie Callaway is still on the board, and so is John Rabun. All of those people from the early days. Now they're the professionals. It's good that the Center is located near Washington. There, it's really at the heart of things. From there, we can disseminate information to satellite groups. Now, at least there's one central place where people can go if they need information on a child who is missing, or on how to deal with runaways, or on how to educate their kids about safety. At the Center, they've started something called Kids & Co., an age-appropriate teaching tool that's used from kindergarten to grade six to give kids just enough information to protect themselves. It lets them know about the lines that people use—"Can you help me find my puppy?"—and it teaches them, without scaring them, in a real, matter-of-fact way. That your private parts are your own. That if anybody ever monkeys with you, that's wrong. That if anything like that should happen, you tell a person you trust. If that's not your parents or your stepdad or your uncle Bob, then it could also be your teacher at school. Because now there's legislation that says that if a child confides something like that to a teacher, it must be reported to law enforcement. No one can get away anymore with a simple, "That's nice, Billy. Thanks for sharing, and sit down." The point is that all of these programs and initiatives have happened because they have been designed and implemented by professionals—psychiatrists, psychologists, teachers. Not John and Revé Walsh.

Today the National Center for Missing and Exploited Children is the only nonprofit organization to be hooked up to the FBI's National Crime Information Center computer. In the old days, when Adam was missing, there was always such an aura of mystery about those listings: "This is law enforcement, and that's just too technical for you. This is top-secret stuff here." In the early 1980s one-hundred-thousand names were on that computer. Now there are close to a million.

It always helps to have a poster person attached to an issue. And that's what Revé and I have been—the front people. Kids are still getting the short end of the stick left and right in this country. Nuclear families where everything's hunky-dory are not the norm anymore, and maybe it's time to catch up with reality. To stop thinking that everything is Mickey Mouse in Wonderland. We build theme parks for kids, as if that's all they need. Look at the statistics. There are kids dying of child abuse in this country. Every day.

In the Florida branch of the Center, there is a blowup photograph of Adam in his red baseball cap on the wall. It's still hard for me to look at it, because in it, you can clearly see his hands. But mostly, when I look at that famous picture of Adam, I see a photograph that is a symbol for all children. We don't have that picture in our family album. It belongs to everyone now.

I give the American people more credit than to believe that they need the picture of a murdered little boy to give them the incentive to do something for

children. We're past trying to hold on to
tragedy. Let's not stay stuck on this little gap-
face wearing a baseball cap. It's not just about o
anymore. It's about a lot of people's kids.

Over the years, some things have become clear to
me. Who the evil guys are, for instance. They want to
hurt people, they hate me, and I hunt them. It's black-
and-white. There's a guy out there who's killed a
nineteen-month-old child? He knows I'm hunting
him. People ask me what I think about the death
penalty. For a long time now I have supported the
idea of a federal statute mandating a death sentence
for anyone convicted of the stranger abduction and
murder of a child. These predators are cowards who
don't deserve to be on the planet. I'm not saying they
should be tortured or strung up. But if they're found
guilty, see to it that they're sent into the next world.
Let them come back as a dolphin or a tree.

I have learned to keep going forward. I worry about
my family and my relatives and the people who care
about me. Someone once asked Meghan what her
father did, and she said, "He helps children and
works at the airport." I'd go back to marketing hotels
in a minute if it somehow came to that. I loved the
anonymity of it. People think that I'm a TV star, and
that it's glamorous. It can be very lonely on the road,
especially when you have three beautiful children at
home and know what it's like to go to work one
morning and never see your son again. I'll fly all night,
from anywhere, to get home. And when it's time to
leave again, they have to drag me out of those gates.

Last year I executive produced three television
series—*Manhunter*, an international show which
runs outside the U.S. in forty-five countries; *Final
Justice*, my syndicated half-hour show; and the prime-
time Fox Network's *America's Most Wanted*. I also
executive produced and acted in my first two-hour
movie of the week called *If Looks Could Kill* starring

Antonio Sabato Jr. And the one show I'm most proud of was a one-hour prime-time special called "Smart Kids." It was nominated for an Emmy for the best special in children's programming. A lot of gratifying work. Revé doesn't like it that I'm away so much, but she understands it. I always say, "Look, I'm fifty-one years old. Everything that I had and was before Adam was murdered went out the window." The livelihood, the business, the contacts, the savings. I had to get our lives back on track, earn a living, get us comfortable again.

Because of *America's Most Wanted,* more than 450 criminals are off the streets who otherwise might not be. How many people would have been hurt or killed if those guys hadn't been locked up? In the nine years that the show has been on the air, we've caught twelve men on the FBI's Ten Most Wanted list. Even better is that we've returned twenty missing kids to their familes.

When *AMW* was canceled, the public spoke loud and clear. In the first six weeks that the show was back on the air, we had our highest ratings in five years. We caught seven bad guys in two weeks—our all-time record. I'd love to catch criminals forever. But I don't want to be looking over my shoulder for the rest of my life.

Someday the show will be canceled for good, and I'll move on to other things. I won't regret the day. But no matter what happens, I will never forget the letters that have come in over the years, by the thousands. Sometimes they're on stationery, sometimes in handwritten cards, sometimes scribbled on loose-leaf paper ripped out of a notebook and hardly legible. Hundreds every week. Letters like this one, from a woman in New Mexico:

November 12, 1996

Dear Mr. Walsh,

I have been wanting to write to you since *America's Most Wanted* first aired. These last few weeks, when I thought maybe you were off the air, I realized I should tell you how much of a difference you have made in my life.

Twenty-five years ago I was a student on the campus of Eastern New Mexico State University, and there were thirteen convicts from a prison on campus to better themselves. The University decided to keep it a secret to protect their privacy, and didn't tell the students. I was a very sheltered and innocent eighteen-year-old, and unsuspecting. I dated one of the convicts for about thirty days, and then all hell broke loose.

He stole a car and took off, and after he left the college kept calling me, questioning me, because the State Police and Department of Corrections sheriffs wanted to know where he went. One of the convicts told the others that I was telling the police about the drugs they were doing. They decided to teach me a lesson.

I was kidnapped, held for four hours, strangled and raped repeatedly. It was the most terrifying experience of my life, and one that has affected every facet of it. I escaped out of sheer terror and ran for blocks, with them chasing me. I am sure that they had every intention of killing me. Someone heard me scream, and then I passed out. When I woke up, after being interrogated for four hours, I was taken to the hospital.

They put me in protective custody by hiding me on the empty seventh floor, alone, for one week. A rape victim doesn't need to be alone. They wouldn't even let my best girlfriend in to see me. The town was searched before they found all of them. When I went back to classes, they told me to wear a scarf around my neck to hide the bruises because they wanted to keep it quiet.

I was afraid of my own shadow. I couldn't talk

about it except to my girlfriends, and then with no emotion. Finally, about four years ago I met the warden of the state correctional facility and he told me that the guy was now in prison. I felt better knowing I wasn't going to run into him and have him recognize me.

I have lived these past twenty-five years being ashamed, and it's just in the last two years that I have been dealing with the pain and coming to grips with it. For the last six years I have worked to get rural addressing and to build the data base for Emergency 911 calls in my county. I never made the connection that my drive and tenacity came from that dark night when there were no phone booths, no central dispatch, running for my life not knowing where I was, or if I was running towards help or away from it.

I joined my volunteer fire department two years ago and it was the first time I was ever in constant contact with normal, healthy men who were saving lives, rescuing victims in the night. I have tried to make a difference and have fought to enhance public safety, seek funds for the fire departments, encourage and praise them. I am deeply devoted to law enforcement and emergency medical services because I know from personal experience what it is like to be, as you said on your program, "in the darkness, a victim . . . alone . . . when out of the night come those who make a difference."

I remember the night that little Adam was missing. We were living in New Jersey at the time, and all these years I have thought about you and your family. And you are right. He didn't die in vain. Because through your work his memory is alive, and other victims' families have received justice. John Walsh, you have made a huge difference in this world, and a tremendous influence in my life. I wanted to

take the time to tell you how much I love you
and what your life stands for. My love and best
regards to your family . . .

Wherever I am, I know that I'm not alone. Our little
band of guerrilla fighters is still at it, and they have
never been thanked enough. My brother Joe. My
family. All of the tens of thousands of people who
have helped us.

I never made a conscious decision to move away
solely from the realm of missing children into other,
broader issues. It's just that, over time, I also learned
about all the runaways who are in danger. And
parents kept coming up to me saying, "John, my ex-
husband stole my kid and I haven't seen my baby in
ten years." Then, when I was dragged into VI-CAP by
Pierce Brooks, I learned about how children are
preyed upon by child molesters and pedophiles.

The way I see it, these things are all interrelated. It's
all about exploitation. Reporters always ask me, "Are
you a missing-children's advocate? Or are you an
advocate for molested and abused children? Or are
you an advocate for victims?" Isn't a missing child or
an abused child also a victim? Once I started to make
speeches and appear in public and become identified
with children's issues, it was just a natural evolution.
All over the country, wherever I spoke about children,
women who had been molested or were victims of
incest also began coming up to me. I was given a
lifetime achievement award by the National PTA one
year out in Las Vegas—twenty-thousand people representing all the national chapters. Afterward, I don't
know how many of those PTA mothers lined up to
talk to me. I'll bet fifty of those women said, "I know
exactly what you're talking about. I was molested
when I was a little girl. I was abused. It was Stepdad-
dy. It was Uncle Bill. Keep going on with your work.
God bless you."

It became clear to me early on that we cannot

pigeonhole the exploitation and suffering of people. Once I started to understand the criminal justice system, it all became crystal clear. Many different kinds of people are victims. And the system doesn't serve any of them. It brutalizes them all. Violence against women and children is a symptom. A symptom of how the lofty goals that this society was founded on do not apply to the weak. The system that was designed to protect these women and children— and now men—instead victimizes them and revictimizes them. Reporters may still try to categorize me. But when the average person on the street comes up to me, it's obvious that he gets it. Ask them what John Walsh does, and they'll tell you, "He catches the bad guys. He's the man."

It's clear to them. They get it. My child was murdered, and I'm fighting back.

I have learned a lot in the sixteen years since Adam was murdered. I've learned that the criminals have all the rights in this country—guaranteed constitutional rights—and that victims have none. Twenty-nine states have passed victim's rights amendments to their state constitutions. But it's still a patchwork. Some laws are tough, others weak. So in response to that, a bipartisan group of people has decided to draft the first-ever victim's rights amendment to the U.S. Constitution.

The most important thing about this proposed amendment is what it does not do. It does not take away any rights of the accused. Because the last thing that any victim needs is to have a case thrown out of court on a technicality, leaving whoever hurt them free to do the same thing again to someone else. If there is anyone who wants to safeguard the rights of criminals, it is victims.

This amendment is still a work in progress. It's being drafted and redrafted, and that's a good thing. Everyone ought to weigh in on this issue. People need to think and talk about it. Basically, the amendment says just three things:

1. That victims should be treated with dignity at trial, and be notified of any hearings and procedures—especially if the convicted criminal who hurt them is coming up for parole or release.

In March 1990, Theodore Wolf, a Maryland State trooper, was shot to death in his police car on the roadside by two drug dealers. At the time, his wife, Virginia, was about twelve miles away, at home, asleep, with their three sons. But when the case came to trial, the defense attorneys subpoenaed her as a witness every single day, even though she was nowhere near the crime scene. Why? Because if you're going to be a witness in a trial, you can't also sit in the courtroom. It might compromise your testimony, and the attorneys are afraid the jury might see your pain. These defense attorneys subpoenaed her, so she wasn't allowed to sit in the courtroom and watch the trial that would determine the guilt or innocence of the person charged with murdering her husband.

Then there's the story of Kenneth McDuff, a guy I tracked in Texas, who murdered three teenagers with a baseball bat. Two fourteen-year-old boys and the thirteen-year-old girl who was with them. Murdered all three and put them in the trunk of the car and ate their fast food. He was sentenced to the electric chair in Texas, twice. Strapped in the chair and given a last-minute commute. His sentence reduced to life without possibility of parole. Then the sentence was reduced to life. And guess what? He came up for parole, and the parents of those three murdered kids were never officially notified about it. He hired a former parole board commissioner, who was now a defense consultant, to urge that McDuff be paroled because he was rehabilitated.

I got a call from the office of Ann Richards, the

governor of Texas, who said, "John, Kenneth McDuff got out and we suspect he's killed five women in five months." And what did he do to taunt the Texas Rangers and the U.S. marshals who were tracking him? He buried some women with just their heads sticking out of the sand, as a message: "I'm out and I'm going to keep on doing what I've been doing all along."

Why can't victims be notified of parole hearings? Why can't survivors come in and speak before the parole board? What about the woman in Arizona who was raped by a guy who jumped up and down on her and broke all her ribs, then slit her throat with a beer can. She wasn't allowed to speak at his parole hearing. He got out, raped again—and the second victim wasn't allowed to be at his next parole hearing either.

2. That a criminal may not profit from a crime he's committed, and that wherever possible, a victim should be entitled to restitution.

If a guy makes money off a book about the crimes he's committed, then that money should go to his victims, not to him. Some states have Son of Sam laws, but not all of them. The average time served in the United States for first-degree premeditated murder is 5.9 years. If someone kills some well-known figure in a state that doesn't have a Son of Sam law, it's entirely possible that that convicted criminal could get himself $250,000 for a movie deal. He could then buy sex and drugs in prison, just as Richard Speck did—the infamous mass murderer who killed 8 nurses in Chicago—and have a lot of fun while he's incarcerated. And then, after six years, he can walk out of prison with a quarter of a million dollars. Under this amendment, no criminal in this country would be allowed to profit from his crimes. Any proceeds would go to the victims. For counseling, if they survive. And to help get their lives back on track.

3. Victims should be allowed to speak in the court-room after whoever hurt them is convicted, to say what they think his sentence should be.

They're called victim-impact statements, which are now allowed in all 50 states. But it's still up to a judge's discretion to allow them, and some judges don't want a victim causing a big ruckus in the courtroom. Richard Allen Davis had spent more than a decade of his adult life in prison. He kidnapped and tortured and raped three women on three separate occasions in California and was paroled. He got out and, in 1993, kidnapped and raped and murdered Polly Klaas. He broke into her home and took her from a slumber party in her own bedroom. And we all saw what he did at his trial: he flipped the bird with both hands at Polly's father, the jury, and the TV cameras.

His trial cost California taxpayers about $4 million. During the two-week sentencing phase, after he had been convicted, he had several expert witnesses, paid for by the taxpayers at about $800 a day, who said that Richard Allen Davis should be spared the death penalty because he was fat and he had acne when he was young. He was an alcoholic. They tried to turn him into the victim. California is one of the few states that allows victims to make an impact statement. Mark Klaas, the father of this little girl, got exactly twenty minutes. Twenty minutes to stand up and tell that jury about who his little girl was and what it meant to lose her.

I have seen parents go to sentencing hearings with pictures of their murdered children, begging judges for the five minutes it takes to say, "I will never see this little girl grow up. I will never go to her wedding. I will never see my grandchildren. This man gave her a death sentence. And me a life sentence. But you won't give me five minutes to tell this jury what penalty I think he deserves." Every victim in this country deserves better than that.

All in all, it's a simple amendment. The same way that the Missing Children Act was a simple bill. It wouldn't cost much. It would give justice a new definition. And for the first time in the history of this country, that definition would include victims.

The Founding Fathers made provisions for the Constitution to be amended when necessary. That's why we have the Bill of Rights, which is the very first set of amendments to the Constitution. In fact, the Constitution has been amended a total of twenty-six times—four of those times for the rights of criminal defendants—and not once on behalf of victims. In all of the Constitution and its amendments, in fact, the word "defendant" is used constantly, but there is not a single mention of crime victims or of their rights. There were ten million victims of violent crime in this country last year. They at least deserve the same rights as the criminal who voluntarily chose to hurt them. Isn't it time that someone thought of the victims?

Throughout history, societies have been judged by how they treat their elderly and their children. I think we should also be judged on how we treat our victims. With dignity. To acknowledge them. That's all we're asking for.

No matter how bad things got for us, there was always something that kept us going: our kids.

It was four years ago, and Callahan started it. He told the neighbors that we were adopting a little brother. He figured that if Mommy had a baby, we'd have to take what we got. But if we adopted one, we could go to the baby store and pick one out. Callahan had saved up eighty dollars, and one day he offered to give it to me to help get us a new little brother.

I said, "Well, you know, Cal, I kind of feel like there's no more real Christmas at our house anymore because you kids don't believe in Santa Claus. All you do is ask for stuff all the time, and that's no fun. So, you know, maybe this isn't such a bad idea after all. We can talk to Mom about it."

Revé finally took me aside: "Look, John, this isn't funny anymore. We have to discuss this. Either we're going to have a child or we're not." Since we had always been pretty good at making kids ourselves, we ruled out adoption. By that point, Revé was forty-two, and she said that she had served her time. It was just starting to get easy again. No more diaper bags and strollers.

"I'm too old, John," she said.

I said, "Yeah, you're right. Okay, we won't."

Which is when Revé really started mulling it over. "If I don't have another one, I may very well regret it," she told herself. "But if I *do* have another one, I know that I'll never regret it." Finally, she decided that she was just going to toss this one to the higher power. Not long after that, she got the test at the drugstore, and, yes, the dot turned blue. She called me up on the car phone one day to tell me, and the only thing she heard was me saying "Holy mackerel" and "Oh my God."

Revé had to go to bed for six months. We gave her a cowbell to ring when she wanted something. Boy, was she ornery and I know I couldn't have done what she did. But she was okay, and when I got that glorious call, I jumped on a plane and made it back in time. Hayden John Walsh was born on August 19, 1994. Afterward, Revé was in the big birthing room with Meg, Cal, Gram, and our good friends Dr. Mel Richardson and his beautiful wife, Ginger. The doctor and his wife brought champagne in a bucket. What a celebration.

The way Revé saw it, everything had turned out perfectly. Because the higher power had won.

Our old neighborhood in Hollywood isn't quite as well-kept now as it was when we lived there. The Hollywood mall has been rebuilt since we lost Adam.

There is no historical marker to tell about what happened there on a hot July day more than sixteen years ago.

But a mile or so away, in a schoolyard, just outside the door of the second-grade classroom that Adam would have walked through for the first time that fall, a bronze plaque reads, "In memory of Adam Walsh, a student at St. Mark's. Oct. 8, 1981."

The plaque rests on a big granite stone at the base of a black olive tree. One that was planted by Adam's classmates and his teachers. I have not been back to the old neighborhood to see it, but a friend tells me that it has grown. It was just a spindly little twig when they first planted it. Now it stands nearly thirty feet tall.

16

The Ending

I THINK BACK ON THOSE TWO WEEKS, WHEN HE WAS FIRST gone. Of how hard we worked to get him back, and of all the things we did to find him. In my whole lifetime I had been so successful at everything I ever did. And this was the only thing that really mattered. The only thing I failed at.

We didn't know that he was already dead. He was dead the first day. Because of one monster who was on his own horrible, nightmare cruise. I realize now how many evil, incredibly selfish beings are out there, doing exactly what they want to do, at an unfathomable cost to others—to all of the good people who spend their whole lives trying to be functioning, contributing, positive forces in society. When evil beings are walking in this country, day and night. Everywhere.

Every time I look at all those family photographs that we have on the shelf in the living room, I know that something is missing. There's little Hayden, the baby, two and a half. And Callahan, so gentle, so bright. And beautiful Meghan—all full of life and spirit. But there's always one missing, right where the big brother should be. The strong, tall, beautiful twenty-two-year-old, who should be standing right next to them all. I know exactly what Adam would be like today. He would be a combination of Callahan and my brother Joe.

A few years after we lost him, I was in Meghan's room one night, telling her a bedtime story. All of a sudden, she said, "Who is Adam?"

"He was your brother," I said.

Meghan had always been so curious, so meticulous. And now she wanted to know where her brother was, and when she would see him. I told her that he had died before she was born.

"What does *died* mean?"

"Well, he's not here with us. He's somewhere else. In a different place."

"Where?"

I was floundering. How could I explain it? And then, it came to me. I pointed out the window in her room and said, "You see that one really bright star, way up high? That's where Adam is. He's a star up in the sky."

I never had to explain it to her again. "That's my brother up there," Meghan would say, pointing. "He's a star in heaven." Later on I learned that Meghan gave the same explanation to Cal when he learned about the brother he never met. Now Cal has told the same story to Hayden.

After it was all over, I had to listen to more advice than anyone ever should from well-meaning clergymen and rabbis and priests. Once, a thousand grief counselors gave me a big award down in Miami, all because I told the truth: "There's nothing you can do, except to sit there and listen to these people. Let them pour their hearts out. Don't give them BS. 'Throw away all the toys. Take down all the pictures. Build a shrine. Stand on your head at sunset. Have twelve margaritas. Go on a cruise.' That's all bullshit."

The Ending

If, God forbid, someone you know has something horrible like this happen to them, then there is really only one thing that you can do. You can listen to them. Sit there. Listen. And don't give half-assed advice. Tell them that it is *not* God's plan. That they *will* survive. And that they do not deserve this. Nobody chooses this. This is not a test. We are not Job. This is not Jesus or God or Muhammad testing to see whether someone who is in the middle of a horrible tragedy can deal with it to earn points for the next life.

What God in the world would have planned for Adam Walsh to be murdered and decapitated so that I could become an advocate for children? God didn't sit down somewhere and plan for my little boy to die so that I could be on TV and change hundreds of laws. No way. That's nobody's God—not Hindu or Muslim or Jewish or Christian. Those are just trite things that people say to try to make you feel better. "Time will heal all things." It doesn't heal anything. It lessens the pain, but it doesn't make it go away. It never heals. The day they put me in the coffin is when my pain for Adam will heal.

Our horrible club has grown: Parents of Murdered Children. Mothers Against Drunk Driving. Homicide is big business in this country. Gang-banging and shootings. Death means nothing here. Say you become the victim of random violence. It's unbelievable to you. But you didn't deserve it. People who get cancer don't deserve it, the same as people whose kids get hit by drunk drivers just because they were out on the road that day don't deserve it.

There is no grand scheme and grand plan. These things are random events. And the only thing that matters is how you deal with them. How you get through them. The only thing that matters is the way that you choose to get through life.

Later on, I met a man whose daughter had been murdered, and for years I was sort of his unofficial counselor. He had lost his business, like I did. He descended into alcoholism, and his wife—the mother of the little girl—divorced him. Classic case. Eighty percent of the marriages that go through the murder of a child fall apart. I saw this guy all the time. He got involved with the Adam Walsh Center in Rochester. After a while, he got into rehab, and we were so happy when he came out. We thought, "God, he's back working and everything. He's really going to make it."

Except that he no longer had a marriage, and now he didn't even have drink to hide behind. He didn't have anything but the unsolved murder of his daughter, eating away at his soul. His life became so unbearable and so painful that he killed himself. We lost that fight, and it really set me back.

All you can do for someone like that is to try to understand, even if you don't. Sit down, be quiet and listen. That's what people like my brother Joe and Jeff O'Regan did for me. They said, "We love you, and we know you're hurting. There's no reason. There's no answer. But we'll listen to you. We'll listen and we'll care."

That's what Revé and I did for each other. We didn't have long discussions about it into the night. We didn't talk reams and reams about it. We didn't feel the need to see a thousand counselors. We just sat there and listened to each other. Talked about Adam. Talked about trying to do something. We never said, "Why us? What if?" That's a waste of time.

From the beginning, I spent hours studying and preparing and rehearsing, because I knew that people would look at me and say, "This is a ranting, raving vigilante father with a murdered child." But I was educated, and I knew what I was talking about. I couldn't just go out there and say, "I'm here. I'm hurt. My little boy was murdered. Pity me. Pray for me. Do something for me. Stop it from ever happening to anyone else." That doesn't work. It will never work.

What works is when you say to someone, "We have

a problem here, and this is how we can fix it. This is
what needs to be done." Anybody can piss and moan
and groan. God knows this country is full of pissing
and moaning people. People ask me what I did ten
years ago, and I can't remember what I did last week.
It was always one crisis after another—trying to start
this up while maintaining that. Since Adam died, it's
been one nonstop, fifteen-year blur. We did what we
had to do to survive.

I loved it when Revé refused to let them see her cry.
They always wanted to get the stoic, courageous
father and the crying, destroyed mother. Revé never
bought into that. She did her work quietly. Even after
she stopped running the Center day to day, she
showed up at board meetings with Meghan in her
stroller. Today, she still gets the monthly reports from
the Adam Walsh Center, now the National Center for
Missing and Exploited Children, Florida branch.
These days, she's a figurehead. They trot her out for
fund-raising events and the ceremonial things. She
stands up in front of rooms full of hundreds of
generous, supportive and caring people. And she talks
to them. Tells them what she knows, and how grateful
she is for their foresight, acting for children, not
reacting. She says that when she's standing there
talking to those people, sometimes she can hardly
believe it. Because what she's remembering is that day
when no one would listen to her. Not the police. Not
the authorities. Not a clerk behind the counter at
Sears.

For a long, long time I had the darkest thoughts.
Way down in the deepest, darkest part of your heart
that you don't ever want to talk about. I knew what
had happened to Adam, the details of it. I'd tell
myself not to think about it, because I knew it would
drive me insane. When I advise other parents, I say,
"Don't let the cops tell you. You don't need to know."
Because knowing will take you to the darkest, darkest
part of your soul. It's a hard battle not to let it take

you to the point of being so bitter and angry and devastated that you become someone you don't want to be. That you shouldn't be. Then you become like the evil ones—soulless. Then they win the battle.

I believe that people should be held accountable for their actions. I'll always believe that. At first, I didn't know how to fight back. But I learned. If I look at it from a distance, I guess that ever since those first two weeks, I've been trying to figure out a way to deal with it. With the anger and the heartache, the pain and bitterness and the vengeance. And what I found was a way of dealing with my heartbreak that was not destructive and didn't hurt anyone else. I wanted to make some kind of permanent, positive change.

I don't know. I think I have. Maybe I haven't. But I do know that because of the work I've done, a lot of people are behind bars who deserve to be there. And there are people on death row who are going to be executed and who deserve that, too. I also know that there are kids who are safe at home tonight because of Adam Walsh. Because of the love and kindness of that little boy and the help of my friends. There are children who are sleeping safe in their beds tonight because of all of the thousands of ordinary people who helped.

I only wanted to do one thing in all of this torture that Revé and I and our family and friends lived through. Through all of the work we did, everything that we suffered, the only thing I wanted was to make sure that Adam didn't die in vain.

And now I know for sure that he didn't.

It's Revé's turn to speak now. She was Adam's mother, and she deserves to be heard:

It has all been beyond belief.

If I wake up someday from a dream and it turns out that the dream was my life, I will believe it. If someday I wake up and I am not me, and everything that I know of what my reality has been turns out to have been a dream, I will not be astonished.

I will say, "Oh, a dream. No wonder . . ."

I sometimes think, "I would be the mother of a twenty-two-year-old. There would be a twenty-two-year-old man around the house." I'm so used to having little kids. Twenty-two sounds so grown-up. But then again, if I had the oldest one now, would I also have had Meghan and Callahan and Hayden? It's not a torture thought. Just something that sometimes passes through my head.

I have a little clay manger with the tiny figure of a naked baby in it—Jesus in the manger that Adam made at school. I bring it out every Christmas. And I have a red papier-mâché tree ornament that used to have a paper leaf on it, with his name: Adam. Of course the leaf has fallen off now. But every year I always hang this awful-looking red papier-mâché ornament way up high on my beautiful designer Christmas tree. And if anybody dares ask what it is, I just say, "Adam made that."

I will never forget that we had to bury an empty casket. That we were told that Adam's remains had to be kept as "evidence." They still have the evidence, as far as I know. Then again, it might be lost. Maybe it's with the Cadillac and the carpet samples.

For me, the scariest thing about Adam being murdered was that the world kept going on as it had been. I went outside and the wind was still blowing. People were still driving to work. It was as if nothing had changed. Just another day. It wasn't easy. But our solace was our work. Figuring out what happened and why and what we were going to salvage out of it.

I don't usually talk to people about any of what happened to us. Because where would I start? It's like trying to describe a color that you've never seen. I sometimes say it was like having been in a terrible accident where you lost an arm. You wake up and you're still alive, so you make the most of that day. And over time, you even get happy again. As happy as you can be without your arm.

Today, if someone asks John and me how many children we have, we say, "Four."

And if they ask the age of my oldest, I say, "Twenty-two."

I only give them as much as they ask. They didn't ask, "Did you ever have a child who was murdered?" They didn't ask how long he was here. It doesn't matter that he wasn't with us all that time. Twenty-two years ago, I had a child.

I don't really have very many of his things anymore. Clothes. Toys. A few mementos. Little things he made in school. I have a box that he covered with construction paper, and there's a little flower handle on the top of it that he made. I keep a few little things of his in that box. A zodiac charm that was given to me when he was born. A tiny cross that he made in school. It's just a little jewelry box. Not anything that will last a lifetime.

I can't remember anymore just exactly what it was like to walk down the street with him. I used to have dreams that he was still here—those abandonment dreams that everyone has at one time or another. I don't have a remembrance of exactly what happened in those dreams. Only the sensation of calling him and trying to get to him. But it seems he's riding on the back of something that's moving away from me.

And our fingers are so close.

There is a poem by the English poet Alfred, Lord Tennyson, about a young man, a friend of his, who died at an early age. One verse reads:

> I sing to him that rests below,
> And, since the grasses round me wave,
> I take the grasses of the grave,
> And make them pipes whereon to blow.

On the morning of April 16, 1997, I was in Washington, D.C., to serve as the lead witness before the full Senate Judiciary Committee at hearings on the introduction of the first proposed victim's rights amendment to the U.S. Constitution.

I sat in the hearing room for two hours, waiting for my turn to speak. By the time I was called to the witness table, all the photographers had left. So had most of the senators.

Meanwhile, about a dozen people were sitting quietly in the back of the room, all wearing green ribbons on their lapels, with pictures of their murdered children. People who had come from all over the country, at their own expense. Just to be there.

When it was my turn to speak, I leaned forward to the microphone.

"Thank you very much, Senator," I said. "I have testified before this Judiciary Committee thirty-five times in the last fifteen years. But today may be my most important testimony of all. Because I am not just speaking for myself as the father of a murdered child.

"I hope that I speak for the millions of Americans who are crime victims and have no voice . . ."

Appendix

Crime Victims' Rights
Constitutional Amendment

SENATE JOINT RESOLUTION 6

Proposing an amendment to the Constitution of the United States to protect the rights of crime victims.

Resolved by the Senate and House of Representatives of the United States of America in Congress assembled (two-thirds of each House concurring therein), That the following article is proposed as an amendment to the Constitution of the United States, which shall be valid for all intents and purposes as part of the Constitution when ratified by the legislatures of three-fourths of the several States within seven years from the date of its submission by the Congress:

Section 1. Each victim of a crime of violence, and other crimes that Congress may define by law, shall have the rights to notice of, and not to be excluded from, all public proceedings relating to the crime;

To be heard, if present, and to submit a written statement at a public pre-trial or trial proceeding to determine a release from custody, an acceptance of a negotiated plea, or a sentence;

To the rights described in the preceding portions of this section at a public parole proceeding, or at a non-public parole proceeding to the extent they are afforded to the convicted offender;

To notice of a release pursuant to a public or parole proceeding or an escape;

To a final disposition of the proceedings relating to the crime free from unreasonable delay;

To an order of restitution from the convicted offender;

To consideration for the safety of the victim in determining any release from custody;—And

To notice of the rights established by this article; however, the rights to notice under this section are not violated if the proper authorities make a reasonable effort, but are unable to provide the notice, or if the failure of the victim to make a reasonable effort to make those authorities aware of the victim's whereabouts prevents that notice.

Section 2. The victim shall have standing to assert the rights established by this article. However, nothing in this article shall provide grounds for the victim to challenge a charging decision or a conviction; to obtain a stay of trial; or to compel a new trial. Nothing in this article shall give rise to a claim for damages against the

United States, a State, a political subdivision, or a public official, nor provide grounds for the accused or convicted offender to obtain any form of relief.

Section 3. The Congress and the States shall have the power to enforce this article within their respective jurisdictions by appropriate legislation, including the power to enact exceptions when required for compelling reasons of public safety or for judicial efficiency in mass victim cases.

Section 4. The rights established by this article shall apply to all proceedings that begin on or after the 180th day after the ratification of this article.

Section 5. The rights established by this article shall apply in all Federal and State proceedings, including military proceedings to the extent that Congress may provide by law, juvenile justice proceedings, and collateral proceedings such as habeas corpus, and including proceedings in any district or territory of the United States not within a State.

972842